The Way 2
The Truth
The Journey Within

WRITTEN THROUGH:
CARLA LEE JOHNSTON

Copyright ©2011-2012 by The Truth Movie, LLC
www.thetruthmovie.tv and www.oneteamhumanity.com

All rights reserved. No part of this book may be reproduced, copied, stored, or transmitted in any form or by any means-graphic, electronic, or mechanical, including, photocopying, recording, or information storage or retrieval systems without the prior written permission of Team Humanity Publishing, Inc., except where permitted by law.

The information in this book is intended to be educational, and not for diagnosis, prescription, or treatment of any health disorder whatsoever. This information should not replace treatment with a consultation with a competent healthcare professional. The content in this book is intended to be used as an adjunct to a rational and responsible healthcare program prescribed by a healthcare practitioner. The author and publisher are in no way liable for any misuse of the material.

Library of Congress Control Number: 2012930533

ISBN: 978-1-4276-4939-3

For more information on bulk purchases, please contact
One Team Humanity Publishing, Inc. at:
www.oneteamhumanity.com/bulkpurchases

OneTeam Humanity
P U B L I S H I N G

THE WAY 2 THE TRUTH,
THE JOURNEY WITHIN

TRANSFORMING OUR WORLD
ONE HEART AND ONE PERSON AT A TIME

The Truth is a new story about us…

May your journey within unlock
the infinite possibilities
that await.

CONTENTS

Preface 1
Introduction 5
How to Read This Book 11

THE JOURNEY WITHIN
Chapter I—The Truth Lies Within 19
Chapter II—The Power of Your Thoughts 49
Chapter III—Completing Your Past 87
Chapter IV—The Practice of Mindfulness 125
    Unlocking the Power of Your Own Deepest Truths

REFLECTIONS
Chapter V—Demystifying the Law of Attraction 159
    The Power of Intention & Belief
Chapter VI—The Language of Compassion 187
Chapter VII—Relationships—The Perfect Mirrors 229

EXPONENTIAL INNERNET CONNECTIONS
Chapter VIII—Community Is Strong Technology 277
Chapter IX—Our New World, A Call to Peace 295

Acknowledgements 319
Sources & Endnotes 323

EXERCISES, PRACTICES & WORKSHEETS
Temporal Tap Process 37
My Life Matters Vow 48
The Thought Awareness Exercise 69
Thought Monitoring Process 70
18 Second Thought Monitoring Worksheet 72
Anatomy EFTA of Acupressure Points 77
Freeing Your Limiting Beliefs Worksheet 78
FreezeFrame® Technique 92
Subconscious Clearing Statement 104
Heartmath Attitude Breathing® 111
Judge-Your-Neighbor Worksheet 118
LifeLine Technique—ILS Sequence 119
Breath of Life, Mindfulness Practice #1 144

Reconnecting to Your Life, Mindfulness Practice #2 145
7-minute Innernet Connection to Your Essential Wisdom,
    Mindfulness Practice #3 146
Breathing Practice Technique, Mindfulness Practice #4 . 148
Releasing Anger Peacefully, Mindfulness Practice #5 . . . 148
Facing A Difficult Person, Mindfulness Practice #6. 152
Seeing Your Connection to The Good of Humanity,
    Mindfulness Practice #7. 153
5-minute In-Powering UP for Business Meeting
    Mindfulness Practice #8. 155
Lectio Divina, Mindfulness Practice #9 155
Double-Positive Reprogramming Technique 179
Intention & Belief Worksheet. 184
Expressing Empathy Worksheet. 214
Feelings Inventory 217
Needs Inventory 221
Vow To Share With Loved Ones. 251
Cutting The Cords of Negative Relationships 270

In the space of nothingness everything is created.
THE INSPIRATION

Our destiny is to realize the completeness of our infinite greatness, our potency, our power and capacity to reach beyond to our inconceivable limitlessness, reuniting our consciousness with the celebration of divine love — the eternal, timelessness and truth of who we truly are.

Preface

Within each and every one of us there is truth and there is wisdom. For some it is buried behind the depths of identity. For others, it surfaces as a fleeting vision of an alternate life, a life that could have been had our journey been altered.

Here we stand as unique beings, each possessing distinct desires, commitments, and needs. Are we perhaps afraid to acknowledge that somehow life as it is, is just not good enough anymore? We love our things, our spouses, families and friends. We may also love our jobs, our hobbies, our homes and vacations. But dare we ask, "Does it get any better than this?" Dare we return to the question that sits at the base of our being: "Who am I?" And as for those of us who feel isolated, shackled, separated or alone , yet never at peace, dare we challenge life and seek beyond life as it is, to ask, "Does my life have purpose?"

Yes, we dare! And the answer is "Yes, it does!"

To reflect even deeper, ask yourself this: "Am I living the truth of who I was created to be? Or am I living someone else's truth of me?"

Choosing to dare and awaken your dreamer, the truth of who you are, is the crucial first step to accessing your own intrinsic wisdom, truth and insight into your unique human blueprint and purpose in life. Forget your schooling and forget what Mom and Dad, no matter how well-meaning, told you. The old ways of the world are failing. We stand at a critical crossroads in human history as the fields of modern quantum physics, neuroscience, neuroimmunology, and neurobiology speak to us and elucidate what ancient texts and spiritual traditions have been telling us for millennia. This convergence shows us that the truth is inside every one of us, patterned into the DNA of life itself in a literal message—your truth, waiting to manifest itself into the reality of your world. Yes, you can go out there looking for the answers to life's questions, for our conditioning has always taught us to seek outside ourselves. We've been taught to rely exclusively on our intellectual minds and to seek linear patterns of thinking.

It is the opposite that is true. Everything you need to transform your present life that feels routine and mundane into a life of extraordinary living has always been located within you. You can search and search but you will never find this answer until you listen to the very lifeblood running through your veins, the pulse of truth beating within your heart. Those nagging questions, those dreams, those desires that sit deep within, all serve a refining purpose that is leading you to the truth. Finding your truth and being it is not selfish, anymore than a fish is selfish for needing water. For it is the truth of who you are—a new story about you as well as a new story about us. When you come to know and live in your truth, everything else aligns to serve this purpose. Ease, flow, and clarity arrive and the road ahead changes from a confusing maze into an ever-expanding journey of revelation.

You, just as you are right this very moment reading these words, are a divine masterpiece, within every cell you possess all the power you'll ever need to clear the false programming creating the limitations constricting you to live as your greatness to co-create a whole new life story of reality to affect lasting transformation in every aspect of your life and world.

What if everything you ever need, and more, is within you... to move that which is unseen into the life living reality of your life?

When you encounter your truth, you will know it. You will feel its authenticity as you deepen your trust. And you will see it has always been there to lead you on your journey of a lifetime, where the unexpected now becomes the expected. And your deepest dreams and desires take firm footing in your new reality. As you apply these life-affirming, shape-shifting principles into your life, everything you have been conditioned to believe radically gives rise to a deeper inner wisdom, revealing the truth of who you really are and enabling you to fulfill your highest and fullest expression of life living through you. Restoring and fulfilling your intrinsic and ever-expanding sense of happiness, peace, abundance, and purpose here on this planet, at this unprecedented time in history.

You are the answer and technology you've been waiting for...

Your journey awaits... Let's begin!

INTRODUCTION

We create our world and collective consciousness by the thoughts, emotions, perceptions and beliefs we hold. If we create our world, we must also be empowered to change it. We are not victims of a random world; no, we are its powerful co-creators.

I awoke at 3:13 a.m., a time of quiet which I've learned to honor and trust as a time I can hear that still small voice, the voice of truth within me, which often is drowned out by the drive and pursuits I embody during my day.

I had gone to bed that evening troubled. A matter of the heart had been on my mind and I felt a decision needed to be made. As I lay there, mulling over the series of events, feeling the sadness that accompanied my thoughts, I begin to think beyond the scope of my own relationship and realized that there is a fundamental disconnection between all relationships in general. Earlier that day, I couldn't even drive into my own neighborhood, because of an invading army of news cameras, reporters, and paparazzi waiting to catch a glimpse of a "celebrity" whose infidelity was fueling the media-frenzied belief that we have a right to play voyeur to another human being's personal pain.

My heart went out to this celebrity.

This cultural obsession with over-exposing the private lives of others was deeply troubling to me. I wondered, "Where had we all gone wrong?" I knew the truth. At the core of who we all are, this behavior is the reflection of an unspoken and unfulfilled need that most lack the tools to express, and is not reflective of who we truly are. I know that we are so much bigger than that. I wondered if others felt as I did. That the illusion of success measured by material gain or fame—"The American Dream"—once attained, was worthless and superficial, without the capacity to deeply experience authentic happiness and authentic love that we are all searching for?

Finally, after an hour or so, I went back to sleep, my thoughts sinking deeply into my mind as I slumbered. When I woke in the wee hours of the morning, it was with a loud internal nudging that I needed to get up and write down what I was seeing, hearing, and understanding.

It was a soul penetrating message—an epiphany that rocked every cell of my body. Words and thoughts that needed to be remembered and written. Words that came from beyond and from within; I could not stop recording the answers. I let my pen fly across the paper as I transcribed all I was hearing and as all my senses were brought to acute awareness, more so than they had ever been. In this mindstate, as I processed my own thoughts, beliefs, and perceptions about my particular relationship concern, a lucid clarity overcame me. Suddenly I understood that the origins of my thoughts, my perceptions, and beliefs, were dictating the reality about not only the nature of my relationship (and how it was troubling me) but also my very perception of it. I began to understand that everything in my life was actually predicated on my ability to choose between thoughts and emotions that were either creating love within me or manifesting fear. This "aha moment" of clarity crystallized further into a phenomenal download of understanding that was so comprehensive that I knew, with a knowing that is outside of logic or rational thinking, that this message and its full vision was exactly what all my gifts, blessings, and life experiences had been leading me up to and preparing me for throughout my life. I suddenly knew and understood at this exact moment my life's purpose—to serve and share this message with the world.

Through the download, which is like an entire library of priceless wisdom embedded in a nanosecond within the "innernet" of the cells of my creation mind and heart, what came through me was that the truth was simple, profoundly simple. The truth is that it is our conditioned minds that constrict and limit our ability to be the truth of who we are uniquely created to be in the world. I heard, "It is in the silence that everything is created." I saw a matrix, an interconnected web of information with lights firing off everywhere, squeezing together, condensing down, to represent a convergence of original knowledge. I saw revolutionary quantum and neuroscientific breakthroughs, coming together now, to help us all create a new story about ourselves and our existence in our world. This participatory matrix was asking us to look within— to re-member and reconnect to the truth of who we truly were created to be, and to apply this wisdom to begin to experience life as extraordinary, powerfully living through us, as we were created to experience life; fully connected, present, and "on purpose" in this journey called life.

As I tried to channel this download into a stream of consciousness that would allow me to recount all of the parts of what I saw, I experienced a wave of pure joy and excitement that seconds later was replaced with fear. I knew that what came through me had the power to change the story of our world. I also knew that what I was being asked to do had the potential and power to shake the current "power-over" paradigms of this world to their core. The key to overcoming the obstacles that deny our sovereign birthright for peace and happiness lies within our hearts, as each and every one of us simply aligns to the truth of who we are. As powerful co-creators we can rewrite, together, the new story about us.

What happened next was a series of "God winks" or affirmations from the Universe, nudging me forward, telling me to trust and honor all that the download had communicated to me and through me. One "God wink" was so radical that it crystallized my own acceptance and purpose of this message. I knew in that defining moment, beyond any doubt, that this message was real and needed to be shared.

It was while driving home the following weekend I began to share, for the first time, some of the main components of this "download" I had experienced. Exactly at the time that I was sharing that I knew who was the right person to help me produce a movie to share this message, my engine oil light came on in my car. I pulled over to consult the manual, which was in the trunk of my car. As I opened the trunk, my cell phone was ringing inside the backpack I hadn't realized I'd left in the trunk. Wondering who was calling, I looked to see that it was Timothy Cavanaugh. I hit the disconnect button, distracted by my engine oil problem. The phone rang again and it was Tim calling back. Realizing it was a late hour and concerned that everything was okay, I took the call. Tim said, "Carla, your cell phone has been calling me at least 15 times in the last hour. I heard you talking about something called *The Truth*, and saying that I'm going to be the one to help you produce it!"

"Bleeping impossible!" I thought as I began hysterically laughing, knowing that this was a pure synchronistic miracle nudging me, loudly, to the understanding that this was indeed a message that needed to be shared.

I've recounted that story many times and one day it dawned on me, "How in the world could he have audibly heard, with crystal clarity, my sharing the message, and that it was he who was going to help me produce it, when my phone was in the trunk of my car?" I hadn't spoken to Tim for more than two months. He was in my phone as Tim C., so how in the world my phone could have dialed directly to him, not just once, but more than 15 times, is yet another mystery I may never truly comprehend. Since then, I've learned to trust in the fact that I don't need to understand how it happened but only to know it did.

Throughout the subsequent making of this book and film, these God winks and synchronicities paved the path to draw together the people, science and resources to complete this first leg of the journey without any predetermined effort on my part. In fact, it was only when I was tenacious, overly willful, or interjected my own interpretations or limitations on the path I believed we should take, did I run into resistance. To honor The Truth's message, I had to go "all in" and risk losing every single perception and limiting belief to which I'd become attached. Yet all along there was this deep internal sense of knowing that kept me peaceful, focused and clear even when major life storms came crashing in an attempt to shatter the message and prevent it from coming into the world.

I am not a film maker, nor a writer, nor have I ever had any desire to take on these roles. But, I knew at the deepest level of who I am that this impulse from spirit was real, so I began my journey into what has now become the opening of our journey together—this book and the production of a film.

The details of my story only have relevance if they serve to motivate and inspire you toward your own awakening to the truth and the voice that lies within you. The Truth of who you are is unique to you and can only be discovered from your own journey. What I can share is that no one's journey is ever the same. Your relationships and life experiences are what unveil your direct access entry point, your front row seat to clearing out life-alienating patterns, limiting beliefs and conditioning. Take a pause to inquire into the reactions to life stimuli and your responses that are activated stemming from the reflections of your circumstances and relationships. By doing so, you stir and awaken within yourself and begin to see the access, or the "admission pass" if you will, for co-creating your greatest story of life, as it was meant to be lived, as the expression of your highest and truest passions, purpose, and unique role that only you can play in your world. The moment you choose living in the question of what is possible, from then on nothing is ever the same.

Many well-meaning people have questioned the title for this book, and, in humility, I must explain that I didn't name it—the title was brought to me during the download. I have learned to trust in the download and to honor it. Because this is the title that was brought to me, I have chosen not to question it. As this journey has evolved and unfolded, the reason for The Truth's title has become clear to me. It is the journey within where our authentic wealth, resources of peace, joy and love are birthed from. I understand now with the very same knowledge and understanding that defies and surpasses understanding itself, as encapsulated in The Truth's lucid message: It is in the space of nothingness that EVERYTHING gets created. We create our world and collective consciousness by the thoughts, emotions, perceptions and beliefs we hold. If we create our world, we must also be empowered to change it. We are not victims of a random world, no, we are its powerful co-creators.

We must regain connection to our heart's and body's intrinsic inquisitive nature and learn to listen, to restore, to rest, to remember and expand our awareness and awaken our conscious mind's pure potential. From there, we can access an infinite and true understanding and wisdom from which all true productive original inspiration resides. Ignore the voice of truth within and you lose something no treasure in the world can purchase or satisfy; loss of connection to your interior world, resulting in a life that cannot fulfill its highest and deepest inspirations. It is a life void of passion, incapable of being connected to the truth within you, the "who" you were created to be.

But if you make the choice to key-in and crack your own unique code by choosing love over conditioned patterns and cycles of fear, you choose a path that takes you to the real you've always intrinsically known was there but have been too conditioned in fear to realize (actualize). As your own unique blueprint becomes apparent and you live and act in accordance with this truth, more is revealed to you, for the journey never ends. When we do what we love, what truly makes us happy and fulfills our very reason for being, we create from a place of authentic love and happiness within, which is then reflected in our relationships and collective world. This is the power we've all searched for. A power hardwired within every cell of every single one of us to change our world one heart and one person at a time.

May your journey to your truth be empowered and driven from all the richness within our human spirit, awakening all the love within you, so you can taste, hold, touch, and breathe it into your life living reality, so your senses can actualize the beauty and original design to sow and reap of the abundance and potentiality that is everywhere, if we choose to see/be it.

May your feet be firmly planted...

May you connect to your courage...remembering the courage that lies within your heart...

How to Read This Book

> *The intuitive mind is a sacred gift and the rational mind is a faithful servant. We have created a society that honors the servant and has forgotten the gift.*
> —ALBERT EINSTEIN

The Way 2 The Truth, The Journey Within consists of nine teaching segments, each meant to be built upon the other.

While you may choose to read through each chapter of the book to acquaint yourself from the vantage point of the entire message, it would best serve you to read each chapter and to work with each teaching as a master program, unto itself, without a defined timeline. Work with each teaching as an experiential practice and process, weaving it into your relationships and interactions in your day-to-day life. As you begin to see results unfolding in your life, you'll also see and feel an internal shift within you, then you will know it is time to move onto the next chapter or exercise.

You see, our minds have been conditioned to expect quick answers and results, an intellectual comprehension of the destination before we even take a journey in order to make us feel safe. As such, because you will be pushing yourself into new, unknown, and unchartered levels of higher and higher levels of consciousness, your subconscious fear-based patterns of conditioning will compile all kinds of reasons for you to not stay on your course of intention. *The Way 2 The Truth, The Journey Within* is about unveiling the truth within you, a pathway and process, encompassing no particular destination or specified time-line, and can only unfold without intellectual comprehension. These new life-affirming habits and patterns of choice can take some time to establish. You'll know when you know, as you begin to see and align each teaching with your intrinsic wisdom and understanding, as your reactions and triggers from your own life experiences begin the journey of unpeeling and un-programming the layers of self-limitations that have denied you the full experience of living as you were created to be—potent, powerful, on-purpose and in abundance.

It takes courage to develop a new life and challenge the belief systems that have helped and protected us through this life. Because we are entering into unchartered waters, it will feel scary to rock the boat with our relationships, as every action and thought in life shifts the energy of that system, sometimes shaking it to its core. We've been conditioned to rely on systems outside of ourselves for confirmation that what we're doing is "right," seeking approval or validation from others which is often painful.

We live in a goal-oriented society that supports and encourages striving and competition, the complete opposite of our intrinsic nature to seek quiet and peace, to learn to tap into our own lucid truth. As you entrain your natural ability to hear your inner voice, the voice of truth within you, a space of tranquility opens up infinite possibilities. This quiet space is where we need to be in order to restore peace and dispel chaos and chatter from within our minds. Cultivating inner trust, patience, self-love and acceptance is what this journey to discovering your truth is all about.

The gift of learning to trust your own voice of truth is more precious than any material or external measurement we will ever achieve. Developing your inner constitution is what makes all external abundance authentic and meaningful, creating deeply connected relationships, fostering and magnifying what matters most to you in your journey to embrace authentic love and happiness in the world.

Paradoxically, as you discover your own inner voice and freedom and the unique purpose of the "who" you were truly created to be, these untold riches living within the vibrancy of your soul will empower and stir the passions within you, inspiring and serving every relationship and experience you co-create in your reality and world, in ways which serve the truth and highest good for all!

Whatever option you choose, whether you decide to read this book privately, create an on-line interactive support community, or form a weekly study group, read this when you are present and in a quiet heart place where you will not be interrupted. Begin each reading getting comfortable, breathing in and breathing out, relaxing and in gratitude for several quiet moments dedicated just for you. Ask your heart to speak to you, to remain open to the lesson that best serves your need in this particular moment and watch the truth, your truth, begin to unfold itself within you.

Remember learning any great work or mastering requires individual commitment and discipline, which is 100 percent up to you. There is a community of support, tools and practices available through the website for The Truth, and The Way 2 The Truth's, The Journey Within teachings at www.TheTruthMovie.tv and www.MyHeartConnects.com for your questions, struggles and celebrations to be shared and supported in your choice to create a new reality *within* the experience of your world. OneTeam Humanity is committed to empowering all, knowing that collectively we can celebrate and support one another on our individual journeys exploring our deepest truths, highest callings and understanding of who we uniquely were all created to be.

This book will be of the greatest value to work within an open forum of learning, confirming the powerful and strong technology that a community support platform provides.

HOW TO READ THIS AS A STUDY GROUP

I would suggest an initial weekly commitment of 12 weeks, in two-hour sessions. What we now know through studies in the field of neuroscience is that it takes about 28 days of concentrated focus to begin to establish new neuropathways and life-affirming (or not) habits into our life. An initial 12-week program will set you on the path of seeing the results of your new thoughts, beliefs and truths being shared within the relationships of your life. This will also create the necessary momentum to firmly root and ground new ways of being within you as you encourage others to share their journey of becoming more with you.

Community is the strong technology that can hold and support you when you meet with resistance sure to come your way as others feel the shift in energy dynamics within your life and relationships. MyHeartConnects (www.MyHeartConnects.com) is a guided step-by-step patented Behavioral Change Community platform which supports you on a bio-chemical and neuro-chemical level in repatterning the self-sabataging thoughts, emotions and beliefs, to rewire your internal biocircuitry, changing the way your perceive the reality of your relationships, and world.

There is a collective, exponential power that a community has to support you when you are weak and have lost your way, and visa versa, so you can be there to support and encourage when others have lost their way.

Community is a strong technology and offers a powerful mechanism to hold and support one another in the journey to becoming more.

> *"The journey to becoming more of the "who" as only you were created to be begins when you choose to experience living life rather than life living you!"*

STUDY GROUP SUGGESTION: WEEK ONE

Begin each meeting after a brief visit, by spending 5 minutes in silence together to get comfortable, breathing to relax and open up the field of heart coherence that will prepare your mind to be ready for each teaching. This can be done as a silent or guided mediation. You can transfer the role of guide or facilitator to each member of your group, or remain open to find what best serves the needs of your unique community. Begin your first meeting with each member sharing for up to two minutes each, what they want to accomplish during this meeting as well as sharing any particular celebration or struggle present in their life at the time.

Find at least one person and ask them to be your accountability partner for the week. Commit to one another for a daily five-minute phone conversation. This is for us to outwardly declare and hold one another in intention, prayer and accountability as we build and entrain our minds, create new habits, and develop our inner resources and strength so that we can experience the deepening of commitment and benefits that true community brings into our life.

Begin with *Chapter One, The Truth Lies Within*, reading through the entire chapter aloud. We all learn differently, so seek to honor and value the individual differences we each have, finding ways to meet the needs of each member of your community. Work with each chapter for at least four weeks so you can come together weekly to share the progress and celebrations you are making or discuss and work to support one another on the challenges that you are experiencing.

Each chapter is different. Some chapters are much more reflective and others have many experiential exercises you can share with your community. Becoming more aligned with who you truly are is an organic, unique process, many times different for each one of us. The key benefit of working in a community is to become aware, to see into, your conditioned patterns for competition. Just noticing your own internal judgments and patterns for competition will support you in sharing and releasing your life-alienating conditioned patterns of relating.

Move forward as the group finds consensus of their internal understanding of an exercise, process or chapter. You'll know when it is time to move forward when you know. There is no right/wrong, or good/bad way to experience this process.

Know that there will be an urge to measure, judge and compare the progress of others to our own. There will be some who feel safer in a community to share openly and others who will need more time to become transparent and authentic to what's real and alive within them. The purpose of community, as with all relationships, is to see the reflections that we give one another, as well as learning to release our own boundaries, judgments, and control structures to develop a kindred trust, a growing curiosity, and collective exponential strength. Through community, we begin to see that while our strategies may vary to meet our needs, as well as our conditioning and painful life experiences are unique to each one of us, our commonality exists in the sharing of our same universal interconnected and interdependent needs.

A community offers such an amazing gift for each one of us who are all at varying degrees of wisdom, understanding, and life experiences. Community contributes to life and one another in such a way that supports and holds us each accountable to living as our highest purpose and integrity. As we each do our own work, the exponential power that community provides allows for an organic common vision of truth to be realized.

Share the natural urges for our subconscious mind to resist as you share with your accountability partner the diversions and distractions that always seem to get in the way of disciplining a new habit, practice and commitment that will transform your life experience. As we learn to support one another in non-judgmental and empathetic ways, we encourage our new voice we are finding within to express the language of our inner landscape of truth, strengthening our new muscles and growing trust that is being entrained for the greatest journey and marathon of a lifetime! The journey to becoming more of the "who" as only you were created to be begins when you choose to experience living life rather than life living you!

Life is to wonder...
...and life's wonder is always created in the choices we make between love and fear.

I
THE TRUTH LIES WITHIN

Truth resides in every human heart, and one has to search for it there, and to be guided by truth as one sees it. But no one has a right to coerce others to act according to his own view of the truth.
—MAHATMA GANDHI

WHY WE JOURNEY WITHIN

We embark upon this journey within to truly come to know ourselves as unique, authentic individuals, and to anchor to a greater context, the grand schema of interconnected life that lives through all of us. You cannot do one without the other. We do this to discover the truth of who we were created to be. We do this to discover what it means to live a rich and meaningful life. We do this to cultivate our genuine sense of happiness and well-being. It is only when we remove ourselves from the outward chaos of the world, and turn inward, to address our painful reactions, symptoms, and triggers, that we can then emerge with a greater capacity to experience life more completely, more deeply, connected to all its glorious facets. During the journey, we find hidden treasure deep within the sea of ourselves to enjoy, to create, and share the bounty of our connected life in a way that expresses and experiences our grandest thoughts, dreams, and purposes—to experience the Universe of truth that lies within each one of us.

The Way 2 The Truth, The Journey Within will lead you to your own empowerment, truth, and potency, giving you essential life skills and tools to directly access higher levels of mind consciousness. You will build reservoirs of inner strength and begin to re-pattern life-alienating thoughts, conditioning, and limiting beliefs, to establish your own personal inner Declaration of Independence and Constitution. Truth has a measurable and certain frequency to it, a lightness, which we actually feel and are naturally drawn to. Truth always serves the highest good for all, while also serving and supporting our unique reason and purpose in life. That is why when we hear truth, it resonates within us clearly. We hear the truth, feeling the vibration of it. Truth is something we just know whether science or reasoning can confirm it or not.

Our relationships and life circumstances provide each one of us the perfect arena to set out on our own exclusive, matchless, yet interconnected inward journey to becoming more. The Truth explores the convergence of science and spirituality to discuss, demonstrate, and teach us how to apply these scientific breakthroughs in the fields of modern quantum physics, neuroimmunology, neurosciences, and neurobiology, converging now with our world's most treasured ancient wisdoms, revealing to us a very different way of being. A new story unfolds about us as powerful co-creators—exploring the truth of who we truly are.

We embark on this journey within to reawaken the dreamer within. To awaken your awareness—your truth that knows who you are, before you were constricted and confined by the limitations now governing a false identity and reality of our world that is denying you to live life as your greatness.

What if everything you ever needed, and more, is within you to be the infinite being that you know you are? To move that which is unseen into your life living reality to experience your greatness and live in your highest truth?

What if each and every one of us, living in our truth, together, can shatter this false reality that has limited us to playing small?

Every limitation you have ever had is simply greatness that you have not yet recognized into your life living reality.

Through the silent language of our connected hearts, we have the power to co-create the abundance and happiness we so desire to transform our deeply interconnected world. The true purpose of our life experiences is to all be co-creators of our reality in our personal and extended world. How you contribute as an intricate puzzle piece, a part of the One Power of the All That Is, is completely up to you. You are the bearer of gifts and talents that cannot be found in the blueprint/fingerprint of anyone else. You are an invaluable missing link that can contribute to co-creating a game-changing solution to the greatest challenges facing our world today. Your truth and reason for being here at this unparalleled time in history is what the journey within is about to uncover.

The Way 2 The Truth, The Journey Within will enable you to explore your connection to your highest Self, to our collective mind and consciousness. You are being provided with life skills to access through self-tools a possibility to live in a way that is aligned, energizing, life-affirming, heart-centered, supportive, and forgiving of Self and of others. You don't need a teacher. Your own perfect teacher resides within every cell of You. It is that which is within your relationships and life experiences that together constructs your one-of-a-kind, customized classroom for inquiry.

Ask yourself the following questions and then pause and take time to reflect on your own life and relationships to see reflections and answers:

- Have you become dependent on looking for answers for love, happiness, and approval outside of yourself?

- Do you feel removed from life, not fully engaged, as if you're looking at the world through some kind of screen or haze?

- Are you unable to really feel joy, sadness, or a sense of connection?

- Do you feel as if you are living a "false" life?

Answering "yes" to any or even all of these questions only proves that you too have been steeped in outdated tribal mindsets that have, to date, shaped a false reality and truth of our world. But true exponential transformation is within reach, in fact, it is within! A whole new possibility for seeing, experiencing, and transforming your world lies inside of you, accessible by only you.

Through reading, and applying the life-tools throughout this book, you will be learning how to bring about more heart-coherence and awareness into your life. This means you will have better integration between your conscious choices, wishes, and desires. You will release the subconscious patterns of conditioned reactions that hold you back and block experiencing full-throttle abundant living. You will find greater potency, enrichment of experience, empowerment and deeper, authentic and connected relationships, as you actually *shift* your presence and conscious experience to reality and to life.

This world is not some grand, utopian, pie in the sky. The Truth is...it is the world that lies *within* your inherent nature, your "inner-net." The subconscious conditioning, fears, and lies you've been told wash away into the ocean of your essential nature and Self, where only abstract potential and unbound awareness exists.

Collectively, the reality of our present world is a reflection of the combined thinking of our human race. And what is that reality? Does it not appear as one that is flawed, overrun, and bubbling over with doubt, greed, fear, debt, war, panic, and negative thoughts? We have exactly the peace, happiness, and abundance to match our current modes of thinking, tribal mindsets, limiting conditioning and our resulting behaviors. Our environment reflects the degree of love we offer it. Our geo-economic systems, corporations, and world leaders all reflect our current level of collective awareness, or lack thereof.

Deepak Chopra states, "When a culture is constrained, its predominant emphasis is on profit-making, ruthless competition, economic imperialism, extreme nationalism, military conflict, violence and fear." Sound familiar? But could the reality of this truth actually be creating the essential drivers (motivations) to awaken innovations, stir our yearnings to express our deepest passions, unique gifts, and grandest dreams to co-create new holistic models of relating and working together, which are more aligned to what serves the highest good for all, rather than the elite few?

By evaluating these global economic and political systems collapsing all around us, we can see what is not working, to implement new, emergent systems that do.

Essential to our victory, individually and collectively, we must journey within to make it possible for a different way of being in our world.

We are all co-creators of this reality. We contribute by first starting the journey within oneself, each in our own unique way. Then as we begin shifting our own inner reality, creating more authentic love and peace within, we can then reach out one-to-one, then many-to-many.

For the first time in human history, spreading tools, sharing transparent dialogue, and information to learn, grow, and begin working together as a united power is now possible. In ways that we are only beginning to understand, our "inner-net" within us can now connect to our global "internet" consciousness to co-create the necessary united global community and collective voice needed in these unprecedented times.

A CHOICE TO CHOOSE LOVE OR FEAR

Your first stepping stone on the path to your empowerment and freedom lies in your pause between your stimulus, the "triggers" of your life, and your response. It is in this pause, by choosing to create the "gap," that you can tap into your authentic truth to choose to respond to life with conscious intention vs. reacting through the filters of your subconscious conditioned programming. Emotions aren't just reactions, they are choices. Your freedom, peace, and access to full conscious awareness of choice, comes in this moment between stimulus and response. You have within you the ability to choose to stop being thrown about on the rollercoaster ride of emotions that govern your subconscious reactions in life—the ones that wreck havoc on your emotional well-being and your relationships.

To stop, to pause, between your stimulus and response, creating a "gap," is the key to the mastery of genuine happiness in life. It is this simple, yet profound, understanding and application that you take control of your life to choose to respond in love over fear. When something triggers a negative emotional response from within you, stop and ask yourself one simple question: "Is this emotion arising from love or fear?" Fear is rooted in your subconscious—it's the lie of "truth" that someone told you about you. You will recognize your fear by the vibration, although you may not know the literal *source*. It feels like a "stick"—an "ouch." It feels heavy, creates unease, density, yuckiness, tension, accelerated heart rate, anxiety, or confusion; an incoherence within you.

Love is the feeling of lightness, ease, joy, glory, freedom, celebration and fun. Fear is not the opposite of love; it is the *absence* of love. Anger, resentment, jealousy, hatred, aggression, violence and unforgiveness are just a few of the many disguises of fear. As you become capable of tuning into your awareness and recognizing your fear, you become fluid and empowered to maintain the flow of your inner peace and joy, as you choose to act with love. To make a loving choice, rather than continue in the same cyclic fear-based patterns of reactions, you gain control over your conditioned autonomic (not subject to voluntary control) subconscious patterned responses. The responses that rob you from experiencing the truth of who you are. When you do, you are operating in an aware and conscious manner and you are also creating new neural pathways in your brain that create new possibilities for you. You transform yourself, and your reality, as these new behaviors literally create new patterns in your brain. You will know life is taking on new meaning, as you face the same relationships and events that were previous triggers that tested you, and drawing upon your newfound awareness, you now choose love and possibility. Your expanding capacity to remain in joy, calm, and peace means you are choosing love more and more, re-energizing your awareness, and opening up and creating a new reality as you continue the journey.

Fear governs our current world. It's apparent in policies that rely upon the imposition of economic manipulation and sanctions, preemptive militaristic air strikes, and social dysfunction. "Wayward" nations might revolt. The powers-that-be act as overlords, exercising a power-over paradigm of governing, not surprisingly, that perpetuates more fear and mistrust by those over whom power is exerted. Stock markets are propelled by fear as stocks are sold quickly in anticipation of failure, bought on impulse to not "miss out" on potential profit. In the United States, 70% of all trading is programmed trading. So, at best, the "small guy" can only hope to survive the trends that programmed trading mandates. True awareness into what exactly we are buying and selling (as witnessed in the sub-prime mortgage crisis) is often lost in frenzy and misunderstanding.

We've become a humanity that reacts rather than reflects. On the home front within our families, our jobs, and our world, we tend to let most everything in our lives be governed by crisis management and time pressure. The simple truth is that we've been so conditioned to act in ways that make us feel productive, while suffering the cost of true connection to our creation mind—the source of where all well-being and meaning of purpose are fed from. So life becomes routine as we do what we think we're suppose to do, and be, to feel fulfilled and happy. Yet, somehow we know, deep inside, there's something missing. Untapped within you is the truth of who you really are. This wisdom possesses the power to unleash your fullest potential into the reality of your life. In actuality, all your "doings" have disconnected you from "being" the truth of who you were created to be. "Multi-tasking" has been reinforced by the media and our culture at large. Worn as some badge of strength, these fractured behaviors actually rob us and our families from living from our true power, essence, and truth.

One common example is the "soccer mom" who runs around town in her mini-van or SUV, schlepping her kids from activity to activity. While this is a perfect example of productivity and dedication, where is the heart substance? Where are the examples of Moms (or Dads) creating deep, quality interactions and connections and then modeling that connection to their children?

We are caught up in distractions and living that runs contrary to our inner blueprint and development, our evolution if you will. This dis-ease (literally meaning a lack of ease) and disconnection is reflected everywhere in the world we see today.

On an intimate level, how many of us feel pangs of vulnerability and insecurity when we find ourselves in love? Many buy into romantic love as they get carried away with the highs, only to get dragged down by the draining energy of the lows that resurrect painful hurts and triggers from our past we thought we had long since gotten over. And many of us wonder, at the end of the day, what real lasting love is and is it achievable?

Life and love was not designed to be routine. Life is love and it is designed to thrive, living through you, to contribute, to create, and to evolve your capacity to experience your essence and truest nature; the truth of who you truly are.

Experiencing transformation and authentic love results from tapping into the infinite realm of possibility created as you begin to listen and inquire into what is really alive and true for you. Transformation is the direct experience of understanding and being in connection to part of the one creation consciousness of the "All That Is." An act of bringing forth or inventing, it is inherently infinite and without limitation. This is the ultimate experience and expression of being life. This inward act of listening to your own reactions, through the mirrors of your relationships and circumstances, possesses everything you will ever need to teach you how to experience and create real, authentic love as your reality.

Real transformation is possible. Within the DNA of every cell in your body, you are perfectly wired as a human being to do just that! In our evolution as a species, the greatest opportunity for individual and collective growth comes through analyzing ourselves to transform our conditioned self-limiting thoughts and beliefs. The choice to choose love and commit to living the truth of who you were created to be gives you the power to change the world every single moment of your life!

THE SCIENCES BEHIND WHY WE LIMIT OURSELVES

Neuroscientists around the world have found that our mind processes about 400 billion calculations per second. Yet, at any one time, we are only aware of 2,000 of the 400,000,000,000 bits of information. This all is being processed by the six hundred kilometers of blood vessels linked to trillions of synaptic biophoton emissions between the neurons within our brain[1]. Thus, at any one time, we are only conscious of a mere 0.00005 percent of what our brain is really doing. Ninety-five to ninety-eight percent of our behaviors and choices are actually being run by our subconscious-conditioned programs, located in the limbic region of the brain. It is here that our programming, the behaviors and beliefs taught and demonstrated during our early childhood, are stored. It is our negative programming that undercuts the conscious choices we make to be positive and to live as fully empowered healthy adults.

As young children we were natural explorers of our world and questioned everything—our minds, our world, and lived as imagined possibilities. At some point, that curiosity subsided and we came to believe we knew or understood the world. Well, what do you suppose happened to that curiosity and who or what answered the questions we had that today defines our world? Where were our beliefs, values, and the shape of our character formed? They were formed by nearly everything with which we came into contact through our childhood. In truth, your reality was not created by you.

A profound breakthrough in the field of neuroscience has discovered our "mirror neurons" system. We've discovered that we learn by imitating and mirroring what we are taught. Our mirror neurons explain why when I ask you to hold up two fingers, those most influenced under Anglo Saxon cultural conditioning will hold up their middle and index fingers. However, in rural South Africa, 90 percent of Africans will use their small and ring fingers when holding up two fingers. Why, because their role models, and their parent's role models, mirrored the number two that way. Our sender's motor movements are picked up, visually or energetically, recorded and then stored in our brains as "somatic markers," and mirrored (learned) by the receiver. Mirror neurons

---

1 Ian Rheeder, *Psychologies of Successful Leaders*, 2010

also explain why we yawn when we see someone else yawn. The same goes for when we smile or feel grumpy when we see/feel someone else smile or act grumpy.

> *Ancient wisdom has told us we were created in the image (mirror) of our Creator. Neuroscience has now discovered we learn through mirroring. How perfect—created to mirror, and created in Creator's image. Through the discoveries in the fields of neuro, quantum, and bio-science, not only can you access your subconscious mind's tape player, but you now have the self-tools to access and uninstall these false programs of "truth" running the life negating cycles in your life, to literally re-mirror and reinstall your new programs of truth.*

Another profound discovery in the field of bio-science by Bruce Lipton, PhD., a cell biologist, featured in *The Truth, The Journey Within* film, chose a path less traveled and studied cells by looking at how the environment influences the expression of cells; mass science, working through the lenses of Newtonian based principles, was only looking externally at how genes control cells.

Bio-science had already agreed that we're all genetically identical. So Bruce pondered, what controls the identity the cells take on? The evidence discovered from his breakthrough work has zero ambiguity and is very clear: *"the fate of the cells is primarily determined by the environment that cells find themselves in."*

Bruce's work challenged an entire system of dogma referred to as "the central dogma, which is the pillar of modern bio-medicine today." The central dogma, still being taught in all the text books of modern today, simply establishes this false "truth" of belief: Your life is determined by the fate, and lot, you received from the DNA you received at the moment of conception. This false message has created a mass tribal mindset of belief, reinforced by an archaic science of belief that everything is separate and that our thinking or beliefs have no effect on the outcome, environment, or our experience of reality. This belief perpetuates a false "truth"—we are powerless victims of our DNA, our circumstances, and world. This "truth" has been killing off our intrinsic, irreducibly connected design of nature's "truth;" we create our experience in the reality of our world through our thoughts and emotions.

Did you know that every gene has over 30,000 expressions it can choose at its identity? We now know that through intentioned thought and belief, you can re-write the way your genes express themselves in your health field through intentioned conscious heart/mind coherence. This is good news! We are no longer victims of a random world; we are powerful co-creators.

Albert Einstein said, "The field is the sole governing agency of the particle."

The invisible magnetic field governing existence is coined The Matrix by the founder of quantum theory, Max Planck. Also called The Field, The Divine Matrix, today, this field in modern science is recognized as the convergence of what man has referred to, and known, a point where spirit and the field of creation consciousness are One.

One-third of all medical healings are due to the placebo effect. We also know that what is coined the nocebo effect is fed from a governing field of negative energy thought patterns. These continued negative fields of thoughts and beliefs, science has now confirmed, attributed to physical disease in your mind/body/heart/heart system.

Did you know that 70% of your subconscious thoughts are the negative "truths" downloaded to you from your childhood and are running and feeding the information systems of your mind/body/heart system that are co-creating the expressions of your life? Scientifically, these cellular "somatic markers" of recorded programs are actually affecting and governing the subconscious limiting patterns of autonomic physiological/psychological emotional reactions and false beliefs of "truth" that are restricting you and running the co-creation of your living experience, defined as the reality of your life.

The subconscious mind records the experiences of "truth" you received during your formative years, sending messages like a conductor in the symphony of the trillions of synapses in your brain that directs and fires off messages that govern your mind/body/heart system. The subconscious mind processes information ONE MILLION TIMES faster and has dominion over your conscious mind. Why? Because your subconscious mind runs every single detail that runs your body system that supports life itself.

Ninety-five percent of the day your subconscious is running your life. Until approximately age 6, nearly 100% of everything we're told, see and sense from our primary programmers (parents or primary caretakers), and secondary programmers (relatives, peers, teachers, religious teachings, media influence and environment), is mirrored within us, and then encoded into our mind/body/heart system through our somatic markers, which gets recorded as fact.[2] This feature of our development is simply part of our biological evolution. It is a critical component to our long-term survival and learning. Our subconscious mind is a primitive area of the brain whose job is to keep us safe. To do this, what's often referred to in scientific terms as our "reptilian brain" records this information like "fire is hot" and "falling hurts" as indisputable facts. These Laws of the Universe then enable us to react more readily in the event that we encounter the same threat at a later point in time. In the event that crisis strikes, it is this survival area of the brain that takes over in an attempt to save us. The problem is this part of our brain lacks the cognitive ability to know whether what we are experiencing is really happening at that moment, or if it is simply a memory being replayed from our thoughts.

Just like anti-spyware on our computer senses a potential threat and warns us, if anything we sense with our five senses, as well as our intuitive sixth sense, triggers that recorded "fact" marker within us, our mind/body/heart reacts as though it were happening in real time. So, during your formative years, when someone says something hurtful such as, "Don't be so stupid," "Little boys/girls don't cry," "Life's a bitch and then you die" or

---

[2] Lipton, Bruce Ph.D., *The Biology of Belief—Unleashing the Power of Consciousness, Matter & Miracles*

"You're ugly," our subconscious mind has no capacity to discern or evaluate what is true for us and records that message as fact. From here on out, these so-called "truths" will subconsciously rule your life! No matter how far we believe we've come as adults, no matter how much we've learned and think we've consciously changed, no matter the hours we've spent in therapy, these false perceptions and beliefs will continue to run the show until we make the choice to uninstall, seek, and be, our own truth.

By nature's design these falsehoods continue to bubble up through your consciousness, through your reactions to life's circumstances, acting as triggers to create the impulse to inquire within.

You may think you are in control of your intentioned conscious wishes and desires. You are literally held hostage, as hijacked captives, by your brain's autonomic responses to your embedded somatic markers and mirror neuron systems. To learn anything, you were wired to mirror the programming and conditioning of your role models, which created your belief system—the stories about life—that are passed down to you during your formative years. This creates a fracture between your true authentic Self and the identity self that someone else, or the world's messages, told you that you "should" be. This truth lends a much more profound meaning to the ancient teaching, "do not make friends with an angry man, lest you learn his ways and set a snare for your soul," as well as understanding how the mirrors of false beliefs and tribal mindsets have become passed on from our actions of modeling, and mirroring, both in positive and negative actions, from generation to generation. Paradoxically, what is nature's divine protection mechanism, sometimes necessary for our very survival, also has the capacity to become our greatest ally. By learning to entrain new positive somatic markers, we un-condition the innocently encoded life-alienating messages given to us from our role models that no longer serve the highest truth of who we uniquely were created to be. You have the ability to begin re-mirroring and re-patterning your own beliefs and possibilities. Only you can know or live in the highest truth of who you are. You can end the negative self-perpetuating cycles of illusion once and for all, to co-create a reality and future worth choosing, for yourself and for our future generations to come.

Why do these two minds often appear to compete? If your subconscious is playing a tape recording program of a limiting belief system of "truth" that is currently in your being, for example: "I'm not worthy," "I don't deserve...," "it is weak to express vulnerable feelings," "I'm not strong, beautiful, blah, blah, blah," these false "truths" run in the background—incoherent with your true nature, the real "truth" you are and were created to be.

Your subconscious is simply a tape player, playing back what it knows as "truth," acting as a grand conductor, directing your mind/body/heart from the programs installed from age 0-6, the "truth" as it is, until it isn't. You can talk until you're blue in the face, but your subconscious mind can not hear your positive self-talk unless and until that self-talk, when you press the record button, is in alignment—coherent—with what it knows is true. Period. Your subconscious' job is to govern the systems that protect your very existence, so you have to become the master programmer and re-install new coherent programs of aligned "truth."

The subconscious mind plays a starring role not only when it comes to your psychological well-being, but also in your physiological and biological systems. As the conductor of the 50 trillion plus cells in your body, the subconscious regulates everything from your heartbeat to cellular regeneration to the development and healing of disease. It is here, on this level, that the programmed beliefs you carry actually commune on a cellular level with the very building blocks creating the reality of your life. In this way, your beliefs create your perceived reality and actually have the power to affect and infect not only your body, but how you experience your reality in every relationship and event happening in your life. You can never be anything more, or less, than what your mind believes. Want a different outcome? Change your thoughts and beliefs.

Albert Einstein, in his understanding of our quantum mirrored world, said two critical quotes to link two key components of "truth" that ultimately leads us to our freedom from being ruled by the limitations of false "truths" within our subconscious mind:

> *"A human being is part of the whole that we call the Universe, a part limited in time and space. He experiences himself, his thoughts and feelings, as something separated from the rest—a kind of optical illusion of his consciousness."*

> *"Insanity: doing the same thing over and over again and expecting different results."*

The double-edge sword is that we learn through mirroring, which is the gift, when what we learn is coherent and aligned to our intrinsic design of serving life and love. The critical dichotomy of insanity exists because of how we learn, creating a tribal mindset that has kept us stuck in multi-millenial darkness; perpetuating false systems of belief that all our "answers" of truth reside somewhere outside ourselves with the "teachers." So, as we are triggered and feel incoherence—separation—we have been conditioned to continually search outside ourselves. In pain, frustration or exhaustion, after all these months, even years, of self-help, of counseling, of positive affirmations, do you still find cycles of relating in relationships that have not yielded the fruits of a life you know deep down is possible? Or, in desperation, have you given up or cried out to God or Universe help me change; this tape player is broken!?

Traditional psychology, like old science, wants to study, take apart, and study the external factors, the why and how things are this way, and how these external factors control your life. Even in the awareness of the why, and how, do not all these forms of self-help, counseling, coaching and seminars still find you basically stuck in the same patterns of relationships, experiencing the same life reality? Your answers and freedom lie within you.

You want to truly transform your life? You have to learn how to engage the tape player in the record mode when the subconscious mind receptor filters are relaxed, open, and receptive to listen, hear and install your new "truths." Temporal tapping is your first energy clearing process and self-tool presented in this work. Temporal Tapping is like engaging the super-learning button on your tape recorder.

As science and ancient wisdom converge, we gain access to the possibility of living aligned and coherent to who we truly are, individually and collectively—that deep down, in our heart of hearts we know as "truth." That is why the human spirit has confirmed throughout millenniums man's capacity to rise above adversity, tribal mindset, or even the laws of perceived nature, demonstrating that we can defy the forces of mass conditioned "truth," and watch a 100 pound woman lift a car off a child in the clutches of death, or be cured "miraculously" of a terminal illness through the exponential power of prayer and belief.

YOUR HEART IS YOUR CENTRAL BRAIN INTELLIGENCE

There is a new field of neurocardiology which has discovered that your heart has its own intrinsic nervous system sufficiently complex enough to consider the heart as having its own brain that has both a short term and long term memory. In fact, the same recording techniques that are used to demonstrate memory and neurons in the hippocampus, which is well known for long term memory, have been used to demonstrate the short and long term memory in the neurons within the heart itself.

Research over the last few years has found that the fields generated from our heart are communicating not only as the key brain directing the body's physiological/psychological responses, but we now can measure that our emotional field is radiating this information and constantly sending/receiving information between people.

Everyone has experienced walking into a room and even before you catch the body language cue, you get a sense, or you feel, wow, this is really a nice environment. Or, opposite to that experience, you know someone is in a bad mood or just had an argument, it just feels tense in the room. *What's important to understand is that this information field is going on all the time. It doesn't matter if you believe it or not, or know it or not, this information is still being communicated energetically and is effecting the people around us.*

We now know the heart communicates with the brain four primary ways. In each of the ways, the heart profoundly influences brain function and how we think and feel. To give the power of our heart brain a tangible reference point, the electromagnetic frequencies that the heart generates, every time it beats, are 5,000 times stronger than the field generated by the brain! Science, through the invent of the magnetometer, can measure the heart fields several feet away from the body (only limited by the devices capabilities), whereas the field generated from the brain can only be measured a couple of inches away.

The data in the last 18-20 years of research is overwhelmingly clear; we are fundamentally and deeply connected. Not just with each other, but with the greater planetary environment itself.

Because emotions aren't just reactions, they're choices; you now can choose to become heart-coherent—aligning what your feeling to what your thinking—by syncing your heart's conscious choice of intention through generating life-affirming emotions and attitudes to your conscious mind. This sends new signals to the brain which begins to repattern the brain's limiting subconscious programming markers of false "truth" in your brain's tape recorder.

To really gain true empowerment in your life, choosing to pause between your stimulus and response, creating the "gap," you can align your heart intelligence to feelings like love, care, appreciation, gratitude, and compassion, which then directs the bodies physiological responses to generate neurochemicals that regenerate us rather than emotions that drain us, shifting our entire heart-field in a profound and measurable way.

UNINSTALLING AND REINSTALLING NEW TRUTHS WITH THE TEMPORAL TAPPING TECHNIQUE:

The brainwave state of children from 0-6 years of age is Theta, the state of imagination. Theta is known as the hypnogogic trance state. We know now that a child learns by mirroring its environment. So for the first six years of life, everything a child takes in through its senses, from the environment, become the downloads—the learned "truths"—taught to us by "other" people, both life-affirming and life-negating "truths." These stored markers now become the behaviors that we play out into our adulthood that are sabotaging us from experiencing our authentic "truth" and happiness in our life today.

Here's just one powerful example of how we ensnare a false Western tribal mindset of "truth" into our life. As an adult every time you're sick, your conditioned programming tells you if you want to get well you need to go to the doctor, or reach for a pill. The authentic "truth" is that your body is a fully wired healing machine designed to function at the highest level of creation consciousness, when you learn to listen to it. It is these conditioned negative "truths" installed into your mind/body/heart system that have constructed all of these roadblocks that deny you your intrinsic ability to hear the symptom to locate the point of creation originating source, to clear the limiting belief so you can heal.

Make no mistake, medicine and the monetary body—the multi-trillion dollar game that governs our "healthcare" system today is absolutely focused on us staying sick and not knowing the truth of who we are.

We've been so programmed by these tribal mindsets to be disempowered, devalued, and oppressed by our false "truths" running the programs of our life, individually and societally. Until now... Until we are not!

The way to shift your life today is to delete the life-negating and limiting programs of "truth" and re-install new programs of belief.

TEMPORAL TAPPING TECHNIQUE
This self-suggestion process was developed by George Goodhardt, founder of Applied Kinesiology. This Tapping Acupressure Technique combines an ancient Chinese acupressure technique and modern energy psychology.

The Temporal Tap affects the brain at each meridian by sedating the triple warmer, because you tap in the opposite direction of its natural flow. It is your triple warmer that governs your body system. By tapping, you calm the part of the autonomic nervous system that acts as the spyware that fights (protects) to maintain your "truth" records, bypassing the filter system of your current "truth" so you can release and uninstall the limiting old "truth," and reinstall and mirror into your receptor cellular memory your new programs of "truth."

This meridian-based healing method works at the level of cellular memory at the point of creation of when and where the false and limiting "truth" is stored. This simple self-tool process can be used for the treatment of a large spectrum of problems:

- Allergies
- Emotional and Bodily Trauma
- Anger Triggers and Outbursts
- Fear, Pain and Related Panic Attacks
- Depression
- Addictions and Compulsive Habits
- Eating Disorders
- Building Confidence, Optimism and Self-Esteem
- Building Your Auto-Immune System

THE TWO-STEP 5-MINUTE TEMPORAL TAP PROCESS:
Begin with the left side of the brain hemisphere to calm and bypass the autonomic nervous system's filter that fights (protects) to maintain your current "truth" of being.

It helps to first create the new positive statement, in your own language, so you can reframe the positive statement from a negative view to begin this process on the left side of the brain to relax the filters to receive the new install of positive "truth."

The left side of your brain hemisphere is the critical and judging side. Tapping on your left side of your temporal sphenoidal (TS) will relax and sedate your autonomic nervous system to bypass the filter system, to uninstall your current negative "truth" that is currently running, which opens up the receptor cell memory to create a new somatic marker, to record your new program of "truth."

Begin tapping the left side of your TS bone, beginning just in front of the ear, at the temple, and proceed around the TS line and finish near the base of the skull.

The illustration below outlines the meridian points.

TEMPORAL TAP MERIDIAN POINTS

With your middle three fingers, tap the meridian line hard enough to feel a firm contact and a bounce. Repeat five times, and tap in rhythm to your statement of "truth."

On the left side of your TS, you want to reframe the positive "truth" statement in a negative context, what you no longer are, or are choosing, that you will be installing in the present-tense.

The examples below are your positive statements framed in a negative viewpoint.

Examples:

* Under pressure I no longer respond in fear, or panic when I feel attacked.

* I am no longer choosing the belief I am unworthy or unloveable.

* I no longer am choosing to see money and my work as opposing forces.

* I no longer make choices of food that do not honor my new sexy body.

TO INSTALL POSITIVE "TRUTHS"

Begin tapping the right side of your temporal sphenoidal (TS) bone, beginning just in front of the ear, at the temple, and proceed around the TS line and finish near the base of the skull.

The right side of your brain hemisphere is where you will receive, install and strengthen your positive "truth," in a present-tense (as though it already is) statement. This statement is best framed as simple and in your native language so your mind recognizes it's you.

See positive statement examples below:

* Under pressure, I am calm, alert and grounded.

* I am totally worthy of joy and love in my life.

* I can make loads of money doing what I love.

* I am healthy and can maintain my slim figure.

With your middle three fingers, tap hard enough to feel a firm contact and a bounce. Repeat five times, and tap in rhythm to your positive statement of "truth."

How long shall I do this process? How long will it last?

Begin daily by committing 5 minutes a day, twice a day. It takes your mind 26-28 days to install new energy set patterns of truth habits into your cellular being. It may take many days before you observe and notice that your mind/body/heart nervous system uplevels and reorganizes itself. You should begin to see/feel a deep response in your habit field. Also during the day, if you catch yourself in negative thoughts or feelings, have a compulsive urge, or notice a reactive emotional habit playing out, use the process to quickly shift your default programming.

It depends on how deeply your subconscious "truth" is embedded and how long it has been playing back the recorded "truths" that are manifesting as the reactive patterns in your life. You may want to set a calendar timer in your phone to keep you on track.

Each one of us have a unique blueprint, and we each start from a different place in our overall physical and emotional health field of well-being. If you find that you are not finding success, change the way you're languaging your statement, and make sure your mind is wrapped around what you are saying, not thinking about something else (or that is what you will be installing). Make sure you are speaking in the native language of your age 0-6 child.

As we move forward in upleveling our creation consciousness, individually and collectively, our participatory Universe will continue to bring in new energy frequencies and healing energy clearing techniques to support each new level we choose to bring into our awareness field.

Our hope as individuals, and as a collective humanity, lies in our ability to re-pattern our mind/body/heart to respond, rather than react to archaic, tribal, life-alienating somatic record patterns. By embedding new somatic markers of information, aligned to the highest truth of who we were created to be, everything in life becomes a gift and opportunity of great potential.

Thanks to the quantum leaps we've made in sophisticated measuring systems, like functional Magnetic Resonance Imaging brain scanners (fMRI), we can now peer into how the mind/body/heart connection really works and see how what we think, act, and feel infects and affects the reality of the world we live in. This science is solving the mystery surrounding the Law of Attraction and the power of positive thinking. We now have science combined with a deeper connection to our wisdom teachings that empowers us to evolve past tribal mindsets that have, until now, limited our abilities individually and collectively to bring new experiences of reality into our lives.

As you free your limiting patterns and beliefs, rebooting and uninstalling unwanted programs is really quite simple and easily achieved. With willingness and discipline, you can rearrange the cluttered closet of your subconscious mind to make room in your mind/body/heart to begin dropping its defenses, opening the doors of infinite potentiality to experience the full empowerment, purpose, and totality of you—the truth of who you are!

The human brain is an open system and flow of energy that constantly takes in nutrients, light, air, water and information, as well as input from our senses, adjusting and evolving constantly with our environment. You will learn how to create new neural pathways and set points, encode new positive somatic markers (mind/body/heart memories of experience), and utilize brainwave synchronization methods, among other self-tools, to open up your world and your life. Once believed accessible by only a minute "rare" percentage of the population, (think the Einsteins and Mozarts of our world), you now also have the power to enhance and entrain your learning, intuition and retention capabilities up to thirty times greater than what you currently possess. You can now create tranquility, euphoria, greater intelligence and understanding. You can tap into more creative insight and access greater ability to focus your attention to co-create the life of your dreams. And there is more…

You are a potent, powerful, and infinite being created to function without limitation at a high level of awareness, joy, creativity and abundance. Living life through the practice of question and inquiry, like the curious mind of a child, is the key to unfolding, un-conditioning, and uninstalling the negative programs and limiting beliefs that prevent you from skyrocketing to living the life of your dreams.

You are the only one who has access to your truth, to create your unique purpose and reality. And, all the questions needing answers are within you. Only you can empower yourself to experience being the reality of the full totality of you!

From the moment we take our first breath we feel the innate desire and drive to learn; to imitate through mirroring, and to grow. It is this very essence of life's design, seeking a fuller expression through us, which possesses the power to push the seedling of grass through concrete, seeking and propelling life, to come to know itself.

By practicing the techniques and tools presented throughout *The Way 2 The Truth, The Journey Within,* you will develop a newfound inner trust, resolve, and resolute strength and power. Isn't it time to begin creating your life rather than allowing life to live you?

WHY THIS IS HAPPENING NOW

There used to be two systems of knowledge: hard science (the study of physics, chemistry and biophysics) and religion (which uses a more ephemeral, less concrete explanation of the Universe). These two systems are now converging to become one whole participatory system.

Beneath the appearance of chaos and uncertainty there is a single unified field of intelligence, which is the foundational core of the Universe. At this level all mind and matter are forced together. From the microscopic to the macroscopic, the atomic to the molecular, the sub-nuclear to the nuclear, all these things combine to form the ultimate intelligence and ground of being of life's essential connection to unity. Now we can see that our very essence of unified connection is supported by both science and spirituality. What has been scientifically validated within the last quarter century is that we can now actively and knowingly view ourselves as powerful co-creators communing within our world. The great Mahatma Gandhi serves us well when he said, "Be the change you want to see in the world." For that now we can most definitely be.

Quantum science, at one level of experience, leaps into a world where the observer affects that which is observed. Through this science, we know that our thoughts and emotions emit an actual energy frequency. In fact, every living organism emits energy. We can now measure our thoughts as energy fields extending far beyond our physical bodies, to ranges limited only by science's limitations in measurement itself.

So why is this happening now? Because it is time. The greatest crises in the last 5,000 years of history is happening now, just as human beings are becoming equipped with the knowledge and tools essential to drive and shift into new paradigms of being and understanding. Nature has shown us that life will always seek itself through itself. As systems of life, we are uniquely capable of harnessing all the tools, learning, and awareness at our disposal. Is it so surprising, as participatory human processes that interact and communicate with the very forces that govern the Laws of the Universe, that we also are actually being called upon by the "All That Is" to save it? Gregg Braden puts it this way in The Truth, The Journey Within film:

> *"All of these discoveries are coming to light, giving us a new way to see ourselves in the world, and it's happening precisely at the time, when the experts are telling us that our world is facing some of the greatest challenges in 5,000 years of human history... that for the first time in history, threaten our very existence... our survival on this planet."*

If we have the power to affect our world through the power of our thoughts, might our world also have the capability of communicating its needs to us? Remember, the human brain is an open system, a flow of energy (revisit this on page 58). It is not just we who commune with nature, but also nature who communes with us.

Quantum science clearly demonstrates that we have the power to communicate, through the silent language of the heart, with the atoms of the world, the divine living matrix, in life-affirming ways. The key to healing our own lives, and planet, lies in our ability to harness the incredible power of our human heart. Science has shown us that on the micro-level we can actually rearrange molecular structures in our biology to heal our bodies, our relationships, and our lives. On the macro-level, we can apply this wisdom to heal the damage created by a millennia of living in power-over structures all constructed on a false belief system based on separation. Power-over is defined as exploitative, life-alienating, tyrannical, unsustainable, etcetera.

AN EMERGENT NEW WORLD IS WITHIN YOU

The key to shifting paradigms is unlocking the truth and unique reason for our being—the "Why are we here?" question—that resides in every one of us. As we reach within to see into the window of what connects us, we can build new systems that support all of humanity. One need not tolerate, nor perpetuate, our current way of being. Real change is possible. Read on and you will be provided with all the tools, techniques, and knowledge you will need for lasting transformation in your life. These tools also nurture a dynamic, authentic, and supportive new powerful story of creating a new life living reality for you, and for our community.

By beginning your own journey into fostering and creating healing dialogue in your own relationships, that healing then becomes reflected in all of your daily interactions. This creates new models of dialogue and interaction throughout our communities, nations and our world. The Buddha has said...

- Do not believe in anything simply because you have heard it.

- Do not believe in anything simply because it is spoken or rumored by many.

- Do not believe in anything simply because it is found written in your religious books.

- Do not believe in anything merely on the authority of your teachers and elders.

- Do not believe in traditions because they have been handed down for many generations.

- But after observation and analysis, when you find that anything agrees within reason and is conducive to the good and benefit of one and all, then accept it and live up to it.

These chapters appear in a specific order by design. The purpose of this order is to work with each chapter until you begin to see it manifest in your life. Remember, your life is a journey, not a destination (for we all know the end game). You will know you're stepping into more awareness by the shift that seems to happen all around you. Its origin and source you are experiencing is the shift within you. Once you have gained your "sea legs," your own inner trust and confidence will lead you to proceed to the next chapter.

A NOTE ON DISCIPLINE

Before you turn the page, remember to be compassionate with yourself as well as disciplined. There's a thief in the night that you must stand vigilant watch against to gain victory over—your thoughts—for they create your world.

The word "discipline" can conjure up negative connotations because of our own childhood experiences when we were punished and "disciplined." Developing a kindred connection with the practice of discipline is essential to any achievement. Whether you are an athlete, or a person breaking life-alienating habits, addictions and behaviors, the act of discipline is vital to moving beyond your intellectual linear conditioning and realm of your mind, beliefs, habits, rituals and resulting behaviors. It is not enough to simply have an understanding of a great teaching or scripture to change your life. Through discipline and practice, you expand your awareness to move into and feel the wordless language within your heart. Your feelings, emotions, and senses open a world unto itself. Expanding your awareness will loosen the emotional knots that have become the constrictions of feelings of anxiety, disease, and disconnection within your body, held there for many years, and often decades, until you decide to live a different way.

On the journey, know that the inner voice of your subconscious mind will suddenly throw tantrums, or pout, reminding you of stories and thoughts to make itself heard. The messages you first hear will be denying and self-limiting. Like the Trojan horse stealthily entering the city of Troy, these messages are the enemy. This voice depends upon you not believing in yourself. Your conditioning will call you things like "loser," say "you can't do it," and find other ways to distract you or convince you that change is impossible. Taking control, you must realize that "I am not my thoughts!" Let the mind continue to do what it will do—

run in the background as the chatter that it is. Do not give in or give up... Continue and you will see and experience the change. Actually, you will be the change!

It is essential that you create extra time to extend compassion to yourself at regular daily intervals. When lessons prove difficult and challenging, confusing or overwhelming, that is when you will feel tempted to let the voice make you feel guilty or afraid. Stop and create the "gap" to breathe and let yourself return to your childlike state of curiosity and inquiry. Think and love like a child!

What life do you experience in the morning when you awake? It is what you call reality. Your current reality can only be based on your mind's perception of what reality is. What would life feel like if everything is actually changeable and possible? What would you truly like to change? And, if you changed it, what would make your life truly meaningful and worth living? And... much more than that, what would life look like beyond your current life experiences that have limited your imagination from stepping into the truth of the infinite potential you truly already are?

The truth is simple. It is your mind that won't fathom the truth. You are not your mind. You are an infinite being with the power to change everything and anything.

There are five steps to freedom to create the truth of who you are NOW. On the following page is a vow that reframes your life. Make copies and keep this vow with you at work and at your bedside. Repeat it in moments when you find yourself experiencing thoughts that are rooted in fear. Repeat it several times a day to remind yourself that you are love, peace and wisdom. You have always had the power to generate all that you need from within. If you have a significant loved one in your life, invite them to pursue their own truth. This can reconnect you back to the sacred covenant shared between you at times when you feel disconnected.

When you continue to repeat the words of your vow, you align with the vibration of the words and send them out to the Universe as an intention. These words from your heart align your action, your integrity, and your commitment to live life as you were created to be. Living your life free from the need to judge others, free from the need to judge ourselves, and free to experience authentic love in all of its design and magnificence.

MY LIFE MATTERS VOW

I, _____, am an incredible gift to the world. I give myself full permission to be completely authentic with my truth, and authentic to all those that I hold close in my life.

I stand fully seeing, fully believing, and fully loving myself for the beautiful imperfectly perfect I am.

I release myself from my need to judge or criticize myself or others.

I release my need to control any expectations I have from giving or receiving love.

I fully show up to express my love and my truth in all my relationships.

I walk in truth, committed to stretching myself. I trust my own capacities to express my fullest potential within me.

I offer my truths and I trust you, _____, (your name or loved one's name) to honor the covenant I have made between myself and my truth.

Signature: _____

Date: _____

II
THE POWER OF YOUR THOUGHTS

> *Your worst enemy cannot harm you as much as your own thoughts, unguarded. But once mastered, no one can help you as much, not even your father or your mother.*
>
> —THE BUDDHA

OUR THOUGHTS ARE POWERFUL!

As we re-program (entrain) new brainwave neural pathways, we shift into expanded levels of consciousness. We open up our intrinsic abilities to access and connect to the All That Is, The Field, the Higher Power of the Universe, God's Universal Wisdom, or whatever you like to call that source that most resonates within you. As we connect to our source, we access the unlimited potentiality to manifest our heart's deepest desires and passions, which are unique to who we were created to be.

On the subatomic scale, there is a particle only recently proven, called a quanta (or sometimes a quark) that physicists have concluded to be anywhere between 10,000 to 20,000,000 times smaller than the smallest atom. It is at this level, the quanta level, all matter and energy are virtually indistinguishable. In fact, it seems to be that it is our current level of consciousness that determines whether the quanta will manifest itself as matter or energy. By looking at the brain states and frequencies of healers and practitioners of meditation at the quanta level, science can now gain insight into what is yielding efficacy when it comes to prayer and self-healing, even though previous scientific inquiries had no explanation.

These new discoveries open up a new understanding as to why the power of suggestion and intention works so profoundly. For instance, have you ever noticed someone who will start to get the sniffles and say, "I'm coming down with one of those horrible colds my kids must've brought home from school. I know it will be a doozey." And, it is! But someone else, maybe a coworker in the very same office, will have the very same symptoms and say, "I'm going home early tonight to get a good night's rest. I'll take some extra vitamin C and I'm sure I'll be fine tomorrow." And they are!

Think for a minute, about the many "I am" statements most of us tend to make. Have you ever had the experience of feeling a little tired, then saying to yourself or to someone around you, "I'm so tired" and then that very instant start yawning and struggling to stay awake?

If we expect that we will have trouble sleeping, most likely that will be the case. In the words of Henry Ford: "If you think you can, or you think you can't, you're right!"

Be mindful of what you say to yourself!

OUR THOUGHTS ARE NON-LOCAL: THEY AFFECT ALL OTHERS AND EVERYTHING ELSE

Scientifically validated through applied kinesiology, known as muscle testing, our thoughts literally make our bodies weak or strong. It's also true that our thoughts affect others and that we can protect ourselves from the negative thoughts of others. Powerful examples of this are in a live portrayal and exercise on-line at our website, www.TheTruthMovie.tv or www.OneTeamHumanity.com, or in *The Way 2 The Truth, The Journey Within* book, supported by a media series of expanded science, tools, and practices that accompany *The Truth, The Journey Within* film.

For much of this chapter I will draw upon the work and experiences of Dr. Henry Grayson who first encountered just how profound the power of thought is to change behavior and mindset was while he was conducting weekly self-help sessions at a state prison in Massachusetts. One prisoner, prior to his incarceration, had become very distraught due to financial troubles. In a state of desperation he purchased a gun and held up a convenience store. While robbing the store, he became nervous and accidentally pulled the trigger and shot the clerk. The wife, sister, and best friend were so appalled and disturbed by his behavior that they did not visit him in jail, nor did they come to court for the trial. As a result he was deeply hurt. His hurt festered, and he started concocting stories about why they never visited him, which then grew into anger, then rage, then outright hatred. His hatred became an obsession, as he thought about how he would kill each of them when he was released from prison. This obsession was increasingly disturbing to his fellow inmates—even first-degree murderers who listened to his ranting day after day. So, when the word got out that Dr. Grayson was coming to the prison, the fellow inmates insisted that he see the doctor. He refused, and they insisted further saying, "If you know what is good for you, you'll go."

Well, the inmate went, along with a "buddy" to ensure attendance, sitting right beside him to demand he speak up about his obsessive thoughts of killing his family and best friend. Learning of this, Dr. Grayson gave him an assignment to work on for two weeks. Every time he would have the obsessive thought about killing his wife, sister, and best friend, he was to let the thought go, and instead shift his focus, and heart, on a memory of a good time with each of them. The inmate reacted saying it was the dumbest thing he had ever heard and refused to do it, until his "buddy" prodded him saying, "You'd better do it if you know what is good for you."

Feeling the pressure of the threat, the prisoner agreed. All the while, his fellow inmates made sure he kept up with his homework, which he did. Then, a most amazing thing happened. On the tenth day of doing his assignment, the prisoner received three letters—one from his wife, one from his sister, and one from his best friend, each written and mailed independently. Each letter began with very similar openings like: "When you shot that man in the convenience store, I was so hurt, embarrassed, disturbed and angry, I never wanted to see you again. That's why I never came to see you. But just a few days ago, I started remembering our good times together and decided I wanted to write to you."

Think about the mathematical odds of this happening. How could this be? Because of the power of thoughts!

In the Kabbalah (the ancient Jewish mystical tradition), it is believed we live on seven different planes at the same time, much like current theories in physics of the coexistence of multiple universes. Everything that one thinks, says, or does on this worldly plane affects their lives in the other six planes. In recognition of our interconnectedness, they are very conscious about what they think, say, or do so as to not affect their other lives.

Our thoughts affect not just other people, but also plants as well as other living organisms. Cleve Backster, one of the world's greatest authorities on the polygraph (the lie detector test), spoke at a professional conference in New York City over 25 years ago, and told a story which started years of research, much of it reported later in the book, *The Secret Life of Plants*, by Thompkins and Bird. He was working in his laboratory late one evening doing research with the polygraph. Getting tired, he decided to make a cup of coffee to help perk him up while finishing his day. While the water was heating, he looked over at the corn plant in his office and wondered if it might react to a threat the way human beings do. He then wired the polygraph to the plant and tried to deduce what would be a threat to the plant. He concluded that a sufficient threat would be to burn a leaf. Finding some matches, he approached the plant, and held a match with the intent to strike it and burn the leaf. Before the match was even lit, the polygraph reacted loudly. Thinking that his wiring might not be connected properly, he re-checked it. Seeing it was connected properly, he took out the match with the intent to strike it and burn a leaf. Once more, the polygraph reacted. Subsequent studies have shown that plants will even react when someone enters the room whom has previously harmed the plant. Next, something happened which totally blew his mind. When his water boiled and he made his coffee, he poured the left over water down the drain. As he did, the polygraph on the plant reacted. Being curious, he boiled some more water and poured it down the drain. This time the plant did not react. After replicating these experiments several times and bringing in a biologist friend, they concluded that the bacteria in the drain were killed when he poured the first boiling water down the drain, but the second time, they were all dead, therefore no reaction. The polygraph uncovered that the bacteria and plant, being interconnected in The Unified Field, as part of the One Ultimate Consciousness which unites all forces and particles, mind and matter, resonated with the other's pain.

This experiment is consistent with major studies done by the Transcendental Meditation (TM) groups in several major U.S. cities: like Washington DC, Detroit, San Antonio, and others. In this study, a large group of TM practitioners were asked to come to that city for the weekend and meditate. When told of this experiment and the expectation that the crime rate would go down 25 percent during the meditation, the mayor of Washington, DC at the time said, "There will be a snow storm in July before the crime rate goes down 25 percent here." He had to eat his words. Police statistics and hospital statistics for crime rates, murder rates, accident rates and catastrophic illness rates, as compared with the week before and after, a month before and after, and a year before and after, found that the crime rate did indeed go down 25 percent for that weekend. And no, there was no snow that July.

How can this be?

In our old Newtonian world view, everything is separate, everything can be observed and measured, and everything has a linear cause and effect. But in the quantum world, as in the spiritual world, things are quite different. There is an amazing infinite source of power not visible to the naked eye. In this world, there is no separateness. There is just one Unified Field, a total Living Matrix of pure consciousness, of which we are all a part. This Unified Field of consciousness could be what we know as God. In the Bible, God is referred to as One "[I]n whom we live and move and have our being." No one and no thing is disconnected from the Universal Field. The Nobel Prize winning physicist of the early 20th Century, Erwin Schrödinger in *Mind and Matter* said:

> "Consciousness is never experienced in the plural, only in the singular. Not only has none of us ever experienced more than one consciousness, but there

> *is no trace of circumstantial evidence of this ever happening anywhere in the world... Mind by its very nature is a singulare tantum... The overall number of minds is one."*

Similarly, David Bohm, another eminent physicist of our time, expressed this interconnectedness in *Wholeness and the Implicate Order* when he said:

> *"It will be ultimately misleading, and indeed wrong, to suppose... That each human being is an independent actuality who interacts with other human beings and with nature. Rather, all these are projections of a single totality."*

Albert Einstein proclaimed a similar perspective when he said:

> *"A human being is part of the whole that we call the Universe, a part limited in time and space. He experiences himself, his thoughts and feelings, as something separated from the rest—a kind of optical illusion of his consciousness."*

Einstein has quite clearly been the closest akin to what our revolutionary quantum discoveries have confirmed—our thoughts and feelings are not separate. It is our individuated parts that create the illusion of separateness. And now science has confirmed what Einstein came to understand.

THINKING AND BEING

The wisdom of the ages has always recognized the importance of our thoughts. In the Book of Proverbs in the Bible it states: "As a man thinketh, so he is." Hundreds of years later, the Buddha said, "You are what you think. With your thoughts you make your world." Six hundred years later, Jesus said, "As a man thinketh in his heart, so he is." And in the late 1700's, the wise Hasidic master Rebbe Nachman of Breslow put it this way: "You are where your thoughts are. Be sure that where your thoughts are is where you would like them to be." Meaning, be sure you would like to be where your thoughts are. The correlation between your thoughts and your being are interrelated and defining your experience to reality. How can you, therefore, change your thoughts to thereby improve your experience to reality and way of being in the world?

Now we come to the first step in the journey on the path to *Your Truth*. You will learn to monitor your thoughts and gain awareness into any life-sabatoging beliefs and associated traumas you may carry. This process is one that is continuous, since the beliefs and traumas may be embedded at a deeper creation point than previously thought, and many times the exact originating source of pain or trauma is never known. To change your life reality, it is not necessary that you access your encoded traumas. You have the power to change your reality every moment of your day. For this reason, perpetual thought monitoring and clearing is essential. Otherwise, your good intentions, conscious wishes, dreams and desires, will all be unwittingly blocked by limiting beliefs and thoughts operating below the surface, in your subconscious as the congealed life-alienating beliefs inhibiting you from experiencing your true power and natural intrinsic capacity to create your life.

How our brain operates is incredible. Our subconscious mind affects the way our brains and bodies function. Thought patterns, both negative and positive, become physically ingrained (as somatic markers) in our brains and bodies, forming the actual neural inner-net structure of our brain. These somatic markers carry encoded information throughout our entire central nervous system. Our mind/body/heart is constantly monitoring our environment. As our inner and outer senses take in information, our subconscious sends signals to all other areas of our brain's neuropathways and markers, which then make us, physiologically speaking, much more likely to think and act in a routinely negative or positive "default set point" cyclic way. It is our somatic markers that go to work, accessing our environment and previous life experiences to communicate messages to us. Our mind/body/heart then responds and relaxes by opening (love) or moves our body into the fear-based responses of flight, freeze or fight, flushing our mind/body/heart with the neurochemicals that influences everything in our system, head-to-toe, extending outward to the world all around us. To change your experience to life, you must first re-pattern and entrain new neural pathways, creating more positive "set points" that expand your capacities across your infinite consciousness, to create and live more aligned to your highest thoughts, dreams and passions.

To better understand how the process works, think of how your computer operates. In order to retrieve whatever file you want, you need to input a command to call forth that information which is then instantly decoded and appears as the document, picture, or whatever it was you wanted. It's the same with our subconscious mind. The command to call forth certain information from your subconscious could be something you see, hear, touch, smell, feel or otherwise experience. Once that command is sent, the subconscious locates the corresponding file or program and launches your mind/body/heart into action. Whether it was a most pleasurable event that happened during childhood, or a trauma or negative experience that incurred at any time of life, your mind/body/heart runs the program. Consider what is being run is not words, memories, or language, but rather a series of chemicals that "trigger" a deep emotional response experienced by the entire mind/body/heart. Now remember, all of this is happening at the subconscious level. For example, if someone shares information with you, if it bothers you, you have just triggered an untruth, a negative somatic marker that is running an old encoded trauma or program. Your heartbeat begins racing, your face gets hot, you feel the pain again as if it were brand new because, for the subconscious mind, the pain is brand new.

It is here, at this moment of stimulus, that this old program begins running and your mind/body/heart triggers the physiological responses and subsequent emotions, and you will become aware (conscious) of feeling hurt. Your subconscious has already appraised the stimulus, taken over to step into action to protect you, making the connection to your old program and "hurt." Untrained, what we will most likely do is correlate the stimulus, in this case the information being said, as the cause of our pain. The extremely intense, "over the top," feelings you sometimes experience in the middle of an argument is a prime example of how these old-patterned responses react. We instantly establish blame, create an internal "story" (for example: he/she doesn't love me), and become the victim, by saying or believing they are responsible because of what they said for the sudden and intense hurt we feel.

In actuality, any number of things could have triggered that reality; they just happen to be the one who pulled the trigger, but the wound, the lie about you, was already there. That trigger could be a facial expression, a word, a smell, an action, something we see, sense or hear. It could simply be a person's mannerism or a non-verbal feeling. It could be almost anything. When there is encoded pain or trauma, any number of triggers will cause our subconscious to run these old programs until we learn how to put a stop to it and take control of creating our life. Unless you learn how to create the "gap" immediately between your stimulus and your response when being triggered, your subconscious mind, believing you are in great peril, will signal chemicals to hijack the part of your brain where reasoning and logic resides, effectively turning off your conscious capacities to learn and choose your response to create a new experience to life. Working up to 800 times faster than the conscious mind, it then responds with one of three possible reactions: fight, flight or freeze. Evolutionarily speaking, this protective system is a gift when facing a real threat, like a wild animal staring at you, thinking you are their next meal. However, it hardly serves you when attempting to live a happy, fully on-purpose, conscious, integrated life of empowered choice.

When you have trouble monitoring your emotional reactions and disturbing thoughts, it means there are encodings of trauma that need to be cleared from your limbic system or subconscious mind. And it is due to such programming that we continue attracting certain people who are not essentially positive for us, yet to whom we feel a sense of familiarity or kinship.

Why would we do this?

Well it is part of nature's grand design to bring us back to our truest nature, to re-member that which we most need to learn in our journey to becoming more. The same type of people or circumstances will return, again and again, creating the picture you have believed reality is. It will come in different packaging, as gifts that lead you to your truth, if you choose to see each experience and stimulus as an opportunity to turn inward, to question and access the infinite possibilities you are. Your power and freedom comes as you choose to inquire within to clear the old programming to re-program new "set points" that, ultimately, raises your default vibration which allows you to then respond with love, compassion, forgiveness, and gratitude.

Remember, each trigger (person or event) is only the stimulus, never the cause of your reactions!

Because the human brain is an open system, when pushed past its current limitations, it has the capability to reorganize itself into higher and higher levels of intelligence and functioning. A runner for example, gives more physical input to his body than it can handle, and the body responds by reorganizing itself at a higher level that can handle this increased input, which we call "getting into shape." When we consider our minds are capable of all of that, and more, it becomes clear that repetition of the same problems again and again does not have to be a life sentence. We can choose to get our minds and hearts healthy and fit.

THE HUMAN BRAIN IS AN OPEN SYSTEM
1977 Nobel Prize winner, scientist Ilya Prigogine, reconciled two seemingly contradictory laws of nature[3]. The second law of thermodynamics states that the amount of randomness or chaos, called entropy, in the Universe is always increasing. On the other hand, many things, including life itself, are obviously part of a process of increased ordering and less randomness. So, scientists wondered, why is it that some things evolve and grow when the overall tendency in the Universe is for things to break down and become less ordered? His discovery was what he calls "open systems." These are systems that are able to exchange energy and matter within their environment. They are able to maintain their structure and even grow and evolve into more complex systems of intelligence and functioning because they actually have the ability to dissipate entropy to their environment in such a way that the total amount of entropy, overall, does increase, obeying the second law of thermodynamics. These

---
3 *Mind-Science Report*, New Life Enterprises, Allen Koss

systems maintain their orderliness, and even increase it, at the expense of their environment.

Open systems are very plastic and can handle all kinds of fluctuations and variations of input from their environment. Each system has an upper limit of how much randomness or entropy it can dissipate to its environment. This limit is based on the system's structure and its degree of complexity.

If fluctuations from the environment exceed this limit, the system cannot dissipate enough entropy to maintain its structure. The example of how runners can push the limits of their systems shows us if a condition persists, at a certain point the system is pushed to reorganize itself at a higher level of functioning in order to create a new structure that can handle these increased fluctuations.

This point, which Prigogine termed the "bifurcation point" (bifurcate means to divide into two branches), is when the system spontaneously re-orders itself in an entirely new way. The new structure will be totally non-linear with what existed before. This change is a true quantum leap, a death and rebirth, and the outstanding characteristic of the new system is that it has the capacity to handle all the fluctuations and input from the environment that the original system could not handle.

We, as human beings, are capable of such transformation. You must be willing to experience this capacity within yourself. By doing the exercises in this chapter and the ones that follow, you will witness the experience of just how radical the change can be when you choose to access pure infinite consciousness to operate without the finite limiting beliefs that create a false reality about you.

OUR THOUGHTS AFFECT OUR MOODS

We have been told by our nation's pharmaceutical companies that the depression we experience is a chemical imbalance which they believe to be innate. While it is true that there is a chemical imbalance, they do not understand the actual cause of the imbalance. They do not convey that the serotonin and norepinephrine chemicals in the brain are changed by each thought we think and emotions we carry. This is why numerous studies have shown that cognitive behavioral therapy is equally effective as antidepressants in relieving many forms of depression, without the negative spiraling health and side effects! You can entrain your own healing capacities within your mind/body/heart.

Professor Irving Kirsch, at the University of Connecticut, used the Freedom of Information Act to require the FDA's release of alarming data regarding clinical studies from six leading pharmaceutical companies[4]. This study showed only a 3 percent difference in effectiveness between a placebo and the actual anti-depressant medication. The damaging side effects that pharmaceuticals do to our bodies can be irreversible. When one stops the medication the depression often returns, because the root originating trauma or belief has not been cleared from our mind/body/heart. Also documented in so many instances is that after awhile, the medication stops working altogether. The truth is medication can relieve the symptoms, but not cure the problem. The imbalance is a result of the thoughts themselves. If you do not change the thoughts upstream, you cannot cure the imbalance downstream in the river we call life.

Thoughts rule! Changing thoughts, breathing into the diaphragm, and stimulating subtle energies in your heart and your energy meridians, with conscious intentionality is just as effective self-tools for relieving anxiety as tranquilizers are. Most importantly, they are not addictive (well actually, fully feeling alive vs. numbing out is a loving addiction habit) and have no harmful side effects. Choosing self-love supports and encourages building new life-affirming choices and patterns that will create your new reality.

It is not the circumstances of our lives which influence our moods most but rather the stories we create about those circumstances that color our perceptions and experience to life. It is not what someone said or didn't say, did, or did not do (the stimulus or trigger), that disturbs our peace of mind. It is the power you give to what you think about what they said or did. Much of the time you focus on the outside events as the "cause" of our suffering. To stop the pain, we try to change the other

---
4 Mother Jones. *San Francisco*: Nov/Dec 2003. Vol. 28, Iss. 6; pg. 76

person or avoid the circumstance, all the while creating more limits in our life. In doing so, we feel more and more powerless. Only when you see that it is your own thoughts that cause misery and suffering, can you take back your intrinsic power to re-frame your reality to choose and create a different internal experience. Understanding that your thoughts are the cause of your pain is not an occasion to feel guilty. Truth is knowledge. Truth cannot set you free until you apply that wisdom with action. Guilt itself has no redeeming value. Guilt, as a means to re-live a negative pattern does not acknowledge your own power to consciously re-frame everything that comes to you in life, as the gifts in small and large boxes, to open up to the present opportunity that awaits you inside that box.

Compassion to yourself and others comes by allowing every range of emotion to be fully experienced through you. Trusting life to be the transient flow that comes and goes, participating fully in whatever is, allows you to transcend each thought and resulting feeling and emotion. As you open to receive life as a transient river, your compassion expands your capacity to create new default "set points" of more life-affirming thoughts and attitudes. You play the significant role and, indeed, are the only player who can transform your barriers to experience authentic love, peace, and happiness. When you generate these qualities from within, they become the reflection you bring forth into the reality of your world. The choice to experience love is yours alone.

Much of the time, you are just not aware of the thoughts that cause your emotions, which subsequently lead to the roller-coaster ride of fluctuating moods, responsible for creating so much of the disharmony and disconnection within your life, body, and relationships. Without adequate awareness and insight, you cannot distinguish the "ally" (love-based) thoughts from the "enemy" (fear-based) thoughts.

A tragic, yet powerful example, resulting in the highest rate of combat neurosis in history, is the story of the American soldiers who fought in Vietnam, who simply could not distinguish the enemy. Surely there were the North Vietnamese in uniform, but there were also the Viet Cong hidden in plain sight: a grandmother, a mother with a baby in her arms, or even a small child, all of whom might possibly throw a grenade into the soldiers' Jeep as they passed. As a consequence, there were times when seeing a Vietnamese person reach inside their cloak would result in their death, as an American soldier reacted through defensive training. Only when the soldier went to view the body did he discover the person he had just killed was an unarmed civilian. Imagine the shock and horror.

Pivotal to their own survival and mental well-being was knowing who the enemy was. Such is the case with the lies of your fear-based thoughts. One can act quite neurotic when filled with enemy thoughts disguised as thoughts that protect us. In truth, it is these thoughts that take you hostage, and hold you as a victim. These enemy thoughts can try to make you feel misunderstood, powerless, and frozen in the battlefield of life. In reality these thoughts zap you of your power and you end up feeling drained, desperate, unworthy, inadequate, unsatisfied, unloved, disconnected and separate, and just plain bad.

HOW OUR THOUGHTS ACT ON OUR BRAINS AND BODIES

The science of today now has the capability of seeing just how our brain reacts to the stimulus of its environment. Through measurements done in real time, scientists are able to accurately measure neurochemicals released throughout our bodies when we have an emotional reaction, mapping and identifying the powerful role our thoughts and emotions have upon our biology.

Thanks to recent breakthroughs, we now know the role each neurochemical plays in contributing to life-affirming patterns of thoughts and behavior resulting in physical and mental health and a sense of well-being. We also know which ones contribute to life-threatening, fear-based conditioned patterns that create the overall dis-ease within our biological systems. These toxins can be identified as excessive amounts of cortisol, noradrenaline, adrenaline, serotonin, dopamine, GABA and more[5]. Excess amounts of these neurotransmitters can over-stimulate our nervous systems causing excitatory symptoms ranging from mild

---

[5] The toxic mind: the biology of mental illness and violence. *Medical Hypotheses 2000*; 55(4): 356-368 E. Van Winkle Retired Neuroscientist, Millhauser Laboratories of the Department of Psychiatry, New York University School of Medicine

anxiety, to depression, to mania, and even stimulate extreme acts of violence.

Biologist Candace Pert, through her research discovered the important role neuropeptides play as chemical messengers for the whole body[6]. Every thought you think and emotion you feel is communicated instantly via these chemical messengers to all other cells and biological processes in your body. This speaks to how our negative thoughts influence the development of cancer, heart disease, as well as other diseases while our positive thoughts help eradicate and prevent disease.

The following story, again shared by Dr. Grayson, further illustrates how the old maxim "mind over matter" can become true.

There was a patient of Dr. Grayson's who suffered from irritable bowel syndrome (IBS). While on the road making calls, he would often be desperately in need of a restroom. Sometimes he found himself unable to make it there in time. He believed it was a physiological problem which was totally out of his control, and that only a medical miracle could solve it. Since none of his physicians had cured him, he reluctantly agreed to see Dr. Grayson for therapy. People so often think that if they admit that their physical symptom stems from their mind it means they are crazy. Such thinking is the ego mind's way of trying to keep us from embracing our true intrinsic nature and power. Our ego mind wants us to think the cause of our problems are external and therefore that the solution is external, then we can continue to experience ourselves as powerless victims of the circumstances in our life. Hence we remain in the illusion of separation and story of victimization.

Dr. Grayson shared a number of thought-monitoring techniques with the man in the hope that they would help. The next week the man returned ecstatic and told Dr. Grayson: "If I have an anxious or fearful thought for more than thirty seconds, I have to make a beeline for the restroom, and I am lucky if I make it before exploding... But, if I catch that thought before the

---

[6] Pert, Candace B, (1997) *Molecules of Emotion: The Science Behind Mind/body/heart Medicine*, Simon & Schuster

thirty second mark passes and change my thought, my stomach remains totally at peace!"

Using the *18 Second Thought Monitoring Practice Worksheet* tool, the man learned how to identify the harmful thought and take charge again of his thoughts. Learning to embrace the real power of his mind, he was able to not only regain control of his life, he also learned to take charge as the proactive co-creator of his own reality.

THINK THE SAME THOUGHT—EXPERIENCE THE SAME REALITY

Social psychologists estimate the number of thoughts we have each day to be anywhere from 24-28,000 while others suggest it may be as high as 72-74,000. They have also discovered a tendency to repeat the same thoughts over and over again. As much as 95 percent of the thoughts you are thinking today are the same as what you thought yesterday and will be, most likely, the same thoughts you will think tomorrow.

Is it any wonder then that you keep on living the same undesirable patterns day in and day out? The great English poet, John Milton, put it perfectly nearly 350 years ago when he wrote: "The mind is its own place, and in itself can make a heaven of hell, a hell of heaven..." And the vicious pattern goes on and on like this: If we think what we always thought, we will see what we have always seen. And if we see what we have always seen, we will feel what we have always felt. And if we feel what we have always felt, we will do what we have always done. Then, if we do what we have always done, we will get what we have always gotten.

You can break the patterns and cycles of your thoughts ruling your life. You can experience the freedom and power of intentional living by applying the tools and exercises inspired by the work of Dr. Henry Grayson.

Dr. Grayson's book, *Mindful Loving*, is an observation of how relationships succeed or fail in accordance with how we *think* about them. Unlike other books and traditional therapy, Dr. Grayson's teaching didn't concentrate on modifying outward behavior or changing what each party *did*. Rather, he emphasized going upstream to the very source of our separation, your thoughts. Using recent discoveries from the field of quantum physics, Dr. Grayson demonstrated how the quality or nature of your communication with your partners (and relationships) and the way we think about our partners actually shapes the relationship itself. His position, which is now supported scientifically, is that the thoughts we think have great influence on the end result of the relationship we experience.

Ultimately, through his work you will be able to re-pattern your lifelong belief that a relationship is comprised of two different entities that have to "hash it out" to ensure each party gets what they need. All relationships are co-created, interdependent, and reflective relationships. This one understanding alone about relationships can revolutionize your internal experience. Something so seemingly simple, yet utterly profound, can shift your experience of reality, by changing your thoughts! Einstein stated, "We can't solve problems by using the same kind of thinking we used when we created them."

Let's see why Dr. Grayson became inspired to develop his Thought Monitoring Process, also known as TMP.

While in graduate school in Boston, Dr. Grayson had the privilege of taking a class in existential psychology taught by the renowned Victor Frankl M.D., who was a visiting professor. A Viennese psychiatrist and holocaust survivor, Dr. Frankl had been imprisoned at the Dachau concentration camp in Germany during WWII.

While in the camp, Dr. Frankl observed a correlation between the kinds of thoughts people allowed in their minds and their ultimate welfare. While some fellow inmates contracted malaria and died, others remained healthy. While some got depressed and threw themselves into the electric fence, others remained hopeful. It seemed that those persons who focused intently upon some positive thought found themselves befriended by the guards, while those who reflected the abject state of their surroundings and circumstance were the persons most commonly abused.

It does seem to be the case that those whose dominant thoughts were occupied in pain; having emotions like judgment, anger, resentment and other low frequency negative thought patterns, experienced that very same reality as the out-picture of their internal minds. Those who repeatedly fixed their minds upon something positive, a thought with higher vibrations, like expressing gratitude for the bit of moldy bread that had accompanied the soup that day, or who pressed on thinking purposeful thoughts for their future when they were released from Dachau, fared much better than those who succumbed to their environment. Dr. Frankl put it this way:

> *"In the concentration camps where all human freedoms are taken away, the one freedom the Nazi guards could not take away from us is the freedom to choose what we think in our minds. It is the one freedom which remains."*

Influenced deeply by Dr. Frankl's teaching and interning experience, Dr. Grayson has continued the study of the power our thoughts have to shape our world and improve our experience to daily life. The exercises and insights below are all inspired or created by Dr. Grayson. In Thought Monitoring Process (TMP), there are three main categories of thought:

1. **The Constant Chatter in Our Minds.** These are the up to 78,000 incessant thoughts per day that play non-stop in our mind's inner-net computer.

2. **Core Beliefs.** The thoughts that have congealed into our belief system. Inputted from childhood role models and conditioning, once embedded, we will do anything and everything, often unconsciously, to get confirmation of such a belief. These beliefs work much like software in a computer program. These beliefs create your life reality.

3. **Interpretive Perceptions.** These are the thoughts we think in moments of interaction with others and with the world. They give our interpretations to each happening, and these interpretations create the new "stories" that shape

our on-going reality. Prior to doing the work (the journey within), most of our perceptions are largely projections. Our vision is distorted by looking through lenses of the past. Rebbe Nachman observed saying, "We do not see things as they are; we see them as we are."

Our relationships overlap between all three kinds of thought. The constant chatter we experience tends to reaffirm our core beliefs. For example, a core belief of not being smart enough could likely create or manifest as mind chatter about ways of becoming smart. For instance: a man who when he was a boy was told that he wasn't the "smart type" might possess subconscious background chatter that tells him he needs to get smart by mentally exerting himself. This leads him to read certain magazines and pick-up certain hobbies, and maybe even major in a degree at college that requires a great deal of mental exertion. He may then go on to get a good job requiring his intellect and may even go on to become an "authority" in his field.

For the sake of proving his smarts, his entire life has been dictated by him reacting against that someone who embedded the lie governing his actions from the subconscious programming encoded in his mind. No matter how "successful" or driven such a man might become, there will always be an underlying perpetual nagging feeling of dissatisfaction, stemming from the preponderance of negative chatter and deep negative beliefs about his own self-worth. His freedom to experience a peaceful, loving state of mind will never be achieved until he finally clears away the trauma and core negative beliefs that limit his experience to reality.

Right now you can begin the work of clearing and transforming your limiting core beliefs. Expect the chatter of the mind to attempt to distract you. How can the mind ever be anything more, or less, than what it believes itself to be? It is up to you to help your mind relax by expanding its experience of you. As you clear the chatter, deeper layers of old locked-away memories will rise up to the surface of your consciousness. The key to your freedom is to not resist or try to fight the thoughts away, nor give them power by indulging them. Instead, see each thought as a pouting child trying to have their way. Be compassionate as you would with a child and let them be. You'll see why as you read on.

Lastly, our interpretive perceptions are the manifestations created from our core beliefs and fed from our chatter. Your interpretive perceptions change as your internal structure of who you are realigns itself. Leave room to allow the space for this to happen if you tend to operate with a sense of cynicism about the world. For instance, leave that habitual perception aside as you do the interior work on your core beliefs. And the next time you engage in conversation with another person or catch yourself running limiting conversation in your mind, do not opt for one of your old stories or ideas.

Until you've installed the new programming and opened new neural "set points," which takes 28 days of disciplined practice, that old virus will try to reboot and infect your mind/body/heart system. Don't feed into this impulse. Just let things be. Stay in the present moment within your relationships and when the triggers come, choose to create the "gap" between your stimulus and response so you can choose healthier attitudes and patterns of relating and love. Don't let the old programming of fear have its way! Get ready to experience what happens when you expand your awareness into the infinite reality you are!

There is more to learn about the three categories of thought. You will be given all the tools you need to gain awareness of your thoughts and to clear and transform them. This will move you closer to uncovering and discovering the truth of what really makes you thrive. Monitoring your thoughts on a regular basis is extremely helpful to assist you in becoming aware of the enemy thoughts that are holding you back in life.

THE THOUGHT AWARENESS EXERCISE

Copy this page, cut this out and carry it with you to help yourself become aware of your thoughts:

BECOMING AWARE OF YOUR ENEMY THOUGHTS:
Carry this exercise with you for a week. Any time you become aware of feeling anxious or uneasy, something other than feelings of being happy, peaceful or at ease, ask yourself, "What was I just thinking?" Once you identify the thought that disturbed your peace, take a deep breath, place a check mark on the card below, and say to yourself, "There is one of those disturbing ego thoughts."

MONDAY   TUESDAY   WEDNESDAY   THURSDAY   FRIDAY   SATURDAY   SUNDAY

Each day you do this Thought Awareness Exercise you will become increasingly aware of the thoughts that disturb you. It is the limiting thoughts that you will need to be conscious of monitoring. For two days, carry a notebook with you and make a running list of all the thoughts that go through your mind. You will find that many will be repeated. You can place a check mark beside those as they appear rather than rewriting them each time. At the completion of the two days, put all the positive thoughts on one page. Keep the positive or life-affirming thoughts, and throw out the ones which are negative, disturbing, and fear-based. **Thoughts that disturb your peace and feel heavy are not the voice of truth. You will know it is a lie if it sticks you with an "ouch." Even if you think the thought is true about you**. If it is disturbing and sticks you it is a lie, and you need to let it go. Remember, to dwell on it will not change it. It will only reinforce the energy and cement in the limitations denying you the experience of living on purpose and being authentic to you in your life.

The information and exercises that follow are absolutely life-changing. Diligence, patience, and perseverance will expand your conscious awareness of who you truly are. Self-judgment, criticism, and frustration have no redeeming value for anyone. Focus on absorbing and integrating the tools into your life. Remember, your life is a journey, not a race!

THE FIRST CATEGORY OF THOUGHTS: THE CHATTER IN YOUR MIND

THE 18-SECOND THOUGHT-MONITORING PROCESS

The chatter in your mind takes on all forms. It appears from nowhere. You've become so conditioned to be accustomed to its presence. The chatter is what your mind seems to do when you're not thinking about anything in particular. Like a radio station we have turned down low, these thoughts accompany us day-in and day-out; and though this chatter may seem to revolve around certain themes, there's usually no conscious rhyme or reason for its existence.

Dr. Grayson developed a simple 5-step Thought Monitoring Process which takes only 18 seconds to calm and clear the Chatter in Your Mind. Dr. Grayson uses it daily and teaches it to thousands of his patients and students. Become a practitioner of this method and you will find it simple and highly effective.

Step 1: Whenever you are being disturbed or have suffered a loss of inner peace, which generally feels heavy or yucky, ask yourself the question: "What was I just thinking?" This is a very important question for it is the first step out of victimization for you to learn how to take the drama out of the equation and become your own Observer. By becoming an Observer to your thoughts, you create a "gap" in the field of your awareness to see into the limiting beliefs keeping you locked into a finite story about reality. By asking this question you are moving away from thinking that the cause of your disturbance is external, or outside your control. The cause for your loss of peace is inside your thought. You can do something about that.

Step 2: Label the thought. Become the Observer to your thought. Once you've observed the thought as an "enemy thought," you can get rid of it. The following command will speak to your higher authority: "There is one of those disturbing thoughts, which has no redeeming value."

Step 3: Remind yourself of the truism: "Whatever I focus on will surely increase. It will increase as my internal reality and my external reality." Then ask yourself the real motivating question: "Do I want this thought I'm focusing on to increase? If I focus on it, it surely will!"

Step 4: Use an action word and issue an executive order saying, "I cancel," "I dismiss," "I banish," "I stop" that thought, "you are not the truth of who I am." Say it with authority and mean it! Remember, this is a command issued from the Higher Self · the one who is taking charge.

Step 5: There is an Aristotelian and quantum principle that says, "Nature abhors a vacuum." When there is empty space, something will rush into it. As we empty our mind of disturbing thoughts and the beliefs that are feeding them, we need to fill the space with positive thoughts, leaving no room for yet more negative thoughts to rush back in. For example, if your negative thought was "I am no good," replace that thought with, "I am a wonderful human being, a child of God!" Or you might choose a mantra, repeat a scripture that means something to you, or sing or listen to an inspirational song that rocks your world. Continue this as long as you need to in order for the negative thoughts to cease. Then go on with whatever you were doing before.

The 18 Second Thought Monitoring Process goes like this:
1. When your peace is disturbed, ask, "What was I just thinking?"

2. "There is one of those disturbing thoughts and lies about me."

3. "Whatever I focus on will surely increase. Do I want this thing I'm focusing on to increase?"

4. "I banish, cancel and dismiss that thought!!"

5. State your affirmation to yourself.

18 SECOND THOUGHT MONITORING WORKSHEET

What was I just thinking when I noticed my peace was disturbed?

Acknowledge and observe the thought as though you are looking at it from the outside.

1. Identify this thought above as a thought that doesn't serve you.

2. This is one of those disturbing thoughts. Add the declaration, "This thought has no redeeming value and is only here to disturb my peace and joy."

3. I acknowledge and trust that whatever I focus on will surely increase. Do I want my thought of (insert thought) to increase?

4. I cancel, banish, dismiss this thought of (insert thought). Demand it, with authority.

5. State your favorite affirmation or the exact opposite of the thought framed as an affirmation. "I now declare…" Example: "I am an amazing wonderful human being capable and determined to create my reality." (Thought: "I am no good at…")

Hold your affirmation as long as required so the negative thought does not re-enter. Shift your energy and replace the thought with a positive thought or feeling, song, or memory that makes you smile, laugh, and feel happy.

For additional copies of this worksheet go to: www.thetruthmovie.tv/thoughtmonitoring

THE SECOND CATEGORY OF THOUGHTS: CORE BELIEFS

CHANGING YOUR CORE BELIEFS

Our core beliefs are the thoughts that create the basic system we live by. Once in place, we will do anything and everything, often unconsciously and even to our detriment, to get confirmation of that belief. That is the reality we know. Here's an example from Dr. Grayson: Catherine inherited a reasonable sum of money from her father. She and her husband agreed to set that money aside for their children's college education. But in spite of their agreement, Catherine was spending it like crazy. Having spent nearly half of it, her husband insisted that she seek therapy for their children's sake. In therapy with Dr. Grayson, Catherine discovered that she possessed the belief that she did not deserve abundance. This belief worked much like a set-point on a thermostat with the temperature calibrating to that particular set point, not higher, not lower.

Catherine's set-point of reality was more of scarcity rather than abundance. Because we unconsciously will go to great lengths to match our belief system, Catherine began compulsively spending the money to bring the amount of abundance down to her set-point. The good news is that such beliefs can be deleted, much like computer software, and new "software" or positive beliefs can be installed. And once the new positive beliefs were installed, Catherine did not feel compelled to spend the balance of the inheritance, and could align herself to the integrity and agreement with her husband to save it for their children's college.

Often we carry beliefs that limit us, and many of these beliefs may be shared by most everyone we know. Such tribal mindsets are culturally conditioned, passed down from generation to generation, which then become your "reality." Subconsciously, you have tactily been brainwashed with constant reinforcements from our "commercialized" environment the moment you turn on the television or listen to the radio. This tribal mind thinking actually limits your potential to create a reality aligned to living from the truth of who you are, NOT from the conditioning of limitation programmed into you.

Maynard Ferguson, jazz trumpet player, accomplished the "impossible," when he learned to play impossibly high notes no other trumpet player before him could play. How did this happen? Ferguson grew up in a very poor family, but was exposed to jazz musicians. Falling in love with jazz, he yearned to play the trumpet. His family could not afford to buy him one, but eventually someone gave him an old discarded trumpet. There was no money for lessons, so Ferguson taught himself how to read music. What he did not know was that he was playing everything an octave higher. Therefore, he thought the incredibly high notes he was playing were the way he was supposed to play. As a result he played higher notes on the trumpet than anyone had ever played before, accomplishing what had long been deemed impossible.

Do you know the beliefs you live by? Do you know the beliefs that serve your highest truth and potential? The limiting beliefs you want to discard? Do you continue to struggle? Then you most likely have a belief that life has to be a struggle. Do you find that those you love go away or leave you? You most likely have a core belief that you will inevitably be abandoned. Do you experience material scarcity in your life? Then you probably have a belief, like Catherine, that you do not deserve abundance or that it is not safe to have abundance. Do you suffer from on-going physical illnesses? You may have a belief that you do not deserve abundant health or that it is not safe for you to have abundant health because doing so would mean missing out on some secondary gain, probably one you learned in childhood.

For instance, if your parents only gave love and nurturing when you were sick, you might find it unsafe to give up sickness, for fear you would give up your intrinsic needs for love, nurturing, and the comfort of knowing that you matter. Do you often feel like nobody listens to you? Then you probably have the belief that no one hears you, understands you, or will not acknowledge your needs. Do you always find yourself engaged in conflict or fights? You may carry the belief that fighting is a way to connect, or that fighting makes you strong, or that you have to be loud, angry, or pout to be heard. Do you continually not have close relationships? Then you may have the belief that closeness is not something you deserve, might not feel safe, or feel comfortable, receiving, and trusting.

You may have missed the memory experience (creating your somatic marker) of your early childhood maternal bonding. During this bonding, the hormones dopamine, oxytocin and vasopressin have been found to be involved in facilitating trust and attachment, which activates the reward centers of our limbic system during this early developmental progress.

What do you often feel? Pausing to inquire within when your relationships provide you the stimulus and emotional reactions will provide you the perfect path to find the answers to this question. You can then start to address any originating trauma that led to the establishment of your limiting core beliefs. Do you often feel afraid, bored, unhappy, lonely, attacked, judged, angry, rejected, inadequate, powerless, unloved, selfish, non-assertive, or mistreated? Each of these feelings, or any other fear-based feelings and emotions, will give you an important clue as to what you have been conditioned to believe.

Identify your limiting core beliefs to free yourself and experience a life of greater abundance in all areas. Jesus shared, "I came that your joy might be full" and "I came that you might have life and have it more abundantly." You are an infinite being with the full capacity to create your reality and live the truth of who you are!

To clear a negative belief, you need to assess how strong it is. Following are instructions that will allow you to quickly assess the strength of your negative beliefs so that you may then move on to properly clear them from your mind/body/heart system.

ASSESSING THE STRENGTH OF LIMITING CORE BELIEFS

Once you have identified a negative belief you wish to clear, you'll want to make an assessment of how strong that belief is on a scale of 0 to 10. The first way is just to ask yourself how strong it is and see what number comes to mind. A "0" means that you do not believe it at all. A "10" means that the belief is very strong. Your self-assessment and intuition you will find is fairly accurate. Be alert that your ego-mind can deceive you, and make you think the belief is much weaker than it really is.

The real truth lies in what is happening or being out-pictured in the joy and connection you experience from your relationships, events, and circumstances in your life or the absence of such things. For example, if you are not manifesting abundant health or success in your life, chances are that you have a belief that you do not deserve it, it is not safe, you're not worthy, or you have the secondary benefit of receiving nurture. To further confirm your assessment:

1. Sit up straight, close your eyes, and breathe into your diaphragm. Then, maintaining your straight posture, relax with your head balanced on the fulcrum of your neck. Say the word "yes" and see if your head feels like nodding "yes." Your head may move or may just give you the sensation of moving. Either way is perfect. Now say the word "no" and see if your head feels like moving left to right, shaking a "no." Once you have a clear sense of movement, pick a number on the ten point scale and say, for example, "It's a 7." If you get a "no" move higher or lower on the scale, following your intuitive gut-reaction. When you get to a "yes," you now have an accurate measurement of the strength of the negative belief in question.

2. Ask for someone to test the muscle strength in your arm. The easiest way to get a clear reading is to extend an arm out to the side. Testing the strength after each statement, have the other person press down on your arm as you resist his or her pressing. Then have them state a few true and false statements. And if you know from your innermost wisdom for a statement to be true, your arm will be strong. If you know from your innermost wisdom for a statement to be false, your arm will become weak. Examples are: your accurate age vs. a false age; an accurate color you are wearing vs. a color you are not wearing. Another example: the accurate town you are currently in vs. a town anywhere else. Get a clear distinction on these and you will most likely get a clear answer to the strength of your limiting belief(s). Have the other person ask the question phrased this way: "Is the belief you have a (insert number)?" If you think that the strength of your belief is an "8," for example,

and your arm stays strong, check the next higher and the next lower number and see if your arm goes weak. Find the number where your arm is the strongest. That will be your accurate reading of your belief. A demonstration of the power of our thoughts is provided for on our website at: www.TheTruthMovie.tv/muscletesting.

You are now ready to begin the process of clearing the belief. Doing so will sustain the shape-shifting transformational experience available to you.

CLEARING NEGATIVE CORE BELIEFS

The Freeing Limiting Beliefs Worksheet™ provides you with a technique that focuses your conscious intention to change and clear unwanted negative core beliefs. This powerful exercise utilizes the Chinese system of acupressure points, which enables you to release the negative emotions and core beliefs connected with a particular pressure point on your body. By breathing as you discharge the unbeneficial belief or emotion, you fuel the brain with oxygen which aids in healing, relaxation, and focus. Such a combination of acupressure, intention, and breathing is very effective in clearing negative beliefs you have stored. The Anatomy Pressure Points Illustration below will assist you in finding the correct pressure point and clearing the limiting belief.

EFTA Acupressure Points
An Adaptation of the Emotional Freedom Technique
By Henry Grayson, Ph.D.

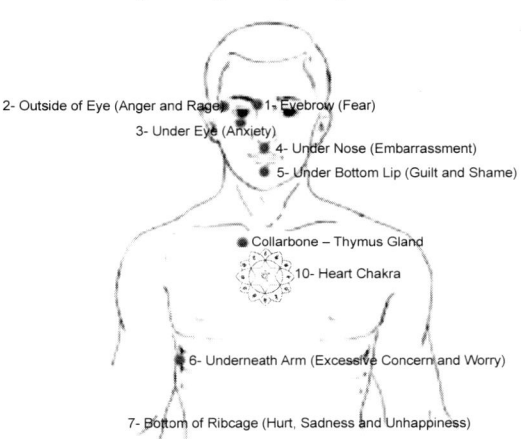

FREEING YOUR LIMITING BELIEFS WORKSHEET

An adaptation of the EFT (Emotional Freedom Technique) Accompanied by Anatomy Acupressure Points Illustration

Oxford's Dictionary defines belief as the certainty that comes from the accepting what we think is true in our minds, coupled with what we feel is true in our hearts.

My limiting belief (or trauma) is:

Write here how you feel your belief (or trauma) has affected you:

On a scale of 0-10, with 0 representing what you don't believe at all, assess how strong the belief is (you may use your intuition or gut feeling for a number or see Assessing the Strength of Limiting Core Beliefs page 75).

0   1   2   3   4   5   6   7   8   9   10

1. Think of the limiting belief and then take a deep breath placing your right hand over your thymus gland and rub your hand in a clockwise circle, and repeat the following statements: "I deeply love and accept myself even though I carry this limiting belief of (insert limiting belief)."

2. Place the fingertip of either your right or left hand to your forehead. Take several slow deep breaths and focus on that limiting belief. Allow memories or scenes which represent that belief to come into your mind. Notice which emotions come up with the memories and/or scenes. Identify where you feel them in your body and focus on these places.

3. Move your fingers to point 1 tap your fingertip there while you say: "I now release all fear related to (insert limiting belief)." Take a slow deep breath. Repeat 4 or 5 times.

4. Place your fingers on point 2, tap your fingertips there and say: "I now release all resentment, anger, and rage related to (insert limiting belief)." Take a slow deep breath.

5. Place your fingers on point 3, tap your fingertips there and say: "I now release all anxiety related to (insert limiting belief)." Take a slow deep breath.

6. Place your fingers on point 4, tap your fingertips there and say: "I now release all embarrassment and humiliation related to (insert limiting belief)." Take a slow deep breath.

7. Place your fingers on point 5, tap your fingertips there and say: "I now release all shame and guilt related to (insert limiting belief)." Take a slow deep breath.

8. Place your fingers on point 6, tap your fingertips there and say: "I now release all excessive concern related to (insert limiting belief)." Take a slow deep breath.

9. Place your fingers of both hands on point 7, tap your fingertips there and say: "I now release all hurt and sadness related to (insert limiting belief)."

10. Place your fingers on point 8 and while taking several slow deep breaths imagine you are breathing love into your heart and exhaling fear out through your solar-plexus, point 9.

11. Place your fingertips back up to point 1, tap your fingertips there and say: "I release any remaining fear of releasing (insert limiting belief)."

Once complete, check your progress by running through the assessment test again or muscle testing your arm to see what numerical value strength your limiting belief is now. Repeat the EFTA process until you get a "0" on the ten point scale.

For additional copies of this worksheet, go to http://THETRUTHMOVIE.tv/freeinglimitingbeliefsworksheet

Now that you are freeing yourself from negative core beliefs, you will find that it is easier to monitor the negative thoughts that arise from the presence of that formerly held belief. Once a negative belief is cleared, the dense energy holding it releases and goes away, opening up a feeling of lightness. It can, however, reappear over time if you allow thoughts back in that could support or reinforce that limiting belief. Continue using The 18 Second Thought Monitoring Worksheet (page 72) daily as a means to keep yourself cleared.

WHAT IF YOU STILL FIND IT DIFFICULT TO THOUGHT MONITOR?

This means that the subconscious mind's limbic system, located deep within the human brain, has encoded information which, acting like a firewall on a computer, can be overriding the rational and conscious part of your brain. The subconscious mind etches in somatic markers which encode memories of the painful past. These markers get triggered through your relationships and events which can unconsciously destroy your joy, happiness, and true sense of power. They can be remembered or forgotten traumas or they can be insidious on-going painful developmental experiences. If this is true for you, you need to first clear out certain encoded memories or traumas to ensure neurochemical responses are not hijacking your rational brain and interfering with your ability to thought monitor which is an important life empowering component to experience living with continued peace and discovering your truth.

Refer back to Assessing the Strength of Limiting Core Beliefs (page 75) and use the Freeing Limiting Beliefs Worksheet™. Replace the word "belief" with "trauma" as you go though the steps. Once you have assessed the level of disturbance from that trauma, you can go about clearing it until you get a reading of "0" on the 10-point scale.

THE THIRD CATEGORY OF THOUGHTS: INTERPRETIVE PERCEPTIONS

There is no such thing as a purely objective thought. Physicists tell us the moment we have observed anything, we have already influenced it. Conditioned as we are, we only see through the filters of our perceptions and the eyes of the past. Or as Rebbe Nachman said: "We do not see things as they are. We see them as we are." A Course in Miracles puts it succinctly: "Projection makes perception." Even when we think we are seeing accurately we are in actuality projecting only from the current beliefs we carry. Even in law it is now recognized that if 10 different people witness an accident or a crime, most of them will have quite different perceptions and descriptions of what happened. Change your beliefs and you can release the shackles of your limiting perceptions to experience a new reality.

Clearing the effects of traumas and negative core beliefs helps by opening awareness to enable new experiences, creating new set-points, to create the confidence needed to build inner trust and proceed with life-empowering practices. Monitoring negative thoughts is a key component of co-creating higher levels of awareness, change, and consciousness. Following this, you can at any time choose to make a perceptual shift in real time, right in the present moment, at the trigger point of interaction.

So how do you do that? First, recognize that there are just two basic emotions in the world: love and fear. Such simplicity is of enormous help in a moment of trigger and interaction when you do not have time to analyze dozens of possibilities. Love feels light and great. Fear feels heavy and sticks you with an "ouch." It helps to remember that everyone is reacting from fear or responding from love. There are no other options. If one is not behaving or speaking out of love, then they are behaving or speaking from fear. And if they are speaking out of fear, there is only one antidote which will help heal, and that is love.

By knowing this truth, the words or actions during acts of anger, rage and violence, can help us to not take the reaction as personal. Instead, we can openly ask our heart's intelligence, what need is crying out as a clear appeal for help and for love?

This allows you to find compassion within yourself to ground yourself to pro-actively choose to respond with love. If you can become the observer, you can see that every act of anger, rage, or violence is simply a tragic expression and appeal for love. Instead of seeing only the nasty or objectionable behavior and judging it, you can choose to remove yourself from a place of weakness or victimization by realizing you're just the stimulus but not the cause of another's behavior. This powerful wisdom alone can allow you to practice remaining peaceful and calm to open the heartspace to choose love. Your choice to act from love, rather than mirror the fear being projected on you, allows you to act as the powerful co-creator which transforms your experience in your relationships. This process is one that is generated from the intention we choose from within. Though invisible to the human eye, this is the greatest tool you will ever apply, capable of turning the raging tides of fear that cause all reactions of violence and war in life.

MAKING A PERCEPTUAL SHIFT

Jennifer was a senior vice president of a major multi-national corporation. The division she headed was down in profits for the quarter, since products are cyclical. But, in spite of the cause of profit-loss being cyclical and not due to some incompetence on her part, her boss was giving her an extremely rough time about it. In the weekly meetings of the vice presidents, she would be criticized and ridiculed in front of the other 75 vice presidents. It was so painful, Jennifer was considering hiring a lawyer to find a way to break her contract and leave the company. I asked her if she would like to try an experiment first. "Of course," she said. "If it works that's far better than all the legal hassle of trying to break a contract. What do I do?" she asked.

She was quite aware that her boss was running scared, fearing the loss of his job if all divisions were not profitable. He had locked himself into a very expensive lifestyle with a chauffeur-driven Rolls Royce, three children in boarding schools, and another two in expensive Ivy League colleges.

Just before the next weekly meeting, Jennifer went into her office for a few minutes to take some deep breaths to center herself. Then, she tried to keep in mind how afraid her boss was, picturing him standing in front of the group, but at the same time, imagining a very frightened little boy inside him. Relaxed and centered, she was able to feel a certain amount of compassion for the scared little boy inside, as well as the frightened man who supervised her. She also had an awareness that like herself, her boss may also feel boxed, afraid, and stuck because of his lifestyle. Still thinking the experiment was somewhat silly, Jennifer continued to hold this image of her boss as she sat in the meetings, regardless of what was going on. After one meeting she came back saying that her boss only ridiculed her about half as much as usual. She was not sure whether it had to do with her exercise, but decided to continue and see. Within a few weeks he had reduced his treatment of her to about 3 percent of what it had been. And within a couple more months, he started to make her his personal confidant, and was inviting her to his home to have dinners with his family. The only thing that was different was that Jennifer was seeing him differently. You too can make a perceptual shift and make yourself feel stronger and less vulnerable. Your different energetic signals will impact your relationships in a drastically different way.

Know that you cannot make the perceptual shift in the hope of manipulating someone into changing. If you choose to genuinely see someone as reacting in fear, you can choose to move into their feelings of fear, which creates a genuine compassion for them, as you accept their actions as an appeal for love. Practice this and watch what happens in your life.

YOU ARE NOT YOUR THOUGHTS

At the very root of all your pain and suffering are your thoughts. Any thought that hurts or sticks can be changed. No matter how long they've been part of your mind/body/heart system, you can transform any limiting, life-negating thought into thoughts that open you up to creating an experience of reality where the feelings of joy, peace, love, health, happiness and abundance are the governing feelings in your life.

Continue to diligently monitor your thoughts and as you discover another negative belief or trauma, clear it from your system. Practicing this allows you to build inner trust to grow and expand your capacity for learning and transformation. Only you can take time to quiet your thoughts to listen to the silent language of your heart, a conversation that only you can hear. As you feel and tune into the impulse to become more, feel more, and live more in alignment with the authentic truth you were created to be, your journey and reality unfolds in a life of limitless possibility.

What you think not only affects you, your body, your emotions and your moods, it also affects everyone and every living thing around you. You are constantly affecting the world around you more profoundly than you can imagine. Such awareness makes Mahatma Gandhi's famous quote even more poignant: "If you want to change the world, first be that change." Where that change in the world begins is not "out there" but rather within you, beginning first, always, with your own thoughts. Gandhi further said, "Always aim at complete harmony of thought and word and deed. Always aim at purifying your thoughts and everything will be well." If you try to change behaviors without changing your thoughts, you will be at war—incoherent and in discord within yourself. To change your thoughts, you must turn inward and become conscious of all the thoughts that disturb your inner peace—which then also disturb your body, other people, animals, plants and every living system around you—the irreducible universal whole. Once you have your own thoughts aligned with the truth within yourself, then you can be effective in bringing about real transformation within not only your living reality but within the world at large.

Govern your thoughts wisely by choosing to embrace positive, life-affirming thoughts that are within you and you will realize the power of mastering your thoughts. By consciously and continuously pursuing the development of your heart/mind coherence, you will attract whatever is necessary to bring you into greater alignment and continued discovery of the infinite being within you. To connect to the inherent kingdom of love and happiness within you is to awaken from the illusion of separation. When the awareness of this truth of you living and being a part of a unified participatory reflective reality awakens within you, life takes on a whole new meaning; shifting your experience of reality in a blink of an eye.

We needn't look very far to see examples of people who seem to have it all: wealth, power, beauty, and fame, yet still play out their life running from an insatiable thirst for more, never seeming to have enough.

Genuine happiness and well-being is an ever-changing, tantalizing, sensuous, delightfully blissful, timeless experience which never becomes stale or old. The inner experience we are all seeking is to live from this joy within. This entire journey called life is to discover this joy of abundance within. Once you drink from this cup, everything and everyone, with or without material measure, unleashes their power of magic from within. The rhapsody of great bounty is found as you discover and live the one purpose we all came here for—to learn to be love, to give that love and to receive that perfect reflection. This truth is the one universal truth that our masters have shared all along—unending bliss is created from the reservoir of authentic love residing within you.

III

Completing Your Past

The unexamined life is a life not worth living. It is time to re-evaluate your past as a guide to your future.
—SOCRATES

THE ONLY WAY OUT...IS IN

By applying the tools in Chapter II, those feelings of more openness and lightness, being more positive, and having more energy are the result of opening up more space within you. You've just unloaded tons of mental and emotional energy that was poorly invested, fueling negative thoughts and stories of your past that have kept your broken records stuck in repeat mode. The vibrations you are feeling, the lightness, the sense of renewal, and your interest in other human beings, and them in you, happens when you lighten your load. These vibrations are felt by everyone. As you erase the stories of the past and free up the power you formerly invested by keeping those thoughts on repeat, you begin to operate on a whole new frequency. Naturally, those capable of operating at the same higher vibration will find themselves attracted to you. As your awareness expands, celebrate building enriching and positive friendships and connections as you enjoy a deepened sense of community around you. If indeed you find you are on the brink of an intimate love relationship with someone, it may be best to delay until you have moved into the "you" you are already becoming, so you don't get trapped in the distractions of the old patterns that keep you locked and constricted. Preserve time, sacred time, to dedicate and honor each crucial step of turning inward and completing your past. Remember, you've spent a lifetime building walls and stories and it will take discipline to re-pattern your new default set points. You may experience old relationship patterns wanting to take over to deflate your sails. Stay vigilant. What you are experiencing is real. Growing your awareness is what matters to construct the life of your highest dreams. You deserve to give yourself this time to learn how to be present, to listen, to tap into your infinite potential, to access the experience and fullness of interconnected life.

The Truth is... the only way out, is in!

Everything you get from the external world, including pain and painful circumstances is both a symptom and a gift, directing you within, waking you up to becoming more of the truth of who you really are.

Creating everything you can ever imagine, and more, is possible now. As you continue to let go of the finite stories and false beliefs about who you've been conditioned to be, you open up the infinite truth of who you are! This is not an exercise of sheer willpower, but of simply doing the work. Using your triggers in life as the tools and building blocks to re-pattern and build new neural pathways, you attain higher and higher levels of awareness and intuition, which allows you to access the truth of who you truly are!

WHO WOULD YOU BE WITHOUT YOUR STORY?

The stories we have told ourselves have been with us for the better part of our lives. Everywhere we look, and often, nearly everyone we know is steeped in some false identity and story. Television, movies, and literature perpetuate this drama while our closest friends, lovers, and family members all feel they know us based on knowing our stories. Well... you are not your story.

"Mom doesn't love me," "My dad was never proud of me," "My partner doesn't understand me," "My children don't care about me," "I'll be happy when I...." These stories have been with us for so long, they feel like a second skin. Doing the clearing work, you now know what that feeling of lightness feels like within your *being*, as you've begun to release the heavy weight and energy needed to run these stories.

Congratulations!

Next, you'll clear out old residual *patterns* of thinking that lie below the surface of your conscious awareness. One neuron in our brain can connect with as many as 15,000 other neurons[7]. This establishes a complex series of connections between neurons that trigger certain negative reactions within us when we experience certain stimuli. After a lifetime of living in response to our entrained core beliefs, these patterns work to maintain particular modes of thinking. Like grooves in a record, our tendency is to slip into such grooves or patterns of thinking or stories. Hence, clearing this level of programming and instituting healthier responses to cut new groves or patterns into our circuitry is essential for long-term successful transformation. This way, when life presents you with something challenging, perhaps the loss of a loved one, the loss of a job, or a separation of some kind, you are better equipped to remain aligned in your truth and operate from a place of authentic love and real potency.

Your stimuli and emotional reactions from relationships and circumstances provide the perfect opportunity to see into yourself. A very powerful exercise provided at the end of this chapter, The Judge-Your-Neighbor Worksheet, is based on and created by the transformational teachings of Byron Katie, author of *The Work*. By judging you neighbor, you begin to understand that the judgments we hold toward others and ourselves serve as starting point for greater self realization; providing greater glimpses into false stories, to see the truth of what is really operating below the surface. Complete the worksheet prior to any further clearing work, and you will gain greater awareness of your own patterns and stories. You'll open up a newfound compassion towards yourself and others as you come to see that all of your personal experiences are, in reality, interconnected and co-created, and are nothing more than mind believing the thoughts and beliefs you hold within. The interior and the exterior are the same. Even in the most chaotic of situations, how you co-create your reality becomes nothing more than a reflection of what is alive within you.

---

7   Shonkoff, J.P., & Phillips, D.A. (Eds). (2000). *From Neurons to Neighborhoods: The Science of Early Childhood Development* National Academies' Press.

WE DO NOT KNOW WHAT WE DO NOT KNOW, UNTIL WE DO

To see into this truth, think about how it is you truly learn anything in life. You only possess the awareness your current life's experiences, to date, have brought into your field of understanding. It is only when you become triggered by someone or something happening that you can expand your consciousness to come to know more than the moment before. Put another way, "We simply do not know what we do not know, until we do!" When your experience has created enough pain, rather than turning inward, our conditioning wants to go to the mind to do what we think we need to do—"solve" or understand the "problem." Do you find that you also try to figure out your "whys" still using your conditioned linear patterns of thinking?

You're not alone!

Pain is a powerful and potent gift. Pain is the impulse whereby you can learn to search within, gain clarity, and unlock answers leading you to live aligned to your truest nature. Remember, *everything* you get from the external world, including pain and painful circumstances is both your symptom and your gift, directing you within, waking you up to re-membering more of the truth of who you really are.

Freedom from suffering and discovering internal peace comes as you surrender and experience the gift of learning to love what is. Suffering is a direct result of thoughts about what someone said or did, viewed through the lens of limiting belief and perception, which then becomes the so-called "reality" experienced in relationships.

Who's writing the story of your life?

Are you living *it* or is *it* living you?

Does it have a happy ending?

ANGER IS A PLAGUE

There is a story of a man so plagued with anger that he went away to work out his "problem." He turns away from the world and moves to a hut alone in the mountains. Choosing to be completely monastic, he dedicates his full practice to working out the anger addiction that has caused much suffering and prevented him from experiencing deep authentic relationships and connections in life. Every morning he wakes and meditates. He then has a simple meal and meditates again until night has fallen. He sleeps, wakes the following day, and does the same thing all over again. Ten years pass. Convinced of his enlightenment, he finally comes down from the mountaintop of his isolation, ready to experience the reality of a peaceful life only to find the town's people have forgotten him, his wife has married another man, and they are living in the house he built! Seeing this, he's instantly engulfed in fury, at which point the town's people suddenly recognize him and they laugh saying he's the same crazy man who'd run off to the mountains years ago. Moral of the story: There's nowhere to run from yourself. At some point you must reckon with the world and reckon with you. The only way out is in!

Your relationships, and life circumstances, provide the perfect experience and mirror in order to turn inward, inquire, and heal negative thoughts, beliefs and conditioning that have lead you down an abyss. Thinking, "If only he/she would ... *then* I'll be happy," makes us the hostage and victim of an external world, giving someone or something else the responsibility to provide feelings of happiness and peace. And, how do you really feel when you try to change, manipulate, or control someone? Do you feel frustration, anger, anxiety, or stress? How do you show up in that relationship when you believe your story that someone "should" be a certain way, or "should" do a certain something, to create your happiness? How does existence feel when you are thinking life should be something other than it is now, in this present moment? Power, peace, love, and happiness lie within you as you inquire within and surrender to what is. It is in the letting go of your resistance to surrender to not knowing anything, that we find the infinite possibility to see without the filters of limitations. Your relationship to life, in the present moment, becomes extraordinary and beautiful when you make love to the lesson that comes from each experience before you.

CREATING THE "GAP" USING THE FREEZEFRAME™ TECHNIQUE

John Symes, featured in *The Truth, The Journey Within* film, mentions one of the biggest game-changing illustrations he received from the Stephen Covey book, *The 7 Habits of Highly Effective People*, which talks about the "gap" that begins to occur when you stop and become aware of the stimuli that trigger your responses. Creating this gap frees you from the victimhood stories that keep you stuck in vicious patterned cycles of relating. As you gain awareness of your typical autonomic response (your usual conditioned response behaviors, thoughts, or attitudes), you then become capable of making different choices. You can choose to no longer respond in the negative, self-defeating ways you have been conditioned by. When you feel triggered, you can stop, magnify the gap, and choose to respond differently. Symes says: "When we create a gap between stimulus and response, we've created the opportunity for freedom." Being in the gap is something we are all capable of once we have a little know-how and practice. This high level of conscious functioning while interfacing with others can restore "broken" or troubled relationships while also giving you a newfound sense of sovereignty, peace and empowerment experienced as your wants and needs make contact with the heart of another.

FREEZEFRAME™ TECHNIQUE

The FreezeFrame™ Technique, created by HeartMath and demonstrated in *The Truth, The Journey Within* film, helps you create more moments of "gap" between the stimuli encountered in your life and your responses. When you are triggered, you can stop, like a movie editor, and freeze the frame on that particular moment of your life. Then, with the frame frozen, you can actually edit that frame by going within, to listen to your heart, and make the choice to experience a different outcome.

For example, someone you love has a loud emotional outburst. During this outburst they might yell, and even call you names, getting right in your face. You feel triggered (the stimulus) with a flood of emotions.

Emotions aren't just reactions, they're choices.

Reacting with anger is certainly one option, as is closing down your heart and ears by your own internal rebellion. Neither choice represents a loving one that maintains connection between the two of you. Both are painful and create suffering which hinder and co-create greater disconnection and distance between you. If you can step back, and stop, you don't have to be sucked into the drama of reaction. See the outburst as a Director, an observer. As you freeze the frame on the movie drama of life and go to your heart, placing your hand above your heart, holding your energies there for 20-30 seconds as you breathe deeply, you create the "gap" and choose your response to experience your freedom.

Listen to what your heart has to say, then, go back to your head. Between the two responses, you can see the choice—the gap. From there you may respond in a way that will have a more beneficial outcome. While doing this it may be helpful to remember that there are only two emotions: love and fear. Remember, whatever the other person is saying or doing is actually an appeal for love. Try listening and guessing what unmet need is crying out through their anger and reaction (Needs Identification list is presented later in the Language of Compassion chapter). Your freedom comes as you make the choice to respond from a place of love.

You can always use the FreezeFrame™ Technique to unlock the situation of drama. Whether in the middle of a business negotiation or talking with your spouse or children, the only control you have to co-create peace in your life comes from choosing your internal and external responses. Creating the gap between your stimulus and response creates freedom to not get caught up in the drama of life. Stopping to pause, enables greater objectivity at what just happened, resulting in a conscious choice to exercise and build new muscles for living daily from our conscious choices, wishes, and desires for authentic connection, building a foundation of well-being and inner trust. We can experience relationships in a new space that fosters the trust needed to co-create more beneficial outcomes of deeper shared intimacy.

BRIDGING THE GAP MEANS BEING IN THE QUESTION

Using the FreezeFrame™ Technique is even beneficial when you're by yourself. You've been conditioned into believing that success in life means results. Learning to drive from this false mentality that focuses on results plays the same etched grooves in the record, "faster is better." This programming allows the mind to run amok and generate autonomic reactions in a millisecond that not only block and ignore your capacity to hear your heart's truth and your body's "gift," which come to you as triggers in the reflections of your relationships, but also denies you the freedom to choose your response from the wisdom that is within your heart's awareness.

When you relax, and freeze the frame, and practice going to your heart vs. your head, you will begin to create new neural pathways, which creates new marker set points, that will begin to create a natural resting default in your heart. Reacting allows life to have its way with you. Your freedom will come when you allow the mind to do what it does—chatter. That is what the mind does. You may then *observe* the response your mind has generated. Doing this enables you to create the necessary gap to then consult your heart—the storehouse of the truth of who you truly are. As you do this, breathe deeply into your chest and s·l·o·w the whole process down and see what happens.

Being in the question, and not in your mind's need for an answer, opens your awareness to create new possibilities. By letting yourself be in the question, acting as both mentor and observer, you learn to move past whatever subconscious patterns are blocking you from operating in your authentic potency and power, to claim being the powerful co-creator of your grandest purpose and dreams. From this open space, the answer often spontaneously presents itself with clarity. Einstein said, "There comes a leap of consciousness, call it intuition or what you will, and the solution comes to you, and you don't know how or why."

Beyond managing your responses and behaviors, being in the question of asking yourself what just triggered my emotion, is a simple moment-to-moment choice you have to experience life in a very different way. Questioning your fear-based reactions, that stem from old dogmatic patterns and false beliefs running in your subconscious mind, puts you in the driver's seat of creating your life experience. As you ask the question, your intuition and cognitive thinking creates the necessary open mental space, the gap, which enables you to act from your highest thought and truth. As you continue expanding the gap between your stimulus and response, you will re-pattern new set points, raising your capacity to stay heart-centered and at peace. You will begin to see that creating a gap is becoming second nature to you.

The next exercise acquaints you with a powerful method for clearing out the subconscious energetic patterns that keeps you locked into finite beliefs that limit you from experiencing and living in your greatness, power, and full potentiality. Every emotion is an actual energy. As energy beings, energy is designed to be in motion. Every limiting thought, decision, attitude, and belief you hold locks you into a judgment and energetic pattern that creates an experience of reality that forces you to play out your story from a place of limitation. Locking judgment into how something should be or not be, what someone ought to do or not do, what you or someone has to have, or not have, to be living life happy, and in ease and flow, creates an experience of life that solidifies the energy, boxing you into energetic thought patterns that feeds all feelings of lack and scarcity from within your mind/body/heart system.

If you're looking for results—more money, more enjoyment, and loads of deep connections, which contributes to making life more wonderful and happy in your relationships, then the less you believe you know (creating your finite reality), the faster this clearing process will work for you.

Our conditioning, from childhood has taught us to go to our head (vs. our heart) to figure out problems and access solutions. Trying to solve our problems comes from a place of linear patterned thinking. This creates a contextual, finite box which only allows us access to what has been stored, to date, in our life experiences and current belief system. We've been taught to love a good challenge. If you're living from the experience of wanting and desiring anything, then you are living from the longing of what you don't have, which never feels good, and constricts your mind/body/heart from *being* the allowance that opens the access of infinite possibility to flow into our lives. As you release these questions of inquiry into the Universe, you can surrender and release, to live in the openness of ease, joy, peace, and acceptance of knowing all is accessible in the field of allowance. All resistance creates a finite limitation that is counterintuitive to the infinite being you are.

Pure consciousness is the choice to live every moment of your life in the presence and within the capacity to generate and receive everything, without judgment of yourself or anyone else, accepting the moment and loving what is. From this open space of pure potentiality, you access the power to co-create everything you desire in life, greater than life as it currently is, and in the highest and grandest potentiality of more than you can ever imagine.

In this power of consciousness, you can create everything.

This clearing process was founded and created from the work of Gary Douglas, Access Consciousness™ (www.accessconsciousness.com), who received his understanding of how to clear the finite contextual electromagnetic energetic fields from a download he received over 20 years ago. His work is now being taught all over the world. I was introduced to Access Consciousness through Angela Gower-Johnson, who has added and refined her teachings to include 23 years of training from ancient wisdom passed down from Native American shamans, combined with her training in the science of Neuro Linguistic Programming (NLP) and energy training. Through Angela and her work, I was introduced to Gary Douglas' partner, Dr. Dain Heer, who travels and leads workshops all over the world.

Dr. Dain Heer started work as a Network Chiropractor eleven years ago in California. Having worked with bodies since he was in college, Dr. Heer came across Access Consciousness at a point in his life when he was deeply unhappy and even planning suicide. Access Consciousness changed everything. When none of the other modalities and techniques Dr. Heer had been studying were giving him lasting results or change, with Access Consciousness, his life began to expand and grow with more ease and speed than even he could have imagined possible.

Within Access, Dr. Heer has developed a unique energy process for change for individuals and groups, called The Energetic Synthesis of Being.

Dr. Heer has a completely different approach to change. He teaches people to tap into and recognize their own abilities and knowing. The energetic transformation possible is fast—and truly dynamic. Today, Dr. Dain Heer and Gary Douglas travel all over the world facilitating advanced classes on Access Consciousness. The access process of Being and Living In The Question below invites and inspires people to experience more consciousness from a space of total allowance, caring, and humor which accesses the phenomenal knowing they are.

You are an infinite beings who come into this lifetime fully aware. Then, here comes that 0-6 programming, and slowly, we become blocked by the conditioning of being told what and who we are and are not. This powerful process of Access Consciousness operates at the level of awareness that knows exactly what your limitations are and clears that lie from your being. Remember, as an energy being, whatever imprints of negative energetic conditioning and embedded limitations have been installed into your energy field, you surely possess the infinite power of knowing how to remove them. You now have the tools to re-member the truth of who you are and were created to be. By the way, these are not your limitations, they are the passed down limitations from your parents, role models, and cultural conditioning telling you the "way" life is.

Remember, you are your own perfect teacher—a fully individuated truth, who has the infinite power to live life "on purpose" as only you were created to be.

LIVING AND BEING IN THE QUESTION: SUBCONSCIOUS CLEARING EXERCISES

For the next 30 days, as you rise each morning, and as you end each day, create a new life habit of living and being in the question, by asking yourself at least two of these questions that feel most resonate to you, then running them throughout your day. This will set your energetic level to align with the answers of possibility as you go about your day. It helps to repeat these questions, ideally, 10-20 times per day or anytime you notice fear-based thought patterns, heavy feelings, or actions of negativity popping up into your consciousness. By holding the intention, breathing with mindful allowance, and focusing your attention to just being in the question, you will begin to create and feel an energetic shift of openness.

These questions are not asked from your conditioned logical mind, nor are they designed to be answered by your conscious mind. Ask your questions from the awareness of original inquiry and wonder, with the curiosity of a child asking for the first time why the sky is blue. This opens up the field of allowance and pure potentiality vs. the finite state of resistance of "knowing" why the sky is blue. Remember, if we think something or someone is already a certain way, we have just cemented in a finite box which does not allow for the Universe to uncreate the lie and open the truth for you.

As you run the questions, you'll want to tune into your senses.

Once you've repeated your question a number of times and you let whatever feelings or thoughts make their presence known, you will feel a perceptual shift or sense of lightness. When you feel this shift occurring, repeat the Clearing Statement on page 104, 2-3 times to release any subconscious patterns and limitations that stand in the way of you *being* the potent, powerful, infinite being that you are.

These questions are energetic questions to open and clear the energetic fields that hold the subconscious limiting beliefs. In fact, as an energy being, every emotion and thought is pure energy. Your participation of allowance is all that is required. These questions and clearing statements go to work to uninstall any finite limitations at the point of creation, when they were locked into your mind/body/heart. Our Universe responds to these questions by shifting your energetic field. As you ask the questions, stay present with the *feelings* that are generated from the question and release them to the Universe. These questions are designed to allow you to experience life, functioning at your highest level of awareness and infinite potential. If the chosen words do not resonate with you, customize them to feel more authentic. The questions are flexible, but the Clearing Statement should be memorized verbatim. Doing so will further open and free your energetic space to feel into your senses and formulate the questions you need to ask.

Note: Question #3 is an amazing question when we feel anger or other draining feelings or emotions. There is a lot of energetic chaos today, which as sensitive and aware beings, you are likely at times to be picking up on someone else's energy and then believing it is yours. Do not naturally assume when you feel a trigger or feeling that it is yours. While it may be, this question will help identify that truth in your body system.

LIVING IN THE QUESTION:
1. What secret agendas do I have with not being the infinite being I was created to be?

2. What secret agendas do I have that maintain everything I cannot change, choose, or institute?

3. Who does this reaction, trigger, or feeling belong to anyway? State: Return to sender with consciousness attached.

4. What is the value of having _____ as an enemy? (meaning: having them work against you, instead of with you?)

5. If I had no past, what would I generate today?

6. If my back (neck) was free from holding stress, what would I generate today?

7. What if I nurture and care for me, how much love would I be?

8. Who am I now and what grand, glorious and rewarding adventure will I generate?

9. What willingness can I be to open all the doors of everything I thought was not possible?

10. If my heart had never been hurt, what fun, amazing, phenomenal, rewarding, and totally orgasmic relationship would I be in?

11. What would it take for me to have a relationship with (insert Name) that is filled with ease, joy, and glory and is totally orgasmic for me?

12. How does it get any better than this?

13. Universe, what is it going to take to totally transform my financial situation?

14. What am I going to have to do, have, be, create, or generate today to have success come to fruition right away?

15. What are the Infinite Possibilities of my living in the house of my dreams?

16. What are the Infinite Possibilities of financial abundance to share with my world?

17. What are the Infinite Possibilities of me having the man/woman of my dreams with (insert desired traits)

Anytime you have found yourself giving your power away, made yourself small, limited, finite or lesser than someone else run:

18. WOW, I chose that, now what do I choose?

19. What infinite possibilities are possible here?'

For those of you who are businesses owners, realize your business is a separate entity that wants to thrive. It will, once you release any limitations and beliefs you hold for it. Here are some questions to ask as you begin your day, or as you enter into a partnership with someone. Find a couple that seem to resonate with you.

1. What does my business (insert name) require of me today?

2. What can I contribute to (insert name) today?

3. What space can I be in that would allow my business to be fun, phenomenal, and rewarding?

You can break down areas of thought directed toward a specific need in your business, or project, and ask questions like:

1. (Insert Business or Project), who can you contribute to bring in the financing I need today?

2. (Insert Business or Project), how can you contribute to bring the marketing I need today?

3. (Insert Business or Project), how do you want to show up? In theatres, in DVD, on-line, book, audio?

4. (Insert Business or Project), will this be rewarding (financially, relationally, etc)?

5. (Insert Business or Project), what phenomenal results can we generate together?

6. (Insert Business or Project), what magic can we be, do, generate and create? And what possibilities will be created in the world with that magic?

7. (Insert Business or Project), what generative energy and space can we be and receive today for the consciousness of the planet?

FOR SOMEONE WHO REALLY GETS UNDER OUR SKIN

The following questions provide a powerful way to clear all relationships of any strongholds that limit the relationship's full potential. It goes to the point of origin and begins to clear out limitations in our relationships. Most limitations and core wounds that block us generally originate from our parents. So think of whichever parent you had the most difficult relationship with and ask the following questions to clear judgments.

1. What does my mother/father mean to me?

2. What do I mean to my mother/father?

3. What does having sex with my mother/father mean to me?

4. What does having sex mean to my mother/father?

With the last two questions, I am not asking you to represent or to imagine the literal expression of having sex. These questions are only representative of the point of creation/conception sex, when the programming our parents had as they created us locked into our energy patterns that we hold around them. Do not judge yourself for asking these questions. Such behavior is simply the mind being fearful and defeatist. We are simply releasing energetic holding patterns.

After you have asked these questions that pertain to the parent, proceed to the exercise below and ask the questions pertaining to whomever it is that gets under your skin. If that person is a parent, do both sets of questions. This is a powerful way to begin the clearing on any relationships that trigger you as they eliminate any secret agendas you are not conscious of harboring in your relationships.

The process may take up to 30 minutes to run. Let any and all of the insane thoughts or emotions that come up for you run their course and begin to subside and ease into a more open feeling/space.

1. Who is this (insert name) person?

2. What does this (insert name) person mean to me?

3. What do I mean to this (insert name) person?

Repeat until you begin to feel a shift of lightness or ease, and then repeat the Clearing Statement a number of times. The Clearing Statement may look and sound funny at first, which is just your linear thinking of your conditioned mind. These questions and Clearing Statement do not access anything in our contextual, finite, or logical mind.

SUBCONSCIOUS CLEARING STATEMENT

> *"Everything that won't allow for this, will you destroy and uncreate it all please? Right and wrong, good and bad, pod/poc, all nines, shorts, boys and beyonds."*

Destroy and Un-Create: This is about destroying and un-creating anything that is finite that is keeping you in a limiting belief or subconscious pattern, blocking your success, happiness and joy.

Right/Wrong and Good/Bad: There are no polarities in the Universe. Polarities keep you stuck in a finite, contextual reality and polarity, which keeps you from being the infinite person you are. Speaking these questions and speaking the Clearing Statement, releases the limitations of what you hold locked as good or bad, right or wrong about an experience standing in the way of infinite possibilities.

POD—Point of Destruction. The ways you've been destroying yourself in order to keep whatever is limiting to you in effect and in existence. This releases the limitation.

POC—Point of Creation. The point where the limiting thoughts, emotions, and traumas were created. This releases the limitation immediately preceding what you decided.

All Nine: All nine layers of the energy holding the subconscious pattern in the physical realm of reality. This releases any limiting energy and subconscious patterns that hold you back from experiencing infinite potentiality in your life.

Shorts: Shorts means everything that's meaningless and meaningful, of consequence and gain, for this specific pattern of limitation.

Boys: Boys are jargon for the Nucleative Spears which are the energetic structures, like peeling an onion, that take you to the core of an issue, to break those cycles that keep you energetically bound to not being successful to change anything you would consciously choose, to live in your power, greatness, and purpose. This is where you get stuck, like peeling a layer of an onion. This clears whatever holds this limitation in place.

Beyonds: Beyonds clears any place, feelings, sensations, or circumstance that has kept you frozen in the headlights of time, not knowing what to do, where you closed down your willingness to look at possibilities. This speaks to infinite wisdom and potentiality to unlock and clear any subconscious patterns and limitations that have kept you frozen.

Transformation is more than change; it is a radical inner restructuring, an evolution into a higher order. As you do clearing work, you create space and enable your brain to reorganize itself into a more beneficial state of accessing greater potentiality to experience life greater than you currently can imagine. Such is a state that never ceases. It is always in motion, always thriving and interconnecting with the life around it. Life is always seeking a fuller expression of greatness through you. Through such transformation you enable yourself to reawaken forgotten passions and discover ones you never even knew you had. Such discovery is an intrinsic part of unfolding your unique truth, authenticity, and reason for being. By aligning with your intention you also return to access the infinite, the All That Is, accessed through living present in the highest vibration of thought: compassion, gratitude, celebration and love.

> *"To bring your body and mind into a place of harmony and to fully embrace, observe, and process the emotions that reside within us is what this journey of being human is all about."*

THE IMPACT OF NEGATIVE FEELINGS: ANGER & FEAR

Pain really is a gift when you see it as a call to go within and wake-up to the truth that is calling to be known. Anger is nature's catalyst to create the impulse for deep reflection into what is the source of our pain and to shine the light of awareness onto what unmet need is being brought forth, into our conscious awareness, so that we may speak our truth into our relationships and life, upleveling our moment-to-moment potential to expand our experiences of love.

The most common "remedies" we have been conditioned to use as a means to deal with our anger is to either repress it, or vent and dump our powerful emotions on others. Neither of these options contribute to our well-being (well of being) for ourselves or our relationships. Repression damages our internal well-being and health as the anger becomes lodged within our mind/body/heart system. Unfocused venting re-excites the nervous system and locks in a finite belief and story about something or someone. Dumping our anger can damage the trust and connection of our relationships, sometimes causing irrevocable breaches in our need for trust and safety, which require a lot of energy to restore.

If you were hooked up to a diagnostic brain scanner and were to view the biochemical processes and responses your body has to anger, and any other negative fear-based emotions, you would see a flood of toxic neurochemicals present, wreaking havoc on your physiological and psychological mind/body/heart systems. You would see that anger and negative patterns of thought are the single most lethal weapons you carry. These neurochemicals possess the power to cause rampant disease in our body, destruction of relationships, and feelings of separation, isolation, depression, anxiety and measurable despair.

Dr. Konstantin Korotkov, Russian Quantum Physicist shares in *The Truth, The Journey Within*™ film:

> *"Fear is one of the emotions, together with anger, that totally destroys our energy field. It is very important that of alot of people keep negative emotions and negative attitudes towards people around them, it affects their bodies, their heart, and their health. And, while we understand that we are not angels, all of us have positive sides and negative sides… we have our emotions which is absolutely clear. However, it is critically important to see what the outcome of negative emotions do to all of us. So, it is very important to realize the effect that negative feelings of anger, causing hatred and division have on our entire society*

> and energy field. As a final process, it is the most important step to choose positive emotions. for our self and for our entire field of consciousness."
>
> "Of course, we cannot avoid negativity; it's understandable, because life today is not ideal. We don't live in an angel world. We live in an open vault. We (subconsciously) accept information all the time, and when it is negative information, of course it has a very negative effect on our consciousness and our physical state as well. We have negative news from media and radio all the time. This anxiety that is generated by media, it has a very bad influence to people, very bad. It affects not only one person, it affects the conscious beliefs of an entire society. So, anger and fear generates a very negative (energy) field, collective in society.
>
> "It is very important to restrict yourself from negativity, and forgive yourself and others, and to return back to positive emotions in the end. Through your own efforts, it is tremendously important to process your anger and not to keep this field of negativity within you. There is very clear evidence that all of the body—your heart, your mind, your spirit, is deeply effected at all levels of physiological processes. Choosing between life-affirming or life-alienating thoughts and actions, either choosing light (love) or dark side (fear) is yours alone. It was always, it is always, and it will be always your own choice. Everyone can choose, everyone can organize his or her own life, in accordance with his conscious choice. If we understand that everything depends on our attitude to life, to environment, to other people, to our everyday activity, then we can totally transform our life."

You have been conditioned to repress, to tragically cut-off, stuff, or downgrade your negative feelings including: anger, rage, sadness, judgment, and disappointment. As we are triggered by powerful emotions, we do what we think we're supposed to do—

we try to relax or change our attitude. When you attempt to relax by downgrading (depressing) a powerful feeling, for example, like anger into a less tangible feeling like disappointment, without first embracing the full expression, and message that the powerful gift anger brings you, you deny yourself access to its originating source to clear it as it moves through you. Depressing and downgrading your anger to feelings like disappointment dampens your ability to also experience life's essence of positive emotions. Mathematically, if you repress your feeling of anger by say 30%, you also repress and downgrade your capacity to access anger's dual, positive feelings of passion, excitement, joy, and love by 30%, robbing your life of the experience to live as the full spectrum of experience of ecstasy, bliss, and joy, which is the truth of who you were created to be.

The suppression of justifiable anger is a coping mechanism we've been doing so long, we are often unaware we are doing it. When anger is continually suppressed, the neurons in our brain become clogged. Toxicosis, which is neurochemical poisoning, develops as a result, leading to future physical and emotional disease. It is our intrinsic nature to be in harmony. We were wired with the capacity to fully embrace, observe, and process through the emotions that come up within us. Emotions themselves are not the problem. The problem is simple. Most of our role models, and their role models, did not have tools or skills to access their inner wisdom to transfer powerful emotions. From the place of what is not, we created the opportunity, and necessary drivers, which led to breakthroughs in the fields of quantum, bioscience and neuroscience. This then led us to the discovery of energetic clearing technologies we now all have access to today, changing everything we previously understood about how we exist and co-create our experience in this world. You can now create the awareness of understanding to access effective clearing self-tools to process your negative emotions in beneficial ways that are non-violent, life-affirming, and connected to the highest truth of who we are. As you apply these practices into life, you can model to others how to stay grounded to a natural state of balanced well-being, changing your experience and reality of life.

To fully feel and learn to express all the emotions that embody the human experience is to participate in concepts of duality. For example, without the perception of suffering or pain, you would not be able to recognize the polarity dual emotion of happiness and joy. Suffering is, because happiness is; darkness is, because light is. All experiences are interdependent and irreducible. You can choose which reality you want to live in as you access the truth of who you are—a powerful co-creator of your own life, as it moves and lives and emotes through you.

Do not confuse these emotional polarities with those based on the rigid fear-based doctrines and power-over models, usually consisting of diametrically opposed positions of right/wrong, good/bad, should/shouldn't, blame/shame. To hold these beliefs in such fixed and rigid positions under the guise of "morality" is to feed into the very same tribal mindsets that fuel ruthless competition, division, greed, and deny the truth of our collective, yet interdependent connection to all of nature. To release these judgments is to open yourself up to be guided by your true moral compass and blueprint, becoming aligned to your truest nature, which is love—to live the ultimate act of compassion for both you and the world.

Compassion is an action and choice birthed from the absence of judgment and forgiveness. It is the highest form of love for it gives acceptance and understanding where there is no logical understanding. By first maintaining your connection within yourself, and then embracing behavior and modes of communication that maintain the flow of connection in your relationships, you shift your understanding and grow your ability for allowance of everything that is meaningful and meaningless to co-exist within you, as you release your judgment of how life is or should be. In this way, you co-create your rich canvas and vast ability to feel and experience what makes you joyful, at ease, peaceful, and living in the highest state of truth, being grateful for all that is in your unique journey to becoming more. As you accept and release the need to cling to, push away, or repress thoughts, feelings, and emotions that will come and go day-to-day, moment-by-moment, you invite your subconscious mind to relax into the full state of allowance. As you learn to open and trust in this process, your awareness of what inhibits you will, by divine design, float up to your consciousness to offer you the gift to continue on the journey to accessing your truth and experience living as your fullest potential in this lifetime.

Remember, there is no right or wrong or good or bad emotions. *All* emotions are a part of what it means to experience being human and offer you the powerful roadmap to discovering the beauty and gift of your humanness that makes you unique.

Howard Martin of HeartMath explains:

"Anger is definitely a learned condition. Anger carries a lot of energy. You can't even sustain anger for very long. There's a river of emotion running under our consciousness, or running under perceptions, 24/7, all the time. And, yet, we don't pay attention to it, we allow our emotions to control us. Certainly, we're going to have emotional reactions to things. But, emotions aren't just reactions, they're choices."

Dr. Rollin McCraty, a neuroscientist at HeartMath, further adds:

"One of the big problems in our society as a whole is that people are really disconnected from their feelings. A lot of times, what we're thinking and we're feeling really don't match, they're out of sync, they're out of alignment. And, that creates a lot of pain, a lot of stress in people's lives. Our heart is the "most powerful rhythmic oscillator in the body."

In order to not let ourselves be run by the roller-coaster ride of our emotions, we must be able to make room for our emotions, and to actually feel and process them within our hearts. The heart "pulls the body's other rhythms into synchronization with its own (rhythm)". Denying your emotion by trying to relax, distract yourself, or downgrade the feeling only achieves a conscious disassociation from the feeling, when in actuality it is still present within the rhythmic and electrical impulses of the mind-heart-body. Without processing and honoring your mind-heart-body by releasing your feelings and emotions, you risk subconsciously adding new negative somatic markers, which then act like stowaway pirates that rob you of full engagement in life! Senses of apathy, isolation, heightened stress, depression, and sudden bouts of anger are the end result, as we become stuck in the energetic limitation of unprocessed emotion. By using tools like HeartMath Attitude Breathing™, you can shift from negative emotions to positive ones while retaining psychophysiological coherence. Meaning: your body, mind, and emotions are not splintered off from one another but rather maintain their integrity and coherence. We, as human beings, are naturally equipped to process anger and other strong emotions when we get them raw, intact, as both something we feel in our bodies and something we think in our minds.

HEARTMATH ATTITUDE BREATHING®

Attitude Breathing®, is a very simple HeartMath technique that engages and harnesses the power of the heart to help you recognize the feeling or attitude that's not efficient or not serving love. Once you recognize your reaction, you can process the emotion and then choose a replacement attitude or emotion that offers greater benefit for all.

1. Really feel the emotion in your senses. Do not think about it. Let it stay present in your body. Breathe in and focus on your heart. As you breathe out, focus on your solar-plexus, which is located in the center of your chest, below the heart, just below your sternum.

2. Practice breathing in through the heart and then out through the solar-plexus for 30 seconds or more; however long it takes to gain a sense of grounded-ness to anchor your energy and attention there.

3. Select two positive attitudes or emotions to breathe in and breathe out that will counter-balance the negative emotion or imbalance of the situation you are feeling stuck in. For example, if you are nervous, you might breathe in an attitude of strength and breathe out an attitude of peace. If you are angry, you could breathe in an attitude of balance, and breathe out an attitude of forgiveness, or you could breathe in an attitude of love, and breathe out an attitude of compassion. Do this for 30 seconds (or more). Breathe deeply with the intention of

feeling the shift of lightness within you, into the feeling of the attitude you are choosing to experience.

As you become adept at breathing and shifting from negative feelings into positive ones like love and compassion, try shifting into other positive attitudinal states like gratitude and joy, or forgiveness and love. Doing this more and more will strengthen your neural muscles, naturally opening new neural default "set points," creating life-affirming somatic markers which continually deepen your intuitive ability to listen for, recognize, and appreciate the richness, vast variety, and fluid nature of your own positive and negative feelings wherever and whenever they appear, so you can choose the attitude and co-create your experience to your life.

INQUIRY IS ESSENTIAL TO TRANSFORMATION
Honoring yourself by living in inquiry opens you up to live from your greatness. When you expend energy closing yourself off from the feelings that arise within you, you limit your potency to access the limiting belief that keeps you locked into a finite reality. When you stay closed off in a finite state, transformation is not possible. Remember, as you use your triggers to engage your intuitive senses, you access your awareness of new possibilities, which clears out the beliefs holding your subconscious limitations. As you continue in the inquiry and question, letting go of limitations, your experience to reality takes on an ever-expanding awareness. Loving yourself in this way means standing and being in your greatness. This energy is so contagious that it releases and gives everyone you love permission to do the same.

Want a different experience and reality in life?

Access the creation of a different possibility. Living life from the question of possibility, believing nothing, opens the space of everything, to access your ever-expanding awareness. The choice to live fully alive and connected will only become manifested into your reality when you prioritize loving and seeking yourself as your highest potential, first, always. Meditation, prayer, quiet walks, and time spent in the solitude of inquiry, is the greatest gift you will ever bring into the reality of this world. Being in your greatness and full power is something you choose every day.

The next chapter discusses how to lead a meaningful and mindful life. The truth is: if you cannot show up for yourself, you cannot show up for others. Open the floodgates of love and potentiality flowing by accessing the truth and uniqueness that is you.

It does not end with you. Your true meaning and connection to life happens as you see yourself as the missing puzzle piece in the big picture of life, in which each of us plays an important co-creative role. The belief that one has to choose between being "good" and getting what they want is absolutely 100 percent false! The belief that one has to be "poor" to serve your mission in the world is an illusion. Our Universe is infinite and abundance is your birthright! There is no separation between what is within and what is all around you. Read on and you will continue to learn how you can unlock your deepest truths and begin manifesting your greatest desires into your life!

CHOOSE YOUR STORY—CREATE "THE GAP"
Authentic love is the experience of reality, living through you, as pure potentiality and deep connection with everything that is. This power has only one source—the source that is filled from the reservoir within you. It is through the mirrors of your relationships, which are gifts brought into your life to reflect your present experience to reality. Every relationship, and experience, acts as the impulse and driver to awaken you to the infinite experience of co-creating your reality, living as your grandest expression of truth.

Wired into your DNA, your mind functions within only two capacities: To react from fear, or respond from love. From two completely different hemispheres in your brain, you are either reacting from fear, or consciously responding with love. When you operate from your subconscious mind, which is your fight, flight, or freeze response, you are actually accessing your limbic system, located at the back of your brain, referred to also as our survival brain. Conversely, it is from the frontal cortex region of your brain, that you access your conscious choice to choose love. When you are triggered, your survival mind takes over to protect you. You cannot respond from love, until you consciously choose to create "the gap" between your autonomic fear-based patterns of reactions, signaling your limbic system to relax. Connecting to your heart, your conscious choice opens your access point of infinite possibility to be the generative co-creative partner of your reality: to experience everything that was not even available to you one moment before. When you are living from this space of nothingness and everything, you relax into being the opening where all possibilities can create themselves. This is where you access "the gap" to pure consciousness. This is where you tap into your healing source. This is when you gain access to where all of your creative energies reside, co-creating your life, resulting in living as your unlimited potentiality.

The graphic below illustrates the two parts of your mind and the actual electromagnetic power you generate from your heart vs. your head, when you pause between your stimulus and response to access the consciousness that expands your capacity to experience more than you can imagine, and even more than that!

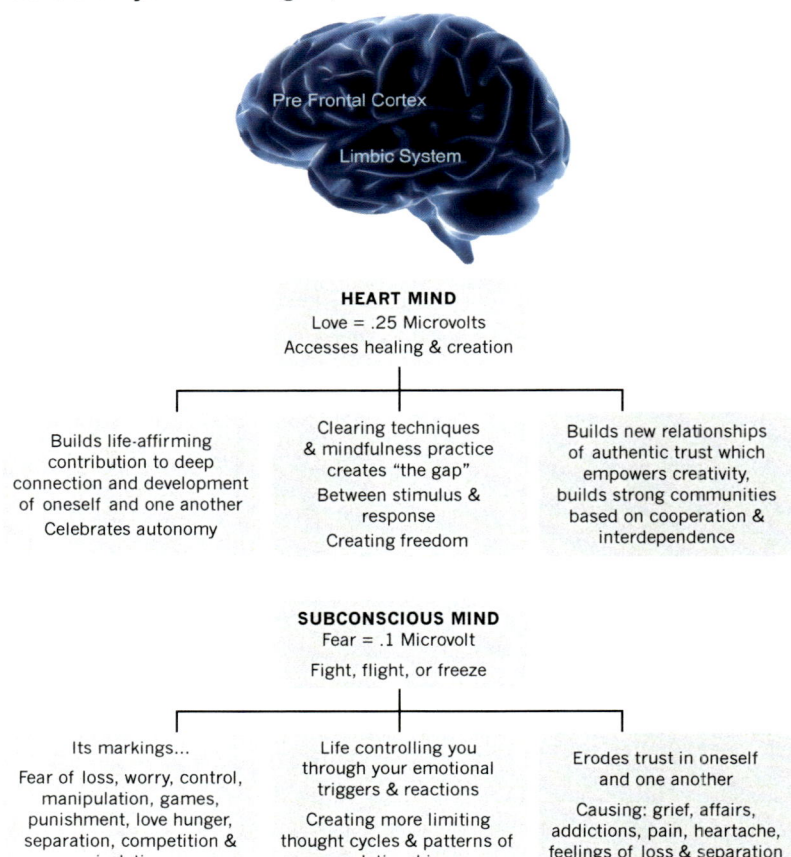

Engaging your heart as your single most powerful organ in your body, which has 40-60 times the power of your subconscious mind (holding your fears, anger, hate, judgments, negative self-limiting beliefs), you can now re-pattern new neural pathways in your brain, to open new awareness that wasn't available to you even the moment before, which creates new set points, moving you into higher vibratory frequencies that access higher and higher levels of intuition, creativity, cognitive learning and intelligence, literally creating laser targeting capacities to manifest your greatest dreams and highest purpose. Learning to move out of your head and into your heart, to make choices driven from what your heart says, and then aligning your heart to your conscious mind, you begin to change your default setting, to one that is naturally coherent and aligned with the truth of who you are as an empowered co-creator of your life and world.

Every millisecond, thoughts and emotions, as well as your inner and outer senses, are constantly monitoring your environment and communicating to you, affecting the neurochemical reactions within every cell of your mind/body/heart. It is the thoughts you think that either rev-up or drain your ability to access the experience of infinite love: your truest nature. By creating "the gap" between stimulus and response by going to the heart and acknowledging life's triggers, you can uninstall the viruses and programs of all perceived limitations. Conversely, expect life to remain as it is if you continue to run the same thought patterns and self-sabotaging beliefs.

You must create an environment to awaken and expand your awareness to create your life as you dare to imagine it will be. This happens through quieting your mind. Downshifting from your usual, programmed mindsets and actions, you create the environment to awaken and access your lucid and creative mind. Your truth and intelligence energetically penetrates and responds within every cell of your body. Think of your thoughts as the radio receptor sites within your body. Through the science of Epigenetics, we now know that through quieting your mind and opening your awareness through your heart, you turn on the bioelectromagnetic power within your heart. This power literally changes your actual gene expression[8], beginning the process of healing and awakening your fullest creative capacity. Creation itself is nature—you are not apart from nature, you are nature.

As you choose love, creating more and more gaps between your stimulus and response, living in the question of possibility, releasing your judgments of how something or someone is, or "should be" for you to be happy, you create your freedom to live an extraordinary and thriving life.

CULTIVATING ON-PURPOSE LIVING
How can I live a fully engaged and meaningful life?

* Choosing to be conscious by creating "the gap" between your stimulus and response.

* Connecting daily to your sacred source, and to revere truth and authenticity above the avoidance of fear and pain to stay the course of living a heroic and meaningful journey.

* Choosing love, moment to moment, is what transforms this experience called life from the mundane into a noble and measurable pursuit of awakening awareness, seeking greater understanding and clarity through the reflective experience, and gift, of relationship. This pursuit naturally leads us in the direction of cultivating virtue; our spiritual eyes of seeing and knowing, past the limitations of our limiting beliefs, conditioning and perceptions into a heightened experience of living which recognizes your highest potential of what it means to transfer spirit into being human.

* Being victorious to align the integrity of what we profess and what we do, and having the courage to take full responsibility for your choices and actions when we do not. Do the work to resolve your grievances, stepping outside of the box to change your limiting mindsets, and release all judgments of yourself and others, asking for

---

[8] Herbert Benson, M.D. and William Proctor, J.D., *Relaxation Revolution: Enhancing Your Personal Health Through the Science and Genetics of Mind Body Healing*

and extending the grace of forgiveness to make amends in your relationship with others, when we have been the source of pain in our loved ones. You hold the master's key of knowledge to what it means to live the experience of co-creating a deeply meaningful life.

✳ To experience true love, we must engage in times of silence to seek an unyielding desire to honor and fight for choosing to live in a way that esteems and co-creates a life-living reality in our relationships to the I AM Self, and others, fully committed to seeking truth and love above our limiting ego and self-sabotaging structures. Living in the silence of the inquiry expands your awareness and reality to open up the infinite you, the you of your highest potential—connected to love.

By staying in the question, inquiring into your beliefs and asking, "What am I holding on to that I don't need to shift into the fully empowered me?" Your intrinsic intelligence responds immediately to attract, with laser-point accuracy, everything you need to expand yourself every moment of every day. Inquiry is the key to your truth and freedom.

Judge-Your-Neighbor Worksheet

Judge your neighbor • Write it down • Ask four questions • Turn it around

Think of a recurring stressful situation, a situation that is reliably stressful even though it may have happened only once and recurs only in your mind. Before answering each of the questions below, allow yourself to mentally revisit the time and place of the stressful occurrence. Don't be polite, kind, or wise.

1. In this situation, time, and location, who angers, confuses, or disappoints you, and why?

   I am _____ with _____ because _____
         emotion   *name*

   Example: I am angry with Paul because he argues with everything I say.

2. In this situation, how do you want them to change? What do you want them to do?

   I want _____ to _____
          name

   Example: I want Paul to see that he is wrong. I want him to apologize.

3. In this situation, what advice would you offer to *them*?

   _____ should/shouldn't _____
      name

   Example: Paul should take better care of himself. He shouldn't argue with me. He should stop lying. He should see that I am only trying to help him.

4. In order for *you* to be happy in this situation, what do you need them to think, say, feel, or do?

   I need _____ to _____
          name

   Example: I need Paul to hear me. I need Paul to respect me.

5. What do you think of them in this situation? Make a list.

   _____ is _____
      name

   Example: Paul is unfair, arrogant, loud, dishonest, way out of line, and unconscious.

6. What is it in or about this situation that you don't ever want to experience again?

   I don't ever want _____

   Example: I don't ever want to feel unappreciated by Paul again. I don't ever want to see him smoking and ruining his health again.

The Four Questions
Example: Paul doesn't listen to me.
1. Is it true?
2. Can you absolutely know that it's true?
3. How do you react, what happens, when you believe that thought?
4. Who would you be without the thought?

Turn the thought around
a) to the self. *(I don't listen to me.)*
b) to the other. *(I don't listen to Paul.)*
c) to the opposite. *(Paul does listen to me.)*

And find three specific, genuine examples of how each turnaround is true for you in this situation.

THE LIFELINE TECHNIQUE AND THE INFINITE LOVE & GRATITUDE SEQUENCE (ILS)

I am often in awe of the simplicity of The LifeLine Technique and its basic premise—love is the bridge between the subconscious and conscious mind; it is the catalyst for healing and transformation, resulting in inner peace. Another pioneer in the field of mind/body/heart healing, Dr. Leonard Laskow, describes it this way: "Love is the energy and awareness of 'between' that allows us to move beyond."

I met Dr. Darren Weissman through my journey of bringing *The Truth, The Journey Within* film and this book into our world. Dr. Weissman received this healing work, also through a download, which is a culmination of fourteen ancient and new energy healing modalities. I have been blessed with many personal clearings and am sharing this work with the world because it is a powerful life self-tool to uninstall the embedded false limiting beliefs and programming we received from our "unknowing" role models, tribal mindsets and from our environment. **Within each one of us is our own intrinsic wisdom for what we need to heal and become integrated to our wholeness and truth.** Applying this LifeLine technique is an effective application skill that allows you to become self-reliant and confident that you possess everything you need to move yourself into a state of feeling and being that empowers you to living aligned to your highest truth and love—your true nature.

When I refer to the simplicity of The LifeLine Technique, I'm talking about the Infinite Love & Gratitude Sequence (ILS) used to harmonize and transform symptoms and stress. Other modalities of healing or treatment use a therapeutic model based upon something or someone being wrong, broken, or dysfunctional. However, The LifeLine Technique's philosophy is deeply rooted in the knowledge and understanding of life's Divine perfection. It recognizes and incorporates the genius of nature; the profound power of allowing rather than resisting; accepting rather than judging; and loving rather than fearing.

When your body or life is speaking with symptoms and stress, as noted earlier, it means there's a subconscious emotion that's ready to be processed. The ILS is a *universal* healing frequency. It uses the power of Infinite Love & Gratitude along with the hand mudra commonly used in American Sign Language for "I Love You."

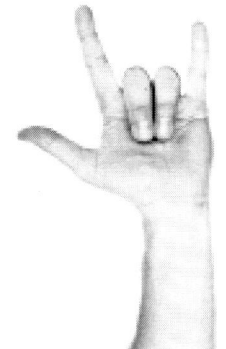 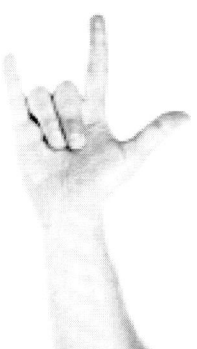

#11-1: ILS

About the words, Dr. Emoto has written that the harmony of Love & Gratitude is the "greatest form of energy." And in *Power vs. Force*, Dr. David Hawkins writes about the potency of hand mudras as a catalyst for enlightenment: "Wherein the palm of the hand radiates benediction (e.g. love), this is the act of transmitting this energy field of consciousness to mankind."

Take a moment and make the "I Love You" hand mudra, as pictured above.

To make that sign, fully expand all fingers and thumb away from each other. Fold down your middle and ring fingers, while keeping your thumb, index finger, and the pinky finger fully extended. Place the "I Love You" hand mudra over your heart. Say aloud, "Infinite Love & Gratitude." What do you feel? Some people say they feel warmth radiating throughout their bodies; others report feeling calm and peaceful.

Can the ILS alone make a difference? Whenever I experience any type of stress in my mind or body, the very first action I take (and I have taught my children to take) is to place the "I Love

You" hand mudra over my heart and say aloud, "Infinite Love & Gratitude."

The following instructions combine the use of the Infinite Love & Gratitude Sequence (ILS) and Muscle Reflex Testing (MRT), is a great exercise to show the validity and power of the ILS. If you don't know how to use Muscle Reflex Testing you can easily learn through an MRT DVD Darren has created. Please go to www.drdarrenweissman.com if you'd like a deeper explanation of MRT.

#11-2: ILS next to body

#11-3: MRT Indicator Muscle

#11-4: MRT "Gives Way"

1. Using the bent-arm indicator muscle to conduct Muscle Reflex Testing (MRT), say aloud, "Hold strong" to feel the "lock out" also known as "zero-point."

2. Now, think about a stressful situation in your life.

3. Once you're tuned into the stressful experience say aloud again, "Hold strong." You will feel the MRT indicator muscle immediately "give way."

4. Now hold your hand in the ILS hand position while saying aloud the words, "Infinite Love & Gratitude." Allow yourself to truly feel the Infinite Love & Gratitude.

5. Now, go back and think about the stressful situation. Recheck the MRT indicator muscle by saying, "Hold strong." You will feel the MRT indicator muscle "lock out" while connecting to the stressful situation.

You may notice that the stressful situation has shifted—that it's more difficult to connect to the story or heavy feeling about it. This is what I call "LifeLine Technique First Aid." It helps you reconnect to your inner peace and truth, disconnecting from the drama and story of the false conditioning that causes the source of all suffering, to empower you in the midst of a stressful situation so that you can move through it.

AWAKENING TO YOUR POTENTIAL FOR PEACE

Remember the ILS is done with intention...for creating an attractor field—a life force of feeling. Seeing someone perform the ILS will provide you with clarity of its simplistic nature.

Learning how to use MRT and the ILS is both fun and exciting. Take your time and practice often. Remember, experience and focused intention is the greatest teacher to embed new ways of being into your life.

If you want a different life, choose a different thought and intention. You may want to begin a new book club or community with the intention of practicing and mastering this art and science of the mind.

If you can drive a car, sing the alphabet song, write a sentence, or perform anything that is simultaneously creative and logical, you'll be able to learn these skills. Anything worth doing and learning requires vision, discipline, and the passion to do your best. Go for it!

Even further, every time you have a negative thought, overwhelming circumstance, pain in your body, or even something positive you'd like to attract into your life, you can simply use the ILS. Transformation, change, healing, and wholeness is your body's true nature. It is the relationship triggers and reactions that are our direct internal guidance system to take us directly to the originating place of creation, where the limiting belief was installed to clear the path for more and more moments of experiencing what it is like to live as the experience of love.

Love is who you truly are! When you are being the truth of who you are, the whole world can see your shining light...and it is contagious!

IV

THE PRACTICE OF MINDFULNESS
UNLOCKING THE POWER OF YOUR OWN DEEPEST TRUTHS

Only when the front of your body is relaxed and open, your breath full and deep... can your fullest intelligence manifest spontaneously in the situation.
—DAVID DEIDA

Between stimulus and response there is a space. In that space is our power to choose our response. In our response lies our growth and our freedom.
—VICTOR FRANKL

In the attitude of silence the soul finds the path in a clearer light, and what is elusive and deceptive resolves itself into crystal clearness.
—MAHATMA GANDHI

In the silence of the present moment, we access the nothing where everything gets created. For only in the present moment can we access original intuition and conception as well as empower authentic love and connection throughout all our life.

Through the practice of mindfulness you can gain awareness of your wandering thoughts and hone your ability to remain in the present. Doing this, you actually commit to being invested in the moments that make up your life. To become mindful is, in essence, to choose life.

At its core, mindfulness is the actualization of Self-love. By coming to genuinely love all aspects of yourself, you gain access to an endless place of wonder, creation and compassion. In the deepest of senses, you return to that place you somehow knew existed, even yearned for, but perhaps only caught glimpses of in your life. This is your place of existence that cannot be touched by your conditioned linear intellectual understanding. It is, rather, a gateway to an ever-expanding connection into the infinite potentiality, and all knowing source of wisdom of the All That Is, awaiting you when you access your pure conscious nature, the truth of who you were created to be.

THE FRAGMENTED MIND

All feelings you experience as isolation and separation actually arise from losing touch with love's pure connection within you. Unless you are deeply connected to the authentic love residing and unbound within you, it is impossible to feel or see love reflected in the external reality of your relationships. Your most sacred and prized possession in life comes from the moments you choose to love and nurture, connecting to your authentic Self, the Self apart from the identities and roles we have taken on. To cultivate Self-love is the greatest and most selfless act of loving-kindness you can bring into your relationships and to the world at large. To fully experience love in this lifetime, we must first be love. This reflection is mirrored in our external reality by accessing our truest nature, which is connected to infinite potentiality. If not, all acts of so-called love become only projections of unmet needs in your subconscious perceptions that have conditioned you into operating from a self-perpetuating mentality of scarcity.

Love in this sense, is treated much like a precious commodity. When you experience love this way, you might feel like you only have so much to give and feel drained or exhausted by giving it. In this scheme, love for Self and love for the other often become pitted against one another, as both parties try to pull (like a tug-of-war) to get enough love. We do this because we believe that someone can return our intrinsic feelings and need to experience wholeness. Reaching out for love without first reconnecting to your source of love within will keep you in an imbalanced state. Our romantic love today is based on a capitalistic commerce of exchange of emotionalism creating a "power over" imbalance. It is for this reason that relationships based on this false definition of love never yield mutual happiness and long-term fulfillment, because a constant emotional undercurrent tug-of-war is what they need to survive.

In this current world reality, opening your awareness of authentic love of Self is perhaps one of the most challenging things to achieve. Reasons upon reasons abound as to why this is the case, many are being identified throughout this book. At the crux of our lack of Self-love is the lie, a false belief that we are separate. Development of your identities in your childhood, into your teens, and young adulthood, is predicated on a mutant fear-based system of separation in the sense that you have learned to create identities for yourself based on what you believe you "like" and don't "like," what you "do" and "don't do," and who you believe you "are" and "are not," all based on an external comparison, with the emphasis often being attached to what you are not.

This is nothing more than your false conditioning and the subconscious flexing its negative somatic-marker-muscles of what someone defined "you" to be, yet it is mistaken for the real truth of one's identity. We are steeped in a culture and bombarded with constant media messages that work to reaffirm this. In this way, a process of external self-definition, based on looking "out there" for answers is mistaken for Self-knowing. In order to delineate oneself, one looks to their family, their peers, their foes, their icons, the constant billboards, commercials and media's messages, and goes through a process of sifting through options of comparison to decide "what I am" and "what I am not." This process of choosing between two diametrically opposed positions of "either/or" does not actual define your truth. Instead, it actually divides you. It is this fractured, false "self" that is lost and unfulfilled, never knowing how to get what it needs to feel happy and at peace. Why? Because it is not you! The truth of who you truly are will only be discovered as you tap into your very own life force and essence.

The "I" of who you truly are has nothing to do with the sum total of your age, your name, or your successes. Who you really are is a Universe within yourself. The discovery of *"feeling"* into you, in the deepest of senses; experiencing emotion, void of any attachment, judgment, or criticism, is the portal to discovering *your truth*. This is your purpose and freedom to experience authentic love. This is where you connect back into the womb, embryo, and gestation place of all creation, where you can release the weight of your past and unlock that which has until now, been un-manifest (not yet expressed potential) into the reality of your life.

Not only are most of us separated from our source, many of us also routinely live in a state of temporal dislocation with our thoughts running amok, occupied with some time other than the present. When you get trapped and caught up in what happened yesterday, last week, twenty years ago, or when you were a child, or when you dwell on what could happen tomorrow, you have lost any ability to co-create your today. This allows your mind to rob you from the gift of the presence and essence of the life happening now.

Accessing pure consciousness is how you employ your true power and potency to live life connected to being in ease, joy, and your full glory!

Anytime you find yourself in thoughts of the past, this means you are dealing with emotions that would best be served to have already processed and moved through them. Conversely, when you run away into the future, the sometime out there (I'll be happy, rich, in love), other than now, you deny the only moment you really ever have to create your reality—now. Now is when you can access the finite beliefs and limitations that have locked you into a reality that is not living the truth of who you are! By fixating on thoughts or trying to intellectually figure them out, often through self-psychoanalyzing, what you are really doing is re-living them, locking and cementing them into your contextual being, exciting and flooding your nervous system with toxic neurochemicals. The resultant frustration and excitement you've just created by revisiting residual emotions, pushes and cements these false stories of who and what we believe back down into the subconscious, resulting in feelings of further isolation, depression, and separation.

Look at how much work the mind is doing in all of these situations. If your mind controls you by your thoughts and you become preoccupied with what you think or believe you are, or "know," this closes the door of discovering your truth, the truth of what your heart truly desires to thrive and live as abundance. Living in the question of present time consciousness allows you to see and hear what your body is really saying to you, so you might come to know the truth beyond the machinations of conditioned patterns of mind. The mind is an open system, but you must create the allowance for it to know nothing, to live with the curiosity of a child. Living life in this awareness and inquiry is the key to experiencing life as the powerful co-creator you are.

A life in which the heart, mind, and body are unified is a life that is mindful. Watch miracles unfold as you discover your truth, as you create the open space to reveal your unique and divine wisdom. The primary way into mindfulness is meditation. The two terms are often used interchangeably. The only distinction is that mindfulness is a way of being, whereas meditation is the access vehicle by which you may come to this state of being. Defined, meditation is a mind discipline where you entrain your mind to cultivate a feeling or internal state of being, such as love or compassion, or create a focal point, such as the breath. Meditation accesses a state of consciousness whereby you access something larger than your existing finite beliefs, to actualize the infinite place of being where everything is possible.

What the practice of mindfulness *is* surpasses definition. You will develop it through practice and through the practice you will come to know yourself.

Focused awareness is difficult for two reasons. Focused awareness requires training the mind and, to date, in the United States we've not allowed this "curriculum" into our childhood training as "education." As parents, we've simply not understood or had the awareness that this is a fundamental foundational life tool to gift our children in developing their own capacities to come to know their true Self, to contribute to life and to create their own life grounded in their own unique gifts and talents in the world. The second reason is that focused awareness challenges our subconscious and ego mind which is threatened by anything that has the potential to release its hold on you. Hence, your ego mind will work against you throwing you all manner of distractions and reasons to thwart your attempts at mindfulness. Do not battle or resist it. Remember what we give our attention to (resist) is what we create. Simply observe the thoughts, returning to your breath, and with discipline and trust, come to know your practice. Come to know your capacity and power of calm observance. Deny the ego's tricks to get you worked up into negative thoughts. A story of this follows:

A Grandpa sits and tells his grandchildren the story of the two wolves. "Inside each of us," he says, "lives a good and happy wolf and a vicious and mean wolf."

The children sit rapt and in wide-eyed wonder at what he was sharing. The grandpa continues, "The bad wolf is always hungry. And, he takes whatever he thinks will first feed his hunger, but it's never enough. But the good wolf, even though he is also hungry, he listens to the voice within his heart. He knows that to be strong and wise, he must only eat that which will make him a true leader and warrior among his pack."

Interrupting and anxious, the young grandson asks, "Grandpa, how do you know which wolf to feed?"

Hearing this, the grandpa smiles, "That's easy," he replies, "It's the one you choose to feed."

Life offers you continual opportunities to choose love or fear. As you patiently persevere and choose, again and again, to feed your capacity for self-love and calm observance, returning your attention to the breath and your heart, you un-program the lies of conditioning that took you away from your truth of who you are and were created to be. By choosing daily times to quiet your mind, in time you will notice that your feelings of inner turmoil and suffering are replaced by more and more moments of quell, peace, and a prevailing sense of equanimity and serenity. Without consciously "trying," you step into the powerful acceptance of loving what is. From here, you access your awareness of the limiting thoughts, feelings, and beliefs that govern your life including those which distract you from being present or being authentically you. You begin to trust and embrace the transient flow of life as it is. All storms rise, fall, and ultimately pass. All life is a constant flow of energy in motion, ebbing and flowing through us.

As you spend more time in the practice of mindfulness, your awareness expands and your life choices align to serve your truest nature and highest calling, which is primordially expansive, almighty, and infinite at its core. To the impulse of your desire, you are no longer governed by the insatiable external quest for more, but rather, become free to choose to serve life-affirming choices, actions, and be guided by your voice of inner wisdom. Now, your natural hunger and intrinsic drive to learn (re-member) is fed and thrives on what is of contribution for all.

The only real valuable thing is intuition.
—EINSTEIN

THE SCIENCE BEHIND MINDFULNESS PRACTICE

When you are truly present within, your brainwaves of Alpha, Theta, and Delta can fully integrate your truth. Under these mindstates, you gain access to tap into your inner peace, calm, healing, tranquility, and harmony. Entraining your brain by returning to the meditative mindstate is the only way you can experience your true presence in your life.

Breakthroughs in the field of neuroscience show that repeatedly fostering an intentional lucid mindstate creates the conditions for brain neuroplasticity, which is an anatomical and physiological change through the formation of new neural connections. Through entering into meditative mind-states, you can literally re-wire your brain at the cellular level changing the way your genes express themselves, allowing you more access into an unlimited field of intelligence, healing, and consciousness. Neuroscience has further shown us that the health benefits of 20 minutes of meditation helps to build new neural pathways, reorganizing your brain, synchronizing your mind to access perpetually infinite levels of intelligence, learning, intuition, tranquility and a myriad of health enhancements. The benefits are not limited to: a reduction in blood pressure, anxiety, depression, enhanced sleep, pain reduction and numerous others physiological changes.

Meditation is essential to unlocking the full potential of who you were created to be.

Binaural-Beat Technology, abbreviated here as (BBT), accelerates positive physiological change. First examined by physicist Thomas Warren Campbell and electrical engineer Dennis Mennerich, under the direction of Robert Munroe, this technology uses calculated rhythms to stimulate all four of the particular brainwaves: Theta, Alpha, Delta and Beta. Whole brain synchronization of these four brainwave frequencies is possible through this technology. These brainwave frequencies have been customized to target specific areas in our brain that neuroscience has discovered create markedly measurable improvements in our mental and emotional health. Benefits include: accelerated healing, behavior modification, enhanced problem solving and learning ability, greater tranquility, pain control, enhanced creativity, greater mental focus and concentration, relief from stress, feelings of euphoria, and equanimity. Through BBT, you can now achieve within 20 minutes of listening to relaxing musical tracks each day the same physiological transformation that previously took Transcendental Meditation thousands of hours to achieve.

In his book, *Megabrain Power*, Michael Hutchison sums up this revolution in neuroscience:

> *"New breakthroughs in neuroscience and microelectronics have permitted scientists to "map" the electrical and chemical activity of the brain in action. Scientists have used the new technology to monitor the brains of people who practice meditation, artists, and others capable of entering so-called "peak domains" when there is a greater amount of activity in the brain. Their first findings were that those peak states are not mysterious and unpredictable phenomena, but are very clearly linked to very*

> *specific patterns of brain activity. These include dramatic changes in brainwave activity, hemispheric symmetry, and rapid alterations in the levels of various neurochemicals. Brain synchronization exercises enable all of us to experience the same "peak states." Mainly 20 minute practices consisting of musical soundtracks of brain synchronization exercises that are not only relaxing but have a tremendous measurable effect...It therefore follows that if we are able to produce the same activity by stimulating our brains with pulsating sound waves, we should all be capable to experience 'peak states.'"*

Incorporating meditations, heart-centered breathing practices, and Binaural Beat Technology (BBT) provides a powerful choice to create a life of equanimity and tranquility, even through inevitable storms of life. BBT enables you to achieve the physiologically transformative results quickly. Disciplined meditation, while also working to transform your mind/body/heart, will provide you with a penetrating view into yourself, beyond all pretense and external measure. Here, you develop your capacity to access profound wisdom and experience a relationship with yourself that establishes the foundation necessary to express your fullest experience of creation love with all that matters most to you. You will grow your intuition and develop a sacred trust in your ability to connect within your heart to the pulse and wisdom center designed specifically for you to express into the world what is authentically true for you.

MINDFULNESS AND EMOTIONS

Mindfulness is the process of deepening your love and acceptance of yourself through accessing optimum mindstates of consciousness. It is not an unengaged, cold, surgical detached examination of life, nor a means of becoming perfect. Mindfulness observes and embraces life as the perfect transient ebb and flow of feelings as they rise up and subside within us; whether they are gentle and kind, or angry and hostile. Acknowledging their presence, without resisting or rejecting them opens the space to allow them to gradually subside.

As you sit quieting your mind, you may hear the all-knowing Sage that resides within you accessing wisdom you never knew you had. You may also encounter the Perpetrator: the harborer of the thoughts of a potential thief, rapist, or murderer.

To access your full awareness is to include everything and exclude nothing including: pain, anger, fear, resentment, frustration, despair, jealousy, rage, desperation, fixation, deceitfulness, insecurity, pride, arrogance, judgment, condemnation, fickleness, mischief, boredom, insanity, nonsense, muddled thinking, laziness, intolerance, acceptance, lust, kindness, compassion, empathy, curiosity, solace, affection, desire, and love. Meditation grounds you to your full state of being, where you experience your equanimity. Whatever emotions or thoughts appear, they are just thoughts, nothing more, nothing less. When I accept that my thoughts and emotions are not who I am, and that they represent a quagmire of all of the thoughts that conditioned me into my current reality and the on-going bombardment of billions of oscillating fear-based brainwave patterns feeding the collective consciousness, I can see them merely as fickle, transient, and ever-changing. I can therefor then chose to embrace love and my capacity to fully relax and settle my mind and body.

Expressed in a memorable phrase, an old Buddhist once shared, "I set the Self upon the Self." Meaning, there is the Self that may be thinking thoughts of despair, but there is also the Self that watches the Self that is thinking the thoughts of despair, and there is also the Self that watches the Self that is watching the Self that is thinking the thoughts of despair, and it goes on and on. This is not to say that you should be remote to what you're feeling but only to say, the truth of who you are is not what you are feeling. As you make allowance within yourself to see a negative emotion as a gift, you free yourself to release it for the lie and limitation it is. *Feeling* is the true gift of the experience of being human. As you breathe into your feeling, you acknowledge its sacred presence for simply existing, while simultaneously not buying into it, nor being consumed by it (this was covered in greater detail in Chapter III).

What follows are the ethical and attitudinal foundations of mindfulness, an illustration of mindfulness, and a series of exercises. The slow and steady transmission to your heart is a million times better than one to your mind. These meditation practices are useful guides. Through the practice of mindfulness itself, you will always continue to explore, to wonder, to come to know thyself—the truth of who you were created to be.

THE ATTITUDINAL AND ETHICAL FOUNDATIONS OF MINDFULNESS

Releasing Judgment—We've been conditioned to have judgments about everything. In Chapter II, The Power of Your Thoughts, you discovered just how many life-alienating thoughts and judgments you carry towards yourself and others. The primary focus of Mindfulness is to become aware. Through awareness you can clear and release any judgment of doing anything "right" or "wrong," "good, or "bad," the way anything should "be" or not "be," so you can open the field of pure potentiality to expand your reality and life experience, living aligned to the truth of who you were created to truly be. Mindfulness is the act of resting in the present moment, when all we have to really "be" is aware.

Developing Trust—Mindfulness develops your inner trust in experiencing the non-contextual knowing—accessing the wisdom and guidance of your own heart. Through the practice, you will come to know your senses of *seeing* and *hearing* in ways that release the finite construction of the mind's limitations. Tuning into what's really authentic for you essentially blasts open your experience of life to live aligned to your truth, unconstrained from the finite beliefs that limit you because you think you already know who you are or what you really know.

The Heart of a Child—Developing the heart of a child allows every experience to be experienced as though it were being discovered for the first time. In Mindfulness practice, this is also referred to as "beginner's mind." By releasing your expertise, beliefs, judgments, and opinions, you can experience the world in all its infinite possibility. Feeling with all your senses the warmth and feeling of sunshine on your face, the smell of a fresh flower, the explosion of taste from each bite of an apple, the touch of soft, hard, warm, hot, the look and the feel of emotions, the feeling of a smile, is what keeps us in the present moment of all that makes life happening around us more wonderful. The spontaneous discovery of embracing real Truth emerges when we know nothing and find everything within this space.

The Gift of Patience—Mindfulness is about the journey, not the destination, as you discover the path to inner peace and authentic love. You have been conditioned into a world where the constant pressure of always having to be somewhere, or endless "to do" lists resulting from the constant electronic chatter permeating throughout your life creates a certain frenzy. From emails, texts, and media (social and TV), all these distractions compete for your attention, adding feelings of overwhelm to the never-ending time pressure of a day. Relaxing and quieting the chaos of your mind is absolutely necessary to access your full greatness. The patience required to simply "be" in the present moment, unlocking the constraints of time, takes a practice of discipline.

Begin by simply acknowledging the thoughts flooding your mind and whatever anxiousness there may be in your body. By doing this, you entrain yourself to return to finding the breath, which expands your awareness so you can listen to the wisdom center in your heart. Establish this new habit and discipline into your life by allowing a set period of time that is just yours. You can relax your mind knowing that, for just these moments, there is no place to go, no right or wrong way to just "be." This is a gift that you give yourself and your relationships that has endless payoffs. By just resting and relaxing in the full "being" of you, you will access a whole new experience of the authentic truth of who you are as an infinite being of pure possibility. Your external world suddenly takes on a whole new meaning as you stay connected within yourself. You reflect loving connection, peace, wisdom, and gratitude into the reality of your life and your relationships.

Non-Striving—Non-striving is the release of the relentless pursuit of "doing" something, striving to reach some unappointed place where we believe happiness awaits. This is the voice of "I'll be happy when: I graduate from high school or college, find my new job, find my new house, get married, get divorced, get the children out of the home, feel better, etc." The foundation established through the practice of Mindfulness is the recognizing and acknowledgment that there's never anything to "get" or "be," no place we have to go to find the deep sense of peace, authentic love, harmony, and happiness. Everything you will ever need to access and create being joy, being peace, being love, being abundant is located where it has always been—within you, right here in this present moment, the only moment that really ever matters.

Surrender and Acceptance—The saying, "It is what it is" or "Que Será Será, "embodies the energy of surrender and acceptance. When you surrender having any attachment to the way things *should* be, you open yourself up to the potential of what *could* be.

From this space you co-create, you re-frame the very constraints limiting you to the world of fixed, finite, and defined parameters of identity and attachment. As you release your limiting beliefs of what you think defines happiness, you unlock the power to discover the very essence of infinite pure potentiality. There are no short-cuts to surrender and acceptance. To get there one must cross the river and wade through the pain of suffering, anger, rage, denial, unforgiveness and fear, diving into the depths of loss, to emerge free of limitations stopping you from creating your life living truth of reality. As you drop the mental debris cemented by the stories of your past, you drop the weight and begin to see things as they truly are, to accept things as they are.

It is what it is. Through surrender and acceptance, you allow real freedom to open up new possibilities in your life. The stories that have previously defined and imprisoned you collapse as you experience a new sense of well-being. Genuine happiness, peace, and authentic love are always an inside job established within, through the internal process of surrender and acceptance.

Non-Attachment—Letting go of all attachments to what you think you know, what you think you like, dislike, hate, believe, what you feel disdain or lack of forgiveness toward, is the key to unleashing the power of true manifestation. How can you know anything at all if you've never really discovered the truth of who you truly are? Through the non-attachment and release of everything you think you ever knew and are, you open your awareness to discover an infinite you, the "who" you were truly created to be.

A STORY FROM MY LIFE

Here is an illustration based upon a true event in my life. The first version demonstrates what would have been my conditioned reaction and response when a "problem" entered my life. The second version is an example of how choosing to remain mindful and present allows me to experience the same event without losing or giving my peace and happiness away to any external event of life.

My Conditioned Mind Living Me

Every morning I enjoy my ritual of a fresh cup of coffee as I start my day. This morning, as I poured the milk, it came streaming out with the consistency of cottage cheese. "This sucks!" Determined to get what I wanted, I grab my coat and head out the door, nearly slamming my doggie's foot in the door as he's trying to join me for a morning walk. "No Shadow, no!" Setting off focused on my mission, suddenly I start thinking about what Gail did and what she said. Pulling into the store, I feel anger lodging in my chest. Looking at my watch, I run into the store to get my milk. I've got a little less than an hour to get to my meeting. I can't wait until my attorney files the paperwork. I can imagine the look on her face when my attorney has her served. Getting into my car, an announcement on the radio jars my attention. Frustrated thinking, "what the hell is this world coming to," I begin my trip back home.

On my drive back I replayed what I said to Gail. I felt gratified by my sharp and cruel imagination as it equaled the same humiliation, hurt, rejection, betrayal, and anger I felt towards her. How dare she violate my rights! She will pay me back for the wrong, illegal, immoral, and false accusations! Surely, justice will prevail against her!

Returning home I'm filled with anger for what she put me through. I'm so filled with anxiety and bitterness that my stomach feels upset. "Ah, bleep the coffee, now I'm going to be late!"

Sound familiar? How many moments in your life are spent similar to this? Unconscious, life lives us as we are completely disconnected to our precious connection to life itself. Why? Because we're consumed by our mind's something, thrashed about by the relentless impulses of our wandering minds. This isn't living. Worrying about what someone said or did disconnects us so completely from the world of laughter, the brushstrokes of color, the beating pulses of sound, the sweet smells present every moment, everywhere, if we but choose to listen and to see. Entrenched and imprisoned by your wandering mind has your world begun to seem routine and dull? A life of routine is what separates us from truth to leave us feeling isolated, numb and disconnected.

The Gift of Mindful Awareness

Now, let's look at the same scenario, but from a different point of view. I brew my coffee and pour myself a cup. Reaching for the milk, curdled… "Yuck!" Determined to enjoy my coffee, grabbing my coat, I notice two tails wagging, excited at the possibility of riding somewhere, anywhere, with Mom. "Let's go boys!" Driving through my neighborhood, I see my friend jogging, I see her singing to the music and I feel joy pour into my heart. She smiles and waves. Feeling tempted to turn on my music myself, I choose to embrace nature all around me. As I take in all the colors and sounds I smile, sensing how blessed I am. Cracking the window so my Gizmo and Shadow feel the wind in their face, I feel the crispness in the air of Fall. Taking in the breathtaking mountain and ocean views, I'm suddenly in awe of life. I see people everywhere enjoying their morning exercise. I so love life!

Pulling up to the store, I look at my watch and see I've got a little over an hour. Suddenly, I catch myself thinking about what Gail did. I feel tightness lodging in my chest. I see her face, her menacing grin, and instantly I feel anger rising up and sense myself beginning to react. Recognizing how I'm feeling, I turn off the car and sit in silence, dropping down into the anger and sadness I feel in my heart. Breathing into what I'm feeling, simply acknowledging it, breathing through it, I replace my thoughts with feelings of love as I breathe in deeply. As I breathe out, I push the anger out. After a couple of seconds of deep breathing,

I regain my center and find myself feeling compassion for Gail. It's not her fault. She doesn't know what she doesn't know, until she does. I know that if she had taken the time to understand the truth of the circumstance, she would likely not hold the same thoughts and judgments about me or my situation. My peace is restored in less than a minute and I go into the store for the milk.

On the short drive home, I rock out to my new favorite song. "How does it get any better than this?" I think to myself. My happiness and attitude is infectious to others. I feel great and totally in touch with me.

I suddenly gain clarity on why I felt hurt by Gail. The reason I'm so hurt is because I care about how others see me. But even more than that, I have come to know that separation is only an illusion and I love to experience connection to that truth.

I love peace in my life. Sometimes, I avoid confrontations even when I now know that compassionate confrontation is the only way to peace. When something or someone triggers me, I understand my hurt is an inner reflection, a gentle nudging to look within, to get to the source of the loss of my own disconnection I feel. When I harbor viciousness or violence in my thoughts, I acknowledge that within me I hold all capacities to feel hurt, disappointment, rage, and judgment, but also I've come to know that all emotions are dualistic. Feeling empowered, I choose in this moment to control my emotions, to return myself to the feelings and attitude of gratitude and joy within me. Choosing love I breathe through the feelings to not allow them to infect my system and affect my day. I have come to trust my capacity to co-create the reality of my life. I am pro-active in removing or bypassing perceived obstacles in my life. Only as I acknowledge "what's alive in me" can I truly be present with life as it is happening through me.

I feel my doggie's anticipation as they see we're home again. "Now, I can settle in to enjoy my cup of coffee." Feeling invigorated, I am present and grateful. The only way to gain real access to the beautiful, caring person I am, is through observing my thoughts. Yes, there is a side of me that would like to launch venomous words at someone who has attempted to hurt me, and even celebrate the cunning of my mind to shame another (I weep inside to see my own conditioning and disconnection and also celebrate my capacity to feel everything alive in me). Trying to restrain, repress, or deny my hatred, rage, judgment, or anger, actually makes me incapable of moving through it or seeing the gift that it provides me on my own journey to discovering more of the truth I was created to be. As I sense my heaviness which is my loss of joy or feelings of ease, I know it is my clue to turn inward. Each time I honor my feelings, I gain access to understanding me. I can see the unmet need, unresolved originating trauma, or false belief triggering my reaction. Now, I'm present to what's alive within me.

Instead of processing my own thoughts, had I chosen to talk to a therapist or download it on a friend, I would deny my own power to change my life. Perhaps, I might have gained some perspective, perhaps I might have felt like I'd gotten it off my chest (even though I'd really only dialed-it-down). But what would I do the next time someone like Gail comes into my life? A therapist or friend may provide some sense of relief for now, but how am I to access my truth? How would my wisdom be strengthened for the next lesson if I'm guided by another's beliefs, projections and perceptions?

My empowerment, my inner constitution, my freedom, and my trust in my truth, begins when I choose to access my infinite potential unfettered by the influence of others. Through my own journey, I allow myself to access and release my pain. It is always my choice, or not, to choose to come back to love.

CHANGING HABITS

The health and healing benefits of living in mindfulness are endless and full of possibility. You have spent a lifetime in the subconscious conditioning of fear-based sabotaging habits, which tightens your muscles and closes and constricts your body systems in defense. Be patient with yourself. Depending on how many years you've lived constricted, it will take some time for your body and mind to begin to relax into its natural open and fluid space, opening new neuropathways that will reprogram and repattern your body and mind. Jack Canfield, co-creator of *The Chicken Soup for the Soul* Series, as well as an author and motivational coach, shares findings from a NASA study and talks about the development of new habits in the film, *The Truth, The Journey Within:*

> "We get locked into habits. It's not easy to change a habit. It takes about 30 days of intensive focus to move a new habit, behavior or belief into your life. There was some wonderful research done at NASA, the National Aeronautical Space Agency, where they had astronauts wear goggles 24/7 that made the world appear upside down... to see how they would handle the disorientation in Outer Space. They wanted to see how they would handle it— would they become hostile? Would they get angry? Would they lose sleep? When you're in outer space, there's no gravity. They wanted to see if they could handle the disorientation. Twenty-six days into the experiment, one of the astronauts' brain flipped the images right-side-up again. Over the next 4 days, all the astronauts' brains in the experiment flipped the images right-side-up. What the neuroscientists took away from that experiment is that it takes about 30 days to create new habits, forming new neuropathways in the brain that then become new, "set points" of more life-affirming habits."

The following suggestions offer support to create new habits into your life:

* Find a partner with whom you can share a habit you want to change. This creates the accountability and community to support you, like a coach, when you feel tempted or weak. Ask them to check in daily with you to share and touch base on how you're doing in keeping your own integrity to your choices.

* Set your phone's calendar to "tone" every couple of hours to help you establish a pattern of refocusing your attention for a couple of breaths as you center your awareness to one of Mindfulness. This can be also be done for any other exercise throughout the book.

* Change the screensaver or wallpaper on your phone and computer to pictures that return your focus and awareness to a place or feeling of peace or love.

* Watch a short video or listen to a song that brings you back to your heart-centered place of joy, peace, compassion and love.

* Choose a Practice you intuitively feel drawn to. Begin to trust your intuition as your best internal guidance system. Practice Mindfulness, or clearing exercises, until you become comfortable and are able to easily recall them any time you feel triggered and want to re-center to find your peace. If you are meditating, it is helpful to set a quiet timer so that your mind is not distracted by your conditioned response of "time pressure." This is your time you've choose to honor yourself.

As you practice these exercises and create new life-affirming habits, your life living reality will dramatically change. In the beginning of your journey, creating new habits can be challenging and you may find yourself straying from the course and intention countless times. This is just your mind's conditioned groove on the record at play. Whether you are installing new affirming habits, or dropping old life-negating habits, they both require determined repetition to set new, or uninstall old, somatic markers into your mind/body/heart system. With disciplined practice, this new awareness of you being a powerful co-creator of a new reality become embedded and integrated into your being, which you will experience the benefits from in every area of your life. The results will come from this internal change within you. Your success is not dependent on the gift of a committed accountability partner, or coach. It does help exponentially to bring these new habits into your life with the love and support of a great friend or partner to encourage you to stay the course.

PRACTICES FOR EMPOWERING A LIFE OF CEASELESS CREATION

The practices of meditation have been with us since antiquity. Passed down from great masters and spiritual traditions, these practices are offered here in a 21st century model. They gift you with a front row pass to transform and co-create your reality in ways limited only by your commitment and practice.

Be gentle with yourself. Discipline is the only path to any form of excellence and mastery! Work with one exercise at a time until it becomes a natural internal default tool that you can access anytime. Choosing to pause, turn inward, to the silent language within your heart regains your sense of centered peace.

These practices will open up your capacity to access your infinite possibilities. We've become conditioned to want a quick fix when we feel pain in our life: popping a pill, using distractions to "feel" happy. Whether we choose physical distractions like exercise or life-alienating distractions of drugs, alcohol, eating, shopping, pornography, or sex, even excessive exercise as a form of diversion (to name only a few), any external means to "fix" an internal condition of the heart ignores the access point to where all genuine happiness and healing happens. The true foundation and source of ceaseless creation of where your authentic happiness and peace resides is—within you!

There is no McMeditation—until you have trained your frenzied conditioned mind's competing thoughts for your time, try setting a gentle sounding timer for 10 minutes. This way you have some peace and reassurance that this time is just for you, so you can relax and not be disturbed by distractions. Ideally, 20-minute practices begin to embed and open up new default mind patterns that entrain your brainwaves into higher levels of awareness and functioning.

Practice #1—The Breath of Life

This is a simple meditation. Choose a quiet place and sit in a comfortable position. Traditionally, meditation is done in a cross-legged position, with your back posture straight to prevent your mind from becoming sleepy. While it is important to feel comfortable, lying down can be a hazard as you are more likely to fall asleep. The place where you access pure potentiality is the brainwave states of Alpha and Theta, which are actually quite alert.

Sit with your eyes partially closed and focus your attention to your breathing. Feel the breath enter your nostrils and fill your diaphragm on the in-breath. Feel the release of your breath through your nostrils on the out-breath. Soon, your breathing will begin to naturally pace itself.

Bring your awareness to the sensation of your breath as it enters and leaves your nostrils and moves through your body. The purpose of focusing your concentration on the breath is to stop distractions and help create a lucid and clear mind. At first, your mind will be busy and full of thoughts. Know that it is possible to feel even more busy and anxious than before you came to meditate, but this is only because you are focusing your awareness, allowing yourself to play witness to the medley of chattering thoughts playing in your mind. You will also begin to sense the constant symphony of biological processes interacting within your mind/body/heart. You will experience a great temptation to get stuck in your thoughts as they arise, but as you learn to resist this temptation and merely observe, you can stay focused only on the sensation of breath. Returning again and again to the breath, your mind will begin to settle. Simply the recognition you make, witnessing how your wandering mind can become lost in mindless chatter when you have chosen to simply sit and breathe, means you already have created a state of awareness. Any time you become aware of your mind's wandering, gently return your awareness to the breath. Do this for the duration of your practice. Gradually, any distracting thoughts you may have will begin to subside and you will feel refreshed, relaxed, and sense a deep inner peace.

Practice #2—Reconnecting to Your Life
The center of all life begins in the heart. In this practice, you will be training your awareness to come to the heart, not the mind, entraining your heart to become your natural default resting place of attention.

Sit or lie down in a relaxed position. Place your awareness on your in-breath and feel yourself breathing that awareness into your heart-center. Maintain awareness on the center of your heart and breathe-in the feeling of receiving love in your heart. To envision this, you may choose to see or feel your arms wrap around your heart. Feel deep love and gratitude for your heart. On the out-breath, push this love out, extending it out through your solar-plexus and say, "I send love from my heart," projecting that love either through your heart by feeling or visualizing it extending out from you, toward the object of your attention. This may be, for example, a deity, person, place in turmoil, passion in your life, feelings you wish to manifest, or simply the world around you.

As you train your awareness to the rising up on the in-breath and the pouring and reaching out from your heart on the out-breath, feeling your mind wander is just your mind being your mind. When you notice that your mind has wandered, gently re-direct your focus and awareness and use that awareness as an opportunity to refocus on the breath, without any judgment for the mind's natural tendency to engage in mindless chatter—it is just your mind being your amazing mind. Remember, you've spent your lifetime being conditioned to focus on your mind, so give yourself time and some grace to begin to attune your heart, to entrain yourself to create more synchronized brainwaves and heart-coherent patterns.

Practice #3—7-minute Inner-net Connection to Your Essential Wisdom

The answers to unlock your highest and grandest expression of you lie within. Located in the inner chambers of your heart is your own internal search engine that can locate whatever it is that you need or want to know now. Using this exercise, you will gain access to your intuition and wisdom.

Have a notepad and pen or pencil handy. Think of a question you want answered. Even write it down; the clearer, the better. You can begin this practice by sitting or lying down. Place a finger in-between the center of your eyebrows, your Third Eye Chakra, to naturally draw your awareness there.

Begin by relaxing your body. With the in-breath, focus your attention on what is known as your Third Eye Chakra, your pineal gland, spending a few minutes to take three deep breaths, noting any sensations you are feeling. Include the sounds inside and outside of your body, the smells, what you may be hearing, whatever the feelings may be that you begin to sense. As you note these senses, on your in-breath and out-breath, refocus your attention back to the Third Eye Chakra and settle there until you reach a place of calm. Once you are calm, guide your awareness down into the inner chamber of your heart, settling your awareness to the moment of now. Envision a door that is your own private entry into the deepest chambers of your heart—the sacred space of wisdom accessible by only you. As you open this doorway, visualize walking into the center of your heart, sensing your surroundings with full awareness. Ask the question for which you seek an answer. If the answer is not clear, ask it again, digging deeper and ask your Sacred Wisdom, "What does that mean?" Even if you hear only silence, your silence will begin to unlock the answers. As you hear or feel your answer(s) bubbling up into your consciousness, visualize yourself packing them up and bringing them with you into your conscious awareness, as you move towards the door from whence you came. As you reach the door, open it and step through, taking a deep breath as you close the door, draw your awareness back to the present, and open your eyes.

As you exit and close the door, remember to:

* Journal or note your answer. This allows your answers to simmer.

* Take action on the answer you received. Keep your awareness focused on the answers to attract, move, and synchronistically open up the paths, people, and events which will continue to emerge into your life.

If you feel like you have not received a clear answer, practice the exercise again, digging deeper, just as you would on a Google search. Rephrase your question. This is about opening the heartspace to allow the infinite wisdom to rise within you. Remember, there is nothing finite or bound in the motion of pure energy and potentiality. Just by asking the question, you magnify the energy, naturally, and automatically set into motion everything you need: the people, places, circumstances, and events to actualize your answers.

Practice cultivating your intuition in this manner for spans of seven minutes initially, building to longer periods as you progress. Even the shortest amounts of time spent honoring your heart's wisdom and intuition this way, builds your heart's wisdom center. Like pebbles in a pond, your questions send ripples of energy into motion toward discovering that which you most need to know now.

Practice #4—Breathing Technique Practice
This practice of Mindfulness utilizes focused attention and awareness on your breath with a mantra or repetitive phrase to center your focus. Your mantra may be centered on a divinity, entity, or a quality you want to radiate from yourself.

Begin by sitting or lying down. Begin relaxing on the in-breath, focus your attention and awareness on your mantra, quality, or simply the breath, whichever feels most calming and peaceful for you. For example, if you are feeling tense, you may begin this practice focusing on the words Calm and Peace. With each in-breath, whisper or speak to your inner wisdom, "Breathing in I am Calm," and with the out-breath, "Breathing out I feel Peace." If your in-breath usually takes 3-4 seconds, pace your out-breath to the same 3-4 seconds, creating a rhythm and patterned flow in your breathing. Continue this practice as you align your inner senses of calm and peace.

Examples for Mantras: On the in-breath repeat the first syllable or word and on the out-breath, repeat the last syllable or word.

| Jes us | Pure Love | Beauty Love | Laughter Joy |
| Bud dha | Calm Peace | Healing Light | God's Love |

This practice is a quick and highly effective way to clear your mind and return your focus to your heart, to create and manifest your desired moment-to-moment reality. Doing this a couple of times, throughout your day, can often make the difference between falling into the fray of negativity and chaos, or maintaining your strength to take charge and be pro-active in creating a life that is free and authentically aligned with your highest truth. This practice may be conducted anywhere. Just be comfortable and free of distractions.

Practice #5—Releasing Anger Peacefully without Damaging Relationships

This technique allows you to fully express and experience your anger or other blocking negative energies, to free it from your body safely and without harm. Doing this, you free yourself from the toxic, violent, neurochemical warfare that locks negative emotions into your neuromuscular mind/body/heart system and heart, allowing them to be released and move through you.

In this meditation you do not focus on the perceived "cause" of any negative emotion as being something outside of yourself, to discover where it is lodged in your body.

Expressing anger and rage has become "taboo" in our society today. As such, our repression of anger is the single most toxic emotion in our body systems, in our relationships, and in our family and societal systems. Learning to allow and trust yourself and give permission to others to fully express and release our most powerful emotions, allows you to fully feel the dual emotions of bliss, connection and ecstasy. When you numb yourself from the fullest expression of what's alive within you, you also numb your capacity to enter into your birthright of creation, ecstasy and connection, in all of its living forms of expression.

Find a place where you won't be disturbed. If you are not at home, don't wait to discharge these toxic emotions from your body/mind/heart, for you'll lose touch with the power, gift, and message they provide you. A park, a public restroom, your car, or any quiet spot are viable options. Also, have a pillow, towel, shirt, or even some tissue handy. This "prop" will be used to redirect and expel your negative energy. To do the exercise, spend a couple of minutes focusing your attention to all the sensations outside your body (what you see, feel, taste, touch, smell and hear). Then do the same focusing this time on all the sensations inside your body. Become aware of your anger and locate where it resides in your body. Intense emotions with whom or what you are angry about may arise. Let these feelings be. Do not resist nor feed into them. As thoughts and emotions rise up, focus your awareness back to your body, locating the anger.

Next, picture a vacuum cleaner suction hose attaching to that place in your body. Focus all your attention toward the suction. The suction hose is the negative emotion, sucking the life force energy and well-being from your body system. Then, take your prop and feel the energy of the negative emotion. Beat, throw, or twist your prop, repeating the statement with the power of the anger emotion, "I am angry," "I'm pissed off," or whatever works for you. As you do this, let the anger rush out through your body and into the end of the suction hose, or throw the towel or tissue, releasing that anger onto the floor. If you are in the restroom, sense the anger flowing into the toilet—then flush it down. The goal is to find, redirect and release the energy from your body system in a way that it is not directed toward another, which then creates separation, fear, harm or violence. If appropriate, using your voice to shout and express the anger at the prop, at the top of your lungs, is a powerful way to release the anger. The key is to just allow the emotion to be expressed where you feel it in your body, then release it. You may cry or feel overwhelmed as the energy of emotions move through you, this is a perfectly natural way your body releases toxins. Screaming is such a powerful way to release the pent up anger that has been stored within you, so if you can create the place for that to happen, go for it. Continue this until you have dissipated all the feelings and begin to sense a lighter feeling of release and calm.

Once you have released your anger, refocus your attention to the sensations outside your body and inside your body at the same time. Ask your spiritual guidance, what would love do to constructively use this energy? Ask you awareness, what unmet need is at the core of my anger or charged emotion? We often feel powerless when we believe that there is only one person or thing that can meet our needs, which creates a finite box that narrows the infinite field of possibility of how that need can be met. Sit and breathe until you feel a sense of clarity and response from your question. You may even shift into attitudinal breathing here. Breathe love or whatever desired emotion you want on the in-breath, and on the out-breath, release any residue of feelings of anger or whatever emotion your anger has transformed into such as sadness or fear. Continue to focus on the breath and the feelings moving in and moving out, through you, until you feel lighter and peaceful.

This exercise can also be done performing a vigorous movement, such as running, swimming, cycling, using the motion itself in place of the prop, releasing the expression of charged negative energy through the movements of your body.

A powerful partner experience and exercise, which will build trust and sexual intimacy, and a mind-blowing connection like you've never known, is to begin to allow our partners the fullest expression of their anger and rage. While this is a practice that may take time to cultivate between you, it is a powerful gift you can give to one another to restore and build trust and intimacy. It helps to hold a safe distance between you to not get trapped up in the energy field of anger's release. Initially, understand and trust that what you might encounter is years of pent up anger and rage, at people and events, that have nothing to do with you. Once that anger has had its moment in the light of release, the softness and open heart that unveils itself creates a powerful trust and safety that yields to a fully awakened mind/body/heart that now has the capacity to unleash our grandest expressions of ecstasy, love and bliss. This is when we can mutually reap the bounty of individual experience that we all desire: to express being filled with the raw, unrepressed expressions of the bliss of raging love and ecstasy.

As a culture, tragically, we've been conditioned that it is not okay to be fully expressive in our anger (or our love). To be fully known, which is our heart's deepest desire, to feel loved and seen, we must restore the full range of emotions moving throughout our body systems. Repressing and turning down the volume of your emotions tightens and constricts everything in your body. As a result, we all pay a price. We lose our fullest experience and expression of creation: our passion and sexuality. When we repress our anger, we repress and tighten all pleasure expression: our sexuality, our capacity to feel and express the love moving through us. Our bodies were designed to be fluid, to feel, and be naturally open to responding with bliss, love, and ecstasy. To trust your capacity to retrain yourself to allow for your unleashed passion (which includes the powerful dual emotion: anger and rage) to express itself, we can each learn to step into what every man and woman has been fantasizing about for millennia.

Although our blueprint and biology as a man or as a woman produces different expressions of fulfillment, we converge at the same deepest longing. A man wants a fully cosmic, powerful, connected, unleashed orgasmic woman Goddess. A man contributes and co-creates that expression when allowing his woman to be fully seen through the expression of all of her emotions, to open up to, surrender to the truth of who she is. A woman intrinsically wants to trust the safety and full embrace of her divine energy, to unconditionally be known, and accepted, in her fullest capacity of expression, which once unleashed, she surrenders and opens herself naturally to express the power she possesses to exchange and move that energy through every cell of both bodies, empowering an intimacy, and communion, thrusting you both into the blissful experience of your connected deepest longings as humans: to be fully known and realized into reality.

While we've been conditioned to fear the full extent of our anger from watching our role models duck for cover when anger comes knocking, once we embrace the shadow of repressed anger and bring light to its powerful message, we access the wisdom and trust that we, in fact, do possess this amazing capacity to hold the gift that anger brings to us. This pro-active choice to listen to what unmet needs that our anger is calling us towards, dissipates the dark and dense energy that anger creates in our body-system, restoring our heart's connection to the fullest expression of love within us and brings that to the experience of shared intimacy between one another.

To date, many, both men and women, have only experienced the appetizer of orgasm, the wetting of our taste buds, not realizing the bounty of the main feast that is awaiting you, just around the corner, once you lift the glass to taste what lies ahead.

When I use the word orgasm, it is not just the sexual act and ecstasy of release, it also is a word that I offer to express our highest pinnacle of experience, as humans, to experience the passions of love that matter most to us. Through this expression, you have the capacity to bring this experience of connection to all of the relationships in your life.

This is what the journey is all about... Life living through us... How does it get any better than this?!

Practice #6—Facing a Difficult Person

Prior to facing a person that is difficult or triggers negative reactions within you, imagine and already know what quality, deity, or feeling you'd like to create within yourself. Bring that awareness into their heart. Communicate and connect to that person's highest truth. You do not have to know the person's belief system in order for this to be effective. Simply breathe in visualizing the person with the intention of connecting to their highest truth. Do this until you have a strong image of them in your mind and your feelings toward them is one of connection and a prevailing sense of compassion. Two to five minutes before you are going to meet with the person is usually sufficient. In the event it is a business meeting, you may also want to allow just a couple of minutes to ground yourself (this is the same exercise mentioned in the story of Jennifer and her boss in Chapter II, on page 82).

As you interact with this person, maintain the image and your intention. Be available to what happens. Sometimes, the vibrational shift you're creating can be sensed, even subconsciously, which may result in skepticism, fear, or strangeness from the other party. Allow for this to be if that is the case. Continue to hold your intention in subsequent opportunities with this person and see what happens. Over time, the person's energy toward you will shift. Trust your co-creative power and stay the course. Allow the other person to come to you. Let the relationship unfold naturally. This builds trust and lets the other person know, subconsciously, that positive connection is achievable.

Remember, all of us are acting out of what we believe we know in the moment leading us up to current life experiences, until we know differently. The relationships and interactions you have in life, as you learn to speak from your truth, with compassion and love, will act as the reflective mirror that allows for the grace that encourages others to become more. You can be a light unto the darkness when you intend and hold real connection as your highest priority in your relationships. Remember the truth: "Judge not, lest ye be judged."

Practice #7—Seeing your Connection to the Good in All of Humanity

This exercise enables you to maintain a sense of humility and remain grounded. Have a particular deity or quality you feel reminds you of our universal good.

When things are troubling you, this will help bring you back to a more beneficial, coherent and connected mindstate. Compassion is often hard to give when we feel rushed, irritable, or have judgment that the "other" is responsible for our annoyance or pain.

Every driver in the world has experienced this pressure. How many times have you been in a hurry and unconsciously been cut off or "slowed" by someone driving 55 mph in the fast lane? How many times have you murmured or had some flippant thought or violent judgment towards that person? Now, reverse the situation. Can you smile knowing that where you have judged and condemned others, you have been both the victim and the perpetrator in this experience of life? The key to your freedom, peace and well-being comes as you release any judgment you are feeling *within* you, towards yourself or others, and return to understanding what unites us—What we all share—my story, your story—my hurry, your hurry. These are our inter-connected Universal Human Needs.

Sit or lie down in a quiet place. Bring to mind a characteristic or a particular deity that radiates the qualities you would like to have. Envision this deity or quality. On your in-breath, focus that quality being written on the heart of the deity. For example, you can envision Jesus with the word "love" written on his heart, or you can envision Buddha with the word "compassion" written on his heart. Then, envision a white light emanating out from their heart. See or feel the light becoming brighter and brighter until it fills the whole body of the deity. Start with a statement that resonates the feeling and connection to love: "I recognize, love, and honor your true nature," or simply put, "Namaste." Originating from India as a common greeting, the word Namaste means, "I honor the spirit in you which is also in me," or "I acknowledge the Divinity in you," or "I affirm your true depth and nature." By silently acknowledging and speaking the word "Namaste" before entering any compassionate confrontation or even as we greet a perceived stranger, acknowledges the kindest, truest part of our interconnected nature to one another and all living things, which grounds us to our connected energy. And energy speaks volumes before even a single word is spoken.

Practice #8—The 5 Minute In-Powering UP for that Business Meeting, Call, or Connection with a Loved One

You can do this five minutes prior to any interaction to create a successful outcome.

First, calm your body. Visualize and feel yourself making that contact, really connecting purely, effortlessly and with the results you desire. For example: This could be anything from the contract being signed, or a potential investor's agreement to meet with you, or a phone call where you need the other party to be receptive and open. Focus your awareness to feelings that you want to motivate and inspire in the other person. Envision the conversation, the laughter, your common connections and the synergy you share. Hold the intention that your common goals and aspirations will be met in a spirit of excitement and cooperation. Express gratitude for the results you will obtain (say this as though they have already happened). Open your heart to celebrate the mutual contribution that you both feel arising from your time together. Focus on your breath and the feelings of gratitude in your heart that you feel when you are connected to what really matters to you about that connection. You have now opened up the space of possibilities to contribute to the outcome you desire.

Practice #9—Lectio Divina (The Divine Word)

This is a powerful practice where you sit quietly with any philosophical teaching or religious guide. Upon opening the book, ask your wisdom to draw your attention to focus on a chapter, a verse, or a particular word that you feel drawn to. Focus your attention on your breath, repeating the word or phrase, over and over, feeling or seeing that message penetrate deep into your body and heart, as you breathe deeper into a meditative state. This allows the word, verse, or phrase to reveal itself to you. This experience can deepen a quality and awareness within you that creates a profound communion and connection that deepens your spiritual practice and teachings. Each time you do this practice, you will gain new insight, heightened wisdom and love. This practice leads you into a deepened peace that surpasses all understanding. When you seek to commune (to become one with) with a word, a verse, or a teaching you move from the contextual linear mind, and grow your capacity to love, day-by-day, moment-by-moment, with the heart of everything you are and the interconnected relationships you engage in.

VAST AS AN OCEAN

Remember, mindfulness is not about the destination, it is about the conscious journey into your sublime Self. This is your all *knowing* you. This is your ever-expanding awareness that opens and connects your reality of experience to the kindest parts of yourself—your true nature. Within you is an ocean of infinite knowledge, passions, potential, and inspiration. Every moment is an invitation to experience the further expansion of your heart and connection to the highest expression of your life, as you open to allow life to live through you.

Living a life of mindfulness offers you everything you can ever imagine, and even more. Only you can access the infinite potential to create the life living reality of your highest dreams. It takes dedication and disciplined practice to master anything in life. To understand, access, and fully re-cognize your greatness, times of silence are needed, to unlock your deepest truths awaiting creation as you listen to the silent language within your heart.

To live a life of meaning, to experience genuine happiness and a sense of well-being, one must be connected to the inextricably interconnected place of nothing and everything, where only abstract potential exists.

In the modern world, the one that we've been conditioned into, we have denied ourselves the only real pursuit that leads us to the truth and answers to the primordial questions of life:

Who am I? What does it take to live a richly meaningful life?

To live a richly meaningful life, these three pursuits are profoundly and inextricably intertwined:

1. The Pursuit of Understanding, of Insight, of Knowledge, of Wisdom: If I let a day slip by and have made no effort, directed no attention to this pursuit, that day is not complete.

2. To Cultivate Virtue: To be wiser, kinder, have more patience...

3. To Cultivate a Deepening Sense of Happiness and Well-Being: From what I am bringing to the world, not just what I'm getting from it.

In the modern world, these three pursuits are often presented as being independent, unrelated and even in conflict with each other. But at the deepest level, the pursuit of understanding must be inextricably intertwined for the cultivation and sake of genuine happiness and well-being. This pursuit leads you naturally to the avenue of cultivating virtue: intelligence, wisdom, sound judgment, and clear observation. So, for the pursuit of understanding to be as rich and deep as possible, it must be entangled, interwoven with the cultivation of virtue, to come to know yourself and the world around you in the deepest sense of Happiness and Well-Being.

How can we do this if we don't know our own minds? The nature of human existence? Our relationship to the people around us? Our connected nature to the environment as a whole? All three pursuits are what naturally give rise to the experience of life in our deepest and greatest sense of well-being and happiness.

We've built a world with systems that deny and repress the discovery of our own essential nature. A world that is searching for love, for meaning; building a false sense of happiness that has led our world into all types of addictions... a craving for stimulus, a certain type of frenzy.

To live a rich and meaningful life we must have times of silence. Times for reflection. Times of simplification. Times of solitude...to come to terms with our own identity, our own being, our essential nature, prior to, the many roles that we adopt and release throughout this reality called life.

Will the truth set you free?

Any discovered truth is simply knowledge. Without application and integration into your being, your life, it is simply wisdom that grows dust on the bookshelves of your life. We are human beings, not human doings. Is it time that we begin to live the truth of who we are...

The Truth is...In every part of you, there's a part of me. It is in the silence... that everything gets created.

V

Demystifying the Law of Attraction

As a Man thinketh in his heart, so he is.
—JESUS

You are what you think. With your thoughts you make your world.
—BUDDHA

To think is to create.
—NAPOLEON HILL

Have you ever really wanted something to happen, so much that it's all you can think about? For example, let's say that for weeks now you've had a thought or question you haven't been able to put to rest. Even though you've sought the answer, it just doesn't seem like you will find one. Then, at a cocktail party, a stranger engages you in conversation and within minutes they give you just the answer you've been seeking. Or it could be that you're working on a deadline and the night before the presentation is due the graphic artist backs out. You are interrupted by a knock on the door. Hesitantly, even frustrated, you answer. It's a young man collecting money for a non-profit. Jokingly, you ask him if he's an artist and mention the pickle you're in. He whips out his iPhone and shows you his portfolio. His work is even better than the artist you had before. This is synchrodestiny in action, one aspect of the Law of Attraction that tells us: THERE IS NO SUCH THING AS COINCIDENCE. When you take control of your own destiny and reality, these everyday possibilities occur everywhere, letting you know you are co-creating your world in everything you think, feel, and believe every moment of every day.

OUR RAS: MIND/BODY/HEART INTELLIGENCE

Recently, in the field of neuroscience, there have been some amazing discoveries that offer scientific understanding to the physiological underpinnings around the recent quantum buzz and phenomena around the Law of Attraction. Located in the medulla oblongata region of the human brain, the Reticular Activating System (RAS) is a system of cells that "control the overall degree of central nervous system activity, including wakefulness, attentiveness and sleep." But this is not all. Thanks to the work of Dr. Antonio Damasio, we now see that our RAS actually works as a kind of data and programming center, receiving the signals sent by our powerful somatic markers which allows for our mind/body/heart to develop a kind of sixth-sense-consciousness or intuition. These somatic markers "are past experiences stored in our body and brain." Wired into every facet of our central nervous system, they act as a very sophisticated laser-like guidance system that enables you to process and store information subconsciously that thereby enables you to think through cognitive thought processes more quickly. Your RAS not only receives signals sent by your already existing somatic markers, but you can also actually emotionally re-program this region of your brain to send signals through your central nervous system that activate your intentions, desires, and highest dreams. When consciously programmed, your RAS begins to hone in with laser-like accuracy to take control of your living reality by opening up the fastest route to achieving your goals.

Abstract thoughts or notions will do little to stimulate this inborn gift. One must clearly define and emotionalize what you deeply want and hold into your awareness, using your whole mind/body/heart system of senses to activate this region of the mind which then arouses the nervous system to literally focus the whole mind/body/heart towards getting what you want.

In Chapter II, we discussed the importance of maintaining psychophysiological coherence when processing one's emotions. The function of the RAS only buttresses this point: Your emotions are meant to be processed by the mind/body/heart not as cold, removed bits of information but as emotions acknowledged, experienced, and moved-through.

When you clear your negative limiting beliefs, traumas, thoughts, and patterns from your mind/body/heart system, you free up an enormous amount of raw energy potential. By arousing your RAS to work in line with what your consciousness and truth want, you enable your nervous system to activate, filtering through infinitesimal amounts of information, responding to your emotional orders, putting your mind/body/heart to work 24/7, firing new somatic markers and neural pathways, opening your super consciousness bull's-eye accuracy, like a 360° radar missile to target your goal. By the end of this chapter, you will have everything you need to put your RAS to work to co-create a new living reality aligned to your highest visions.

Such revolutionary new findings on how your RAS works has led some scientists to conclude that its very existence explains away the mystery around our Universal Law of Attraction. As human beings, we now know we possess a sophisticated bio-system whereby we can entrain our whole mind/body/heart system to tune into what we want to aide us in getting it. This science confirms that you possess an infinite potential to actually commune with the atoms of our world and mind/body/heart system to activate your natural inborn faculties. In no way does the possession of your RAS negate the existence of a larger, prevailing intelligence. This finding merely shows us that we are all powerful co-creative agents that are a part of the irreducible One Power of The All That Is, and possess the necessary physical "wiring" to participate with the non-physical infinite Universe to achieve our grandest desires. You intrinsically play a co-creative role, as a participatory part of the equation. The totality of you—your thoughts, your aspirations, your physical self—is all part of The Grand Unified Field. Your RAS is simply a part of how you commune and communicate with everything that is around and within you.

OUR ARCHITECTURAL BLUEPRINT

That which is *within*: your truth, your guiding system, your inspirations, and your source defining your unique purpose in life is what I call your Architectural Blueprint. Connecting to and having your actions extend from your truth is a vital part of actualizing your heart's desire into your physical world's reality by directing your RAS, your Law of Attraction, to work for you.

Waking up to the truth of who you are involves an active role and intention to align your conscious desires while using your triggers in life to clear the subconscious limitations holding you stuck into negative energetic attraction patterns. This enables the process of possibilities to unfold. The more you align your truth, through your words and actions by engaging a perpetual process of clearing your limitations as you feel them come up, the more real, tangible, active, and fluid your intuitive honing capacities can become in creating the life of your highest potentiality. Your intrinsic desire to learn and thrive, living as your greatest potential is beyond any societal conditioning, any idea, or physical construct of what you currently think you are. It is the truth of why you are here. Living as the life breathing reality of what you are created to be is the driving force that turns on life living through you. It is what excites you to jump out of bed into action in the morning. When you create a world where you are serving what you love to do, then everyone and every living thing that connects to you benefits—for you are serving your highest dream of you and it is contagious!

When you go within, you gain access to your infinite truth. This state of being is achieved through Self-work, meditation, spending time alone in silence, and in silent times communing with nature. As you apply these teachings and skills something extraordinary happens. Your thoughts crystallize into your reality. Thoughts drive the actions that create your destiny. What this seems like under the guise of human linear-thinking and understanding is that the two parts, thinking and action happen together. Thoughts and emotions are what activate and create your reality. Remember, everything that happens to you is happening to serve your highest purpose. Your predominate thought-energy drives your actions, blasting out a message to the Universe of your readiness to receive. To create something into reality, you must emote the energy to co-create it into existence. You were born with this power within every cell of your human divine masterprint.

The Belief and Intention worksheet, the clearing exercises, and your daily connection through Mindfulness practices will clear the runway to access your highest dreams! Thoughts of doubt are nothing more than vestiges of old fear-based mutant programming of energy patterns in your life. Any negative thought only has creative power when you cement them in by giving them your emotional (emotive) attention. Cancel them, state your affirmation, and direct your thoughts to ones that are life-affirming. Do not dwell in doubt. Doubt carries a very low vibration that undercuts your positive vibrations. Any feelings that stick you with an "ouch" are a lie stemming from your conditioning and limiting beliefs. Thoughts that feel "good" create an expansive, open feeling within you, representing your highest truth.

WHEN YOU DO NOT "KNOW"

Know that within you, your highest truth and awareness knows exactly who you are and what you need to thrive in your life. Living in the trust of knowing nothing, creates the open space and allowance for everything that is true for you to come into your conscious awareness, even if you do not intellectually "know" it. Choosing to release your rigidity, finite beliefs, and judgments about how, what or who anyone is, or should be, sends your RAS to work to map out the fastest route to what will fulfill your fullest expression of you. If you don't know what your purpose is, think about what you love to do. Focus on what you love and your truth and purpose will begin to open up the possibilities to discover what your divine blueprint is. The 7-minute Inner-net Connection to Your Essential Wisdom practice in the previous chapter will open up clear answers, visual images, and vital clues. Your RAS is working to bring you clues that lead you back to your source truth.

It is only your false fear-based conditioning that has trained you to want to rush and find something that will explain your reason for being. Closing the past and coming to stand on the razor's edge of the present moment opens up infinite possibilities to live life not attached to judgments or beliefs which limit your experienced reality in life.

As human energetic beings you are constantly changing. You are an infinite part of a dynamic living Universe. Listening to the truth of your heart's grandest desires intertwines your purposes into the energy necessary to create the co-creative energy that designs your life. Stay open to living in the question, "Who am I?" There is a grand plan written in every cell of DNA in your body, being activated as you live your life as an ever-expanding possibility.

Finding your purpose does not have to mean choosing between your heart's desires and doing something out there in the world. Stay true to what you love. Serving your highest desires will always be a connected part that serves what's good and true for everyone. No comparison or living in someone else's possibility for you will make you jump out of bed in the morning, filled with happiness and feeling life course through your veins! Not knowing anything, living in the childlike inquiry, opens the space to allow everything to become a co-creative agent in creating the truth of you!

THE NEWTONIAN WORLD

The Newtonian view of the Universe, the predominant view still enforced today in the created systems that govern our current reality, views our world as an assortment of things that are separate and operate as distinct "parts of the machine." In an attempt to learn about all these various parts, separate branches of science have emerged. It is thanks to all these various areas of scientific inquiry that we have been able to see what's inside an atom, study quarks to achieve an understanding to some of life's primordial questions: What is the nature of human existence? What is our relationship to the people around us? What is our connected nature to the environment as a whole? Who am "I," apart from the roles I have adopted? What defines my reality? Can I change it?

It is nothing short of breathtaking to see just how far we've come and how now, for the first time in history, we have enough of the puzzle put together to know that we are powerful co-creators of the living experience of our reality. All of this has happened in a warp speed momentum of time!

We are no longer limited by an old world tribal mindset that sees us as powerless victims of our conditions, genetics or circumstances. No, the truth is: you are a powerful co-creator of your life living reality, moment to moment, and you hold the capacity wired into your original DNA blueprint, before it was contaminated by fear, to translate your heart's desire into your physical realm of this world.

Now we enter the reality and see the truth of where two paths converge. Less than three hundred years after Newton, modern quantum physics, molecular biology, neuroimmunology, and the neurosciences all point us to an ever-expanding scientific frontier. What was formerly thought of as separate is really part of a grand whole, the Grand Unified Field, a single universal field that unites us all and through which all levels of nature function; the very thing Einstein was trying to locate by formulating his Theory of Everything. Consciousness is not a creation of the human mind; it exists both inside and outside of us. This Living Matrix or Grand Unified Field is the basis of all mind, all matter. It is in this non-material field, united at its core, where all abstract potentiality exists. The Weizmann Institute of Science states that "The observer affects that which is observed." As a *part* of the Field, we are participatory co-creators within the Field.

Discoveries in the science of unified field theories prompted noted quantum particle physicist Dr. John Hagelin to assert a need to rename the elementary particles, the lepton, quark, and electron according to the role they play in a "single self-interacting field." This would simplify our understanding of how everything connects to its respective "unified source in the unified field" so that "each aspect of the discipline would indicate its position and purpose with respect to the whole." This "vision of the whole" explains each part's significance to the grand scheme that forms our understanding of consciousness.

Quantum physicist, Dr. Konstantin Korotkov in the film, *The Truth, The Journey Within* helps elucidate the power we, as humans, have to affect the world around us this way:

> "[T]he power we have has nothing to do with some mystical experience, because it is an absolutely understandable physiological process. As human quantum processes, we have our activity of our brain, activity of our heart, of all our organs, and

> *they are all based on some electrical process, and it means electrons, and as it was once said, photons. So, in quantum principle, our activity is based on [the] exchange of electrons due to narrow systems, due to molecular processes, and electrons and photons, all based on quantum process. And when we came to this understanding all over the world, not only in our team, then a lot of processes got real big scientific ground, because we developed and can now measure through electric cardiogram, and through electroencephalogram (EEG—a test that measures and records the electrical activity of your brain), our human energy field."*
>
> *"This energy field is not just what we produce in our body, but is a constant exchange of energy, determining how we interact with the environment, and this is very important. With our experiments with quantum electrodynamics, we have found without a doubt, that our positive emotions have a tremendous effect on our physiological systems of our bodies and on our environment around us. So, it is absolutely clear, that it is not just our thirst (for meaning and understanding), but it is a strong governing power in our world."*

What Dr. Korotkov asserts, and many of our world's leading quantum scientists concur with, is that we as humans are not distinct from this Grand Unified Field but instead are a dynamic participatory part of it. We are "human quantum processes" in our own right, responsible for contributing to the billions of oscillating brainwaves that not only affect our reality, but create our collective morphogenetic field.

You are NOT the helpless victim of your circumstances. You are a powerful energetic infinite being that through observation and directing your thoughts and emotions, through action, you become the co-creator of your experience to reality and existence.

Within the last quarter century, our scientific exploration into consciousness itself being a part of the irreducible whole of the very fabric that creates all of life changes everything we have ever known about who we are, and how we exist in our world. This knowledge has been written into our ancient wisdom texts, our philosophies, and spiritual teachings for millenniums. When viewed from this quantum perspective, familiar religious and philosophical terms such as: The Holy Spirit, Divine Light, Nirvana, Zen, Buddha-field (a Zen Buddhist term meaning the field of consciousness created by an enlightened being), Brahman (the Hindu term for the non-dual, incorporeal, absolute source of All That Is) are now fully converged to meet our latest scientific findings. These all refer to a dimension of consciousness that is inextricably participatory in nature. Even Plato's Theory of Forms can now be appreciated when he stated that "any human participating in the search for truth through the apprehensible world that the real underlying truth will be known."

Man does not stand apart from nature. Man is an irreducible part of nature.

How does man come to know real truth, to participate in such interconnected exchange to access a larger, prevailing intelligence?

Nearly all cultures speak of men who commune with Nature or God, whereby they access certain truths that they share with their fellow man. Such men have been called: Prophets, Shamen, Healers, Seekers, Messiahs, and Enlightened Beings.

DENIAL LIMITS OUR CAPACITY TO EVOLVE INDIVIDUALLY AND AS A SPECIES

The pressure to push these new findings into the closet, to pretend they have never happened, or deny that they even exist, is great for a number of complex reasons and underlying motives. Simply put, thanks to a legacy of societal conditioning, people have become dependent upon seeing themselves a certain way and on living a certain way, even when it falls short of yielding true and genuine happiness, lasting satisfaction, sustainability, and well-being. Our conditioned tendency for many is to opt for the path of least resistance, for the path that is comfortably "known."

Such is the way it has always been. The majority has always been slow to accept new scientific discoveries. Just think, a mere 400 years ago, man believed the earth was the center of the Universe, and that the Sun, Moon, and stars dutifully orbited around *it*. Galileo proved, beyond doubt, that Copernicus had been right, the earth *did* orbit the sun, even then the most erudite scoffed considering it an absolutely preposterous idea! In fact and tragically, Galileo was persecuted during an inquisition for challenging a belief system that had no foundation of truth and yet governed mass belief.

So here we stand, at another pinnacle moment in history. Thanks to new discoveries in the fields of both neuroscience and quantum science, We, humankind, are on the crux of yet another shift in the way we conceptualize and actualize the very nature of being and our consciousness to affect significant change into our lives.

As these unsustainable systems, built of a false belief system of science, collapse around us, we now know the truth of who we are: we are powerful co-creators of our Universe.

The answers to life's most quintessential question, "Who am I?" and "What is my purpose in life?" empowers the truth within you to go deep, clearing out the limitations, piercing the illusive veil hidden in the lies we've been conditioned into, to effect the models of internal change individually, and collectively to transform the power-over systems that, to date, have defined and limited your individual and our collective perceived reality.

Will truth set you free?

Any discovered truth is simply knowledge. Without application, its wisdom grows dust on the shelves of your life.

Everything you will ever need to unlock your truth and your freedom to live life "on purpose" and in full abundance has always been located within you, written into your DNA, accessible through the silent language of your heart.

Denial limits your capacity to step into living as the infinite potential and truth of who you are.

THE FIELD OF DREAMS

Numerous scientists, philosophers, inventors, and other great minds all credit a certain state of mind responsible for yielding some of the world's greatest discoveries—called the dream state. Thomas Edison has his famous "catnaps." Walt Disney and Albert Einstein, as well, credited a particular state of mind as being the source of knowledge, accessible only once they cleared their conscious minds and dozed off into this alternate mental state. Dreams are credited by numerous other great inventors and thinkers as the source from which they are able to draw revelatory new ideas and visions.

Dmitri Ivanovich Mendeleev, Russian chemist and architect of the first periodic table, retold a dream he had in 1869: "I saw in a dream a table where all the elements fell into place as required. Awakening, I immediately wrote it down on a piece of paper." Thus, the periodic table we all learned in our high school chemistry class was born.

Canadian scientist and physician Sir Frederick Banting had a dream that hinted at a method for extracting the hormone insulin from a nonhuman pancreas. As a result, Banting found an effective way to treat people with Type 1 Diabetes and was awarded the Nobel Prize in 1923 for it, and was eventually knighted.

American inventor, Elias Howe, once dreamed he was being chased by cannibals with spears. While the natives were waving their weapons, he noticed that the shafts all had tiny holes in them and the spears were also bobbing up and down. Waking from his dream, Howe was finally able to complete his invention of the automatic sewing machine, realizing he had to move the eye of the needle to the bottom instead of placing it at the top.

Danish physicist Niels Bohr, progenitor of quantum theory, said he came up with a functional model of the atom after dreaming he was sitting on the sun with all the planets hissing around on tiny cords. At only 28, Bohr published his model of the atom and went on to found and serve as Director of the Institute of Theoretical Physics, now named the Niels Bohr Institute, in 1921. Bohr was awarded the Nobel Prize in 1922.

Author of the timeless story, *Dr. Jekyll and Mr. Hyde*, Robert Louis Stevenson reported the idea originated in a dream, as did much of his best work.

What do you presume these men were really doing? We now know through MRI and other sophisticated scientific measuring systems that view brainwaves in action, they were creating the peak brainstates to access and go beyond their own solitary finite minds and were tapping into something infinite, something that could spark original thought in their minds and hearts only after their subconscious limitations and constructs of mind got out of the way. They were communing with The Field.

ACCESSING YOUR FULL POTENTIAL

We can desire as much as we like, try as hard as we can, but only when we settle our minds can you access that pure ground-state of being where you access the infinite field of potentiality. Going to The Field is not an exercise in will-power, thought or intent. It is a process of conditioning your heart and conscious mind. In this state of being you entrain and align your mind/body/heart which opens your awareness and tunes into the brainwave frequency to create this dream-like waking state of consciousness. The very act of thinking, of a mind engaged in thought, distracts and disables this process by pushing whatever signals you are sending and receiving back through the filters of your encoded beliefs and perceptions. No legitimate or original creative forms of divine intrinsic invention from the phenomena of the participatory Universe can become unveiled through you, unless you access the gates of where pure potentiality resides. Your linear mind must come to rest to access your pure potential.

Tapping into your truth is easier than you might believe.

To do this you will need to enhance and train your capacity to create the necessary brainwave patterns of Theta and Delta, the very same brainwaves present in dream states and responsible for many of the world's greatest inventions and discoveries. Binaural Beat Technology, discussed earlier, more thoroughly on page 132, Chapter IV, is a highly effective 20-30 minute soundtrack technology that stimulates the brainwave patterns of Theta and Delta, enabling you to experience what had formerly taken literally thousands of hours of meditation to achieve.

BBT technology offers you tremendous advantages when it comes to enhancing your natural untrained capacity to access your highest potential. These self-tools are now making radical change possible in ways that are compatible in today's overextended schedules. Your capacity to fine-tune your mind's ability to access this mind-state is only limited by the effort and time you create in your life. Your RAS will allow your passions to fire on all cylinders, channeling your desire through to every part of your body, to transmit the energetic frequency signals, accessing the consciousness necessary to achieve your deepest desires. Our great poet and mystic Rumi said, "Out beyond our ideas of wrong-doing and right-doing there is a field. I will meet you there."

Our infinite greatness lies just beyond our mind's contextual concepts, just beyond our illusions of separateness and limitation.

You now have all the Self-tools you need to commune with the forces that co-create everything you experience in the reality of your world.

INTENTION & BELIEF MEDITATION

Select a place in your house that you can return to regularly. Because of the way vibrational frequencies and your somatic markers work, the more time you spend in this particular place, the easier and faster it will be to relax and open your access point of infinite consciousness and pure potential, because you have conditioned that space.

Set aside anywhere between thirty minutes to a full hour. This is your time that allows your life to be filled with your full potency and truth. This space should be quiet, comfortable, and free of interruption. It may be helpful to have props that act as reminders of what you hold as sacred or what you want to intention into your reality. Bring pictures or scents that help to enhance your senses of experience or whatever it is you intuitively want to create a creative and peaceful space.

Complete the Belief & Intention Worksheet, located at the end of this chapter to be clear on your intention. The clearer your statement is, the clearer your mind's eye will be able to visualize or feel it. For example, *getting* the job of your dreams may be hard to visualize but you can *envision* yourself in action, actually doing the job. You can see yourself helping a client, wearing a particular suit, while also feeling the happiness and great sense of purpose that arises as you do the work you love. You want your heart's truth and awareness to open to the full potential of what that would feel like.

You may be more visual, or auditory, or more able to tune into your senses, so find what uniquely serves you best as you practice.

Before you begin this meditation, it helps to check into your mind/body/heart system to see if there are any built up energy stores that you can discharge. Discharging these blocked emotional stores helps bring your heart into coherence. Spend whatever time is necessary to expand your heartspace and mind to feel open, calm and receptive.

Use your intention statement to state your desire. The space you are creating within your mind/body/heart system is one that is open and able to receive. The more you can tune into your intention using all of your senses to fill and align your mind and heart: to see, touch, feel, smell, how it energetically feels in your heart when you open to receive what you desire, the clearer that message is sent out into the field of possibility to manifest itself into your reality. Stay present with each and every sensory experience, staying on point with the breath bringing into existence the feelings and emotions creating what you are envisioning.

Your Intentions can also become great affirmations for your Thought Monitoring. When you feel a heaviness in your mind/body/heart or catch yourself in a limiting or negative thought, dismiss it as the lie that it is! Returning to your breath opens the space and redirects your thoughts which will keep your "on purpose" in co-creating your reality.

ASSUMPTIONS OF INTEGRITY

In your day-to-day life, you must by vigilant to choose to put your mind towards intentioning your visions into reality. There are certain specific assumptions of integrity that are dependent on maintaining your open access to living your life in your highest levels of potentiality:

1. My inner truth is the spirit and source that generates all abundance in my life. Abundance is my divine birthright and promise from the Universe. It is from a place of compassion and gratitude that I co-create and manifest what I am most passionate about, desire, and aspire to be. I know when I call a vision into action, it is already done. The Universe is lining it up for me, bringing the people, the wisdom, the teachings, and whatever else is necessary for my deepest passions to become reality.

2. My reality and the manifestations of the everyday miracles I call forth are realized in direct proportion to my willingness and my actions, which will open up my awareness to align my highest thoughts, feelings, emotions, and beliefs into the fabric of my being, aligning my deepest truths, of who I am and what I was created to be. I am open to receive everything that is needed to surrender any limitation that is blocking my capacity to be the generative, potent, and powerful co-creator of my life living reality creating through me.

3. I am now choosing to create my world committed to the discipline of discovering my deepest, highest good, and Self. I know that my positive thoughts vibrate at frequencies 1000 times stronger than any negative thoughts or fear-based emotions. In this acknowledgement, I choose to let go of negative and limiting thoughts and beliefs that prevent me from living the life I was created to be. I trust that I am fully capable of seeing deeply, with awareness and intention, into the gifts that the mirror of relationship provides. I am grateful for all of my relationships trusting that every experience I receive holds the keys to overcoming the sabotaging beliefs that stand in the

way of my manifesting a world filled with everything I can imagine, and even more.

4. I co-create my reality by asking for everything I intention into my reality and that it be created with ease, great clarity, and passion. I allow my thoughts, feelings, and all of my senses to commit to actively experiencing every vision as though it has already happened. I celebrate this awareness that it is already happening. I trust and surrender every intention I make, accepting the truth that everything always works out for my highest good; which may not always show up as I desire or believe it should be. Every finite "should" I have created, I release and uncreate them now. I acknowledge that I've chosen all experiences in my life and only I have the power to co-create and change my life. Through my intentions and actions I will be pro-active in clearing limitations blocking my direct path to access the pure potential and truth of who I am and what I was created to do and be in this world. I receive my power to access my complete manifestation and creation of my living reality.

LIVING THE LAW

Living the Law of Attraction means living in active belief or faith that the Universe aligns with you as you co-create the reality you intend. When circumstances in life show up different than what you desire, remember, what you resist persists. Accepting, "Wow, I chose this, now what do I choose next?" opens up your awareness to not cement in any new stories that limit you or keep you stuck from creating the life of your dreams.

Through your thoughts, emotions and actions, you are either living as your highest intention, or limiting yourself into finite patterns of life that deny you from the experience of thriving and living your truth. The more you stay on-purpose and committed to Self-work, the faster you will experience your interior and exterior experience of reality aligning your unique gifts and purpose into the physical reality of your world. Like physical exercise, building new muscles requires diligence, dedication, repetition, and action. If you stray off course, your mind/body/heart and life will begin to show the signs of your choices. This is the case with all mind/body/heart entraining and intention practice.

The process of realizing your truest nature and highest Self is a lifetime journey. Your magic in life unfolds as you stay focused and powerfully choose to direct the course of your life. Like a plane's computer navigational system, the computer is constantly monitoring the plane's coordinates, adjusting and realigning your trajectory. In truth, it constantly veers off course and then corrects because of its navigational design. You are wired with all of the necessary parts to redirect your path any and every time your awareness gives you the WARNING: danger, you are off your truthful and consciously programmed course. You can now avoid that painful crash landing as you listen to the alarms of your awareness that rings.

Your RAS system takes the shortest route and works to align your course. What you allow into your mind's and heart's bio-computer, your thoughts, your emotions, and your actions, become the coordinates that set and directs the path of your life. You can re-program and re-adjust the course anytime you are not living as the ease, joy, and abundance that your life was designed to be.

Remember, the word "action" makes up part of the Law of Attraction. It does require action by you to move that which is in the unseen world to that which is seen. The greatest action you can take is to stay vigilant to monitoring your thoughts, and guarding your emotions (heart). For it is your thoughts, and the subsequent emotions, that drive everything into your world. Remaining grounded and present to what you desire most in life, staying narrowly focused, allows your mind/body/heart connection to become your most powerful vehicle for opening the field of consciousness that will most directly chart the course to living as your most abundant life.

Years ago, before there was any talk about the Law of Attraction, when asked by managers, and others, how I had accomplished the life of my desires, I used to share my mantra that my wise accountant shared: "Fake it 'til you make it," a term many of you have undoubtedly heard. In essence, these are the A, B, C's of the mathematical sequence that unlock the sequential code and instructs your RAS to align your fastest route to creating your desired reality. Stepping into action, watching through the lens of your awareness for the synchronicities that are everywhere, fine-tuning your RAS radar, entrains your mind to remain unencumbered or effected by the white noise of the negative thought patterns limiting your belief. Jesus Christ said, "Ask and it will be given to you; seek and you will find; *know* (knock) and the door will be opened to you."

Living the Law by monitoring your thoughts, limiting beliefs and behaviors, as well as guarding your heart by monitoring your choices and circumstances, becomes most challenging when we are triggered. Guarding your thoughts also means guarding being drained by our friends or loved ones who feel the need to commiserate or unload their hurt or charged feelings into our reality. We have never been taught to ask permission or check in before we dump our toxic emotions into someone else's front yard. Begin modeling the compassionate action to communicate whether, or not, you have the open space to allow for your support. It takes you coming from your strength, and power, to contribute to truly helping them ground back into their own heart-coherence, strength and truth of who they truly are, sharing the truth of your awareness that negative stories and beliefs are what are limiting their reality. Only when you can be truly present to hold the heartspace of compassion or empathy for them do you become a pro-active leader. Model your awareness by redirecting them to their own heart and give them self-tools that guide them to where their wisdom and possibility is waiting. It is not our job to play God in another's life.

Byron Katie shares in the The Truth film, "There are three people's business in the world. There's your business, there's my business, and there's God's business—and my business is a full time job." Who's guarding and co-creating your life if you're busy in the story of someone else's life?

New breakthroughs in science have revealed that we as human beings are powerful imitators. Located within our inferior frontal cortex and superior parietal lobe is your Mirror Neuron System (MNS). This system is hardwired into your brain as a developmental short-cut that causes you to unthinkingly copy just what you see others doing. This inherent learning by imitating and mirroring happens on a pre-cognitive level. To test this out right now, hold up two of your fingers. Most likely, without thinking, you held up your index and middle finger. Wonder why you held up those two fingers? Your Mirror Neuron System has mirrored what you have seen others do who have been conditioned by Western mindset. Had you been raised in rural South Africa, chances are you would have raised up your little finger and ring finger, a result of the Mirror Neuron System mirroring a different cultural conditioning habit. This lends more credence to the teachings, "Do not make friends with an angry man, lest you learn his ways and set a snare for your soul" and "you are known through the company you keep." If you spend your time with creative minds, you will become creative. Our mirroring system is not selective. Our MNS mirrors both the positive and negative attributes of our role models. As the triggers come up through your life, they are the gift that allow you to go back into those negative programs of mirroring and hit the pause button on the drama of your life story, to inquire within. It is from this place of inquiry that you can delete the place of creation where that limiting and negative false "truth" was imbedded into your somatic markers, to reprogram and create coherence between your subconscious and conscious "truth" of who you are.

Wow, a powerful reminder that we lead through our mirrored example! Creating an abundant life is a choice. Guarding your heart of whom and what we allow into our hearts and mind/body/heart is the single most important awareness we can choose to make to co-create a peaceful and thriving life.

By creating the gap to choose a different conscious response, you can re-mirror and repattern your choices to what best serves your conscious and highest thoughts, wishes, and desires!

For this reason, it is mission critical to not allow negative people, circumstances, and negative self-talk or negative talk from others to damage or thwart your intention of Living the Law. This awareness helps you view and guard your interactions with those who tend to perpetuate life-negating behaviors and limiting attitudes to set firm boundaries. It does not serve love to support a limiting set of beliefs or attitudes, believing that your contribution of "listening" can help. In truth, we perpetuate limitation if we allow it. If a friend or loved one seeks your time and wants to unload their negative or limiting "stories" onto you, check in with yourself first to see how you feel about their habit to seek "advice" about their problems. If you are not seeing a shift in the way they are living and choosing their reactions to life, choosing love means we have the courage to speak our truth and awareness, of what will contribute to them also learning how to choose love (for yourself), and be prepared to move on if they are continuing to live in patterns that deny the very thing we cherish, life itself.

Before they begin, it is helpful to say something loving like "I'm happy to be here for you to help you get this off your chest" or "I value you as a friend, so I can listen if that is what you would like for five minutes if that can contribute to you." These statements reassure them of your intention for contribution and support as well as establishes a way of relating that empowers building deep connection, authenticity and trust. Now is a perfect time to begin modeling and support them to focus their thoughts and heart to where their true power lies: in the silent language of their own heart. This is a powerful truth you can offer to help guard your heart from the energetic attack of negative people or limiting patterns of relating: "I'd love to hear what you are wanting to unload because I can tell you are triggered, but right now I am not able to support you as I have some conflicting heart needs. Can I come back to you to contribute to your need for support at a time when I am open and present to really hear your heart?"

We've been conditioned to look for answers outside of ourselves. Redirecting a loved one back to their own power and wisdom is the most loving, compassionate act we can model.

Ask yourself what need is being fed if you find that you often allow others to see you as their dumping ground and it has it become a habit? How do you feel? Does your listening contribute to empowering them? Community is strong technology when we can be there to model new possibilities when we lose our way. Friends offer a support network that have the creative capacity to expand awareness and model new patterns of co-creative, compassionate relating.

Learning to be fully present to listen to the heart needs of yourself, or another, is a conscious act of compassion, requiring us to just be, without judgment. Your gift is to create possibilities of awareness where their current understanding and awareness may not be able to see just a moment before. If you open your heart, your intuitive awareness can offer a powerful possibility in creating a different reality. Now you're serving as a co-creative contributor to awakening a new awareness into the living reality of your life.

If we are not clear on our intention and contribution, then we limit ourselves and the relationship and perpetuate a continued limiting relationship dynamic that is not in alignment with Living the Law.

If you share your life-tools you empower them. An ancient Chinese proverb said, "Give a man a fish and you feed him for a day; teach a man to fish and you feed him for a lifetime."

If you find that they have not empowered their life to the action and change, your choice to remain in the dance of negative relationship patterns denies you from operating in your greatness and potency. Knowing that relationships offer us our most dynamic mirrors for change, speaking your truth, in love, and moving past relationships that are stuck in limiting patterns is the most loving, and freeing, gift you offer yourself and the other person. You may be just the mirror that forces the inward reflection that empowers their heart with truth. Redefining the relationship is how you create change for yourself and for another heart. As energy beings, every action creates a cause and effect. You choose your life... what do you choose now?

The choice to empower yourself or another is yours alone. How many times do you find yourself in thoughts about the business or life of another? When your mind is running thoughts or feelings about their life, who is running yours? Something to think about...

Thanks to our Somatic Markers, and our brains intrinsic wiring to constantly uplevel and learn, we can create new positive patterns every moment. Our subconscious brain only hears what comes after the don't-want-statement. For example, "I don't want to eat that or I'll blow my diet," or "I don't want to be struggling financially all the time." Our brain hears the words eat or struggle. Using the Double-Positive Reprogramming Technique, you can reframe your statement, "I'm choosing to eat foods that help me maintain a healthy weight," or "I am choosing to find work I am passionate about and the money will come." Remember, it is the positive declarative energy of the thought of what we want (vs. don't want) that beacons the signal to our RAS to send out to the Universe what we want. To increase the effectiveness of this technique, wear a thick rubber band and as you say the double positive statement, snap the rubber band hard enough to create an ouch. This registers the pain into our subconscious which embeds a somatic marker, opening new neural pathways and embedding the new positive marker patterns to override the old negative ones.

Our conditioning is what creates patterns of negative thoughts and habitual negative interaction. These patterns can wreck havoc not only on our relationships, but on our overall health and feelings of well-being, which then cements these mindsets into fixed, finite and pervasive limiting mindsets. Locking yourself in a bubble may seem tempting at times when we have a friend or associate who espouses continued negative beliefs or statements. Avoiding any relationship does not allow you to become a pro-active contribution to a different way of interacting in all your relationships. You have the power to set the energetic tone of every relationship you engage in.

It takes courage to be different and challenge a mutant fear-based false system of limiting belief. You are not loving yourself or your relationships if you tune out to someone's negative comments and stories about life, but pretend to listen. The tools in the following chapter will provide you with powerful language tools that equip you to confront difficult relationships in life. When someone says something and that sticks you with an "ouch," somewhere in the statement, there's a lie. All lies carry a stick. All truths feel light, opening, uplifting and make you feel good.

Whether it is you or a friend speaking in negativity, you will know it is a lie because it will stick you with an ouch, a feeling of heaviness or "yuck!" It is important to play a pro-active role in first tuning into your awareness and honoring what you're feeling and then choosing self-love to guard your heart from any lie or negative limiting beliefs.

Positive or negative thoughts are contagious. Remember our mirror neurons. When I yawn, I trigger your mirror neurons and you yawn[9]. Or when someone is angry, stressed or grumpy, have you noticed that you find yourself feeling the same? Trust that when you find yourself feeling yucky, you must consciously tune into the power of your senses to shift your energy and not be drained by the actions of another.

If we all do not know what we do not know, how does our awareness expand? We learn by mirroring and modeling new behaviors. You are the only one that can be responsible for meeting your needs for well-being, safety, and protection from the negative energies coming from your world.

Your subconscious mind is constantly sending and receiving information. It does not know whether what you are experiencing is actually happening or not. It is the negative signals that are perpetuated in society coming from our media, through marketing, and through our conditioned patterns of relating, that perpetuate and attract more negativity and fear that the world is not a safe place. Through neuroscience we can now witness the endorphins released in our pleasure centers in our brains when we watch someone who appears happy when they take that pill, drive that car, or have that new whatever. These insidious, yet powerful forms of brainwashing define an external identity of what will make us happy, feel loved, feel satisfied, or define what success is and will never quench the thirst that comes from the well-of-being we discover when we journey within.

When you find incongruence in your heart, it's a lie. You also now know inquiry is key. Practice awareness in every facet of your choices and behaviors and watch how powerful you are to align

---

9 Robert Provine, "Contagious Yawning and Infant Imitation," *Bulletin of the Psychonomic Society* (1989), vol. 27, no. 2, pp. 125-126.

everything you need to consciously choose where you place your thoughts and energy.

YOUR JOURNEY IS UNIQUE

Your own personal world and external reality is shaped through your constant interaction with your environment. In turn, you are in perpetual communication with our Grand Unified Field, a Living Matrix. From the moment you take your first breath you are born with the power to commune with and take part in this field through the power of human emotion, literally rearranging the atoms in your body and your world. No longer are you the passive observer. You own the responsibility of being the co-creator and participatory agent of change, creating your experience of your life living reality supplied by an infinite Universe.

Science confirms that you are more likely to change your belief-system when presented with either a fact or by seeing a perceived miracle happen. This opens up our subconscious mind that keeps us locked into finite beliefs. By seeing something, or having facts presented, our learning by imitating expands the field of awareness to allow in a new possibility.

Remember the story in Chapter II, of Maynard Ferguson, the jazz player who was able to change the finite mass belief that a human could not achieve playing an octave higher? Because he simply didn't know that he was playing an octave higher an entire paradigm of belief was shattered allowing others to do the same. Throughout history, the impossible becomes possible because one man or woman thinks outside the limitation of belief. Once that possibility becomes realized, then the morphogenetic field of possibility can also be realized by mass consciousness.

Within every cell of you is the wisdom and answers to unlock every limiting belief and conditioning that is keeping you locked into self-defeating patterns of living. Now you have the facts that you are no longer a victim of a random and separate world, over which you have no control. You are a powerful co-creator. Your conscious choice to self-mirror new positive attitudes or beliefs allows you to reframe and overwrite the negative conditioned patterns of the limiting tribal beliefs and mindsets that have, to date, held you locked into a finite way of living.

It will be possible to co-create the experience of a shared experience of living the ultimate truth—as love—when we each contribute our full awareness to access living in our fully empowered truth. This is your individual journey that begins the moment you end the external world of judgment, comparison, or measuring yourself to any other living soul on the planet. To live as your greatness, your truth, and in your full potential of co-creative power, modeling to others through mirroring what living as a new possibility can look like, you contribute to a collective possibility of a new living reality. Your journey to expanding your awareness is spontaneous and ever-expanding, even from the moment before, when you choose to release what you think you know, to open up to the field of living life in the constant possibility of question. You alone possess everything you need to attract everything you need to thrive.

How does life get even better than this?!

We'd love to share with others what's changed in your life, to inspire others to see what is truly possible when we come together to co-create and live the new story of The Truth about us! Let us celebrate with you as your stories encourage others to live as the possibility of being an empowered co-creative, infinite source of nothing but pure potentiality.

Life can never be anything more or less, than what our minds perceive it to be.

Join or create your own support community to connect and share your journey to becoming more with others who have decided to go "all in" to become the new story about us. Visit us at: www.MyHeartConnects.com and www.OneTeamHumanity.com.

The following Intention and Belief Worksheet is a powerful tool to align you to your fastest route to co-creating your life living reality.

INTENTION & BELIEF WORKSHEET®

Go to a comfortable, peaceful, and uncluttered area within your home that you can use as your intention and meditation space. Because all thoughts and emotions carry vibrational frequencies, the more you spend time in a particular place in your home the more your energies create a conditioned field of higher frequency and awareness. You will be able to relax with greater consistency and ease each time you enter into this divine field of pure conscious potential.

Begin by breathing deeply, slowing your mind and thoughts, to bring your awareness to the vision of your desire, aspiration, and intention. Find the feeling or memory which allows you to access the experience of feeling deep compassion and love. During your in-breath, as you begin breathing in, breathe in how it would be to experience your focused intention. During the out-breath, move that feeling and intention through your heart, pushing your feelings through your solar-plexus into the Universe. Experience the sense and feeling of gratitude, acknowledging that your intention is being called forth into your reality.

Continue holding your vision during your in-breath and out-breath, until you've activated all the emotions associated with your intention. Feeling more open, or lighter, or a sense of ease are all good indicators that you've opened the field of possibility. Pay attention now to the people, places, and circumstances that will enter your reality to watch your RAS align your life to your intended experience.

Declare with passion what your desire and intention is:

Now describe here how it looks, feels, smells, sounds, and tastes, as though you're an artist, painting or sculpting the reality of your life…..

Invoke all your senses, emotions and images to focus on your beliefs, passions, and intentions with specific clarity.

State the reasons and needs of your intention. Surrender it to your highest spiritual intelligence knowing your intention is organizing itself into physical reality. Ask intelligence to bring to the light any subconscious beliefs that may be limiting you in creating the reality you intend and then run the Clearing Questions and Statement provided in the Completing Your Past chapter.

Your intention is your Declaration to the Universe, so hold your conviction that you will not allow any belief, person, or circumstance to stand in the way of your intention.

Now surrender your intention completely, trusting that everything is working for your good. Your RAS and The Universe knows your deepest dreams, highest calling, and the fastest path to creating your reality.

Breathe-in the feeling of deep gratitude and love and what the feeling and experience means to you, accepting the wonder, peace, and mystery of just "being" in the spirit of love.

* To receive additional worksheets, go to: www.thetruthmovie.tv/intentionandbeliefworksheet)

VI

THE LANGUAGE OF COMPASSION

The highest form of human intelligence is the ability to observe without evaluating.
—J. KRISHNAMURTI

Have you ever tried to truly express a profound memory or experience and found a chasm between what you would like to impart and what you are actually able to convey? Often, our words do not adequately translate our intentions, deepest feelings, or experience. Do even your sincerest of attempts at expressing the nuances, intensity, and range of emotions alive within you feel nearly impossible to adequately express?

There are two main reasons for this.

The first is that we are locked into a prevailing conditioned "power-over" paradigm when it comes to verbal interchange. Because of our modeled conditioning, nearly all communication takes place within the context of a power-over exchange. Under these dynamics the concern is not communication or understanding per se, but rather, an exchange of who has the power, resulting in a push-pull struggle in an attempt to keep the advantage and be heard. Tragically, this subconsciously conditions you to instantly feel separate even when you are not knowingly in disagreement. Moreover, this mirroring of power-over communication has entrained you to not actively listen because we're busy, oftentimes, forming our own rebuttal in advance. Amplify this when you feel triggered, disconnected and unheard, and we needn't look very far outside our own world, to see the damage that this form of communication yields in maintaining goodwill, trust, authentic connection, and intimacy in our relationships.

Do you find that quite often you don't really feel heard or understood? How do you respond when you feel unheard, threatened, verbally attacked, or judged?

The second reason communication tends to fail us is because we haven't been trained to listen and speak from our own intrinsic wisdom and truth. We are not attuned to listening to what's really alive within us, creating even more of a feeling of separation within. All feelings of suffering, isolation and separation are created from losing our connection to the life, and Source, that lives within us. As you begin to align your heart with your needs, and learn to make clear requests, you find you are more likely to have your universal need to be heard and understood met, as well as share in our interdependent connection to meeting needs in a way that is authentic, fosters deeper intimacy and trust, and contributes to a way of life and being that makes life more wonderful.

The Language of Compassion (LOC) is the most powerful communication process I have experienced that allows you to establish a high level of connection, while maintaining your integrity, your autonomy and trust with others. When you connect with your needs, you can make clear requests which allow others to contribute to meeting your needs. When you free your relationships from judgment or implied demands, you open the flow of connection which allows your natural capacities to contribute to one another, to spontaneously flow. This is what makes relationships more authentic and wonderful for everyone.

What if at the heart of every war and feeling of separation you experience in life, whether between lovers, friends, or nations, you find that it is just the strategies you employ to meet your needs, not the needs themselves, that cause the war of separation between two hearts?

POWER-OVER VERSUS POWER-WITH?

At the basis of the power-over paradigm, is the false belief that we, as human beings, are separate. Conditioned since early childhood we competed for grades, approval, and even love and affection. We have learned to adopt strategies of blame, guilt, shame, lying (or in-authenticity), withdrawal, and even manipulation and control in order to have our needs met. Spend the day observing any typical family and you will see a highly sophisticated dynamic of power-over relations at play, as each member tries to get what they want or need. Such becomes the source of much grappling and self-limiting strategies and sabotaging behaviors which are at the basis of all feelings of division, rebellion and separation. Power-over communication is the root cause that negatively impacts all of your relationships: from the romantic, parent-child, friendships, or in the work-place.

Most have been raised being told what we should do, should say, should be, or not be. Stuck in these patterns of limiting relating, we have been conditioned since childhood to be on the receiving end of this perpetual power-over paradigm, in which power was exercised over us by the "big people." Totally dependent upon your caretakers for survival, you were forced to comply.

Did you learn to outwardly comply, but inwardly rebel against this form of relating? Have you ever met anyone, 2 years old or 100, who does not resent (and often act out either overtly or passively) when being coerced by power? Is it any wonder that by the time we reach adulthood we are more than accustomed to this underlying current of power-dynamics, finding ourselves also vying for control? Perhaps as bosses, we use our hierarchy to also exercise our power over. We come home from work and mirror the same power-over patterns of relating. Ever heard the age 'ole adage: "because I said so?" This mentality is wielded as power-over our children, who pass it on to theirs. Can you see how this relating permeates and shuts down our natural innate capacity and desire to stay connected and authentically desire to contribute to the needs of one another?

> *In the space of demand, healthy human beings will generally respond in a state of resistance. This is natural as it protects our deep needs for autonomy and freedom to choose to love.*

When we look at children, we can see their natural capacity and desire to contribute.

Choosing to stay connected to explore possibilities, as we truly listen to the differing needs and requests, allows win-win solutions to arise that were not available to us before when we stayed locked into these power-over cycles of relating. Choosing to stay connected to the flow of exchange to hear what feelings and needs are being expressed, opens up the space of possibility for co-creative, powerful and thriving relationships of choice.

Let's look at power-over versus power-with relating in action, noting the very different outcomes:

Power-Over Work Illustration

An overworked assistant, Michelle, is angry at her boss for making her work so many extra hours. When her boss Marcia asks her to do yet another task, Michelle seizes the opportunity to ask for more money as compensation for the extra hours she's been working. Marcia, her boss doesn't like being put on the spot this way. Because she really needs the work done, she reluctantly chooses to comply with her employee's request. Michelle feels powerful and victorious for awhile. But since she still feels exhausted and like she is missing the enjoyment of having personal time in her life, she grows increasingly morose. Whatever power she felt is lost now. She feels saddled to her job and to her need for the extra money. The boss grows to resent the employee, feeling she really can't trust her to see the big picture and have a sense of ownership in the company. She begins to see her as only looking out for her best interests. The boss decides that two can play at that game.

Same Work Illustration using Power-with

An overworked assistant, Michelle, is angry at her boss for making her work so many extra hours. When her boss, Marcia, asks her to do yet another task, Michelle completes the task but as she is doing it, she finds she is becoming even more angered. She takes a few breaths and when the boss seems to be between tasks, she asks, "Can we talk when you have a few minutes?" Marcia agrees. An hour later, Marcia walks up to the Michelle's desk and says: "You wanted to talk?" Because Michelle wants her boss to cue-in that this conversation is important, she stands up from her desk and takes a seat at the conference table across the hall. Marcia sees this and follows suit. Michelle smiles at her boss Marcia, looking at her with kindness.

Michelle begins saying, "Thanks. I know you're busy and we have a lot to get done." Marcia nods and takes a sip from her water bottle. Michelle knows her observation needs to be specific.

Michelle continues: "I now have a lot more e-mail, paperwork, and three times more legal-reading to do since we've acquired this new project. I have stayed late nearly every day for the past two weeks to simply stay afloat. Even with the extra hours it seems doubtful that I will be able to catch up and get my month-end reports to you on time (observation)."

Hearing this, Marcia feels defensive and answers, "I know. It's hard for both of us right now. I've been working a lot."

Michelle breathes in, she doesn't want to lose courage or momentum. She also knows her boss needs her compassion. She smiles and responds, "I know you have been working really, really hard. I see what you do and I'm honestly amazed!"

Hearing the enthusiasm in her employee's voice and knowing someone else sees what she is doing makes her feel good. She smiles.

Michelle continues, "With all the work, I feel a significant amount of stress and I've begun to realize I'm even more frustrated and drained when I can't do some of the things that help reenergize me (feeling)."

Hearing this, Marcia is stumped. She was thinking her employee Michelle was going to ask for more money but maybe it's time she wants.

She continues, "I was going to ask for more money but thinking about it, I realized that while more money is nice, that doesn't really speak to or meet my deeper needs for fun, restoration, and play. I need time and my own presence to appreciate the other aspects of my life that I value. I was wondering how that sounds to you (request)?"

Marcia hears this. She's reminded of something she's long since forgotten. She used to be better at balancing her work and her other interests. In a flash, she sees that trail she used to hike every morning before work. She's going to get back to hiking. She always feels great when she hikes. Realizing she's drifted off, she looks at Michelle.

Michelle smiles.

"So what is it you want? More time?" Marcia asks.

"Exactly. I would like to leave here on time at least 2 or 3 times a week if at all possible (request)."

"Tell you what, make a list today of all the more mundane tasks you have to handle and we'll see what we can outsource and what can wait. As for the month-end reports, let's sit down together and get those done first thing tomorrow morning. That way, we won't be stressed about them anymore. Now I think it's time for you to go on and get outta here," Marcia says with a smile. She's astonished at just how astute Michelle is.

Power-over Relationship Illustration:
A married couple, Don and Amanda, are in a dispute over an on-going parenting struggle. Amanda asked Don to not let their 4-year-old, Megan, watch a certain TV show. When she returns home, she finds their daughter, Megan, watching the show. Seeing this, Amanda's face becomes flushed with anger. She sets her dry cleaning down on the living room carpet, walks over to the TV, says something consoling to Megan and changes the

channel to another show. What follows is Amanda calling Don to the mat for failing to comply with her request. Don responds by undercutting Amanda, telling her she has no faith in him as a parent. Amanda feels hurt by this. She tries to reassure him and tells him she does believe he's a good father. Don responds with numerous examples when she has either told him, or implied, that he was somehow lacking as a father. Don ends his tirade saying, "I just can't do anything right for you!" Amanda feels drained and stumped by his accusations, she sulks and remains quiet. Don walks out of the room feeling like he's just won. He's drained thinking, "so much for date night."

Same Relationship Illustration Applying Power-with Relating:

A married couple, Don and Amanda, are in a dispute over an on-going parenting issue. Amanda has asked Don to not let their 4-year-old Megan watch a certain television show she feels is violent. When she returns home, she finds Megan watching the show. Seeing this, Amanda's face becomes flushed with anger. She sets her dry cleaning down on the living room carpet, walks over to the television and says something consoling to Megan before changing the channel to another show.

She feels her anger. She takes a moment to breathe, creating a gap. She takes a moment to center into her heart to see what she really needs so she can make a clear request. Then, Amanda walks into the kitchen where Don is sitting at the table reading the paper.

"I'd really like to talk to you, is this a good time?" Amanda asks.

"Sure," Don responds, haphazardly moving his attention from his paper.

Amanda chooses to not take his split attention personally. Amanda shares her observation.

"I noticed Megan watching the show I asked you not to let her watch anymore (observation)."

Hearing this, Don becomes defensive, slamming the paper down. Seeing this, Amanda chooses to not react. She senses his need to be acknowledged that he is a good father. As she chooses to relax to listen to what need his actions may be masking, she sees his face relax and his expression becomes neutral. She continues.

"When I see Megan watching that show filled with violence, it makes me worry for her well-being. I also feel like you don't trust or value my need to protect our daughter from this kind of conditioning. I want her to feel safe and trusting as she learns to interact in our world. I'd really like to have your support, respect, and some reassurance from you to know that my needs matter to you (feelings and need)."

Breathing again, Amanda made sure to state her request as a question, with the tone in her voice rising at the end.

"I'm wondering if you'd consider my request next time and not allow her to watch that show (request)?"

Don was expecting they were going to have another one of their fights. He's surprised at his wife's succinct manner of getting to the point. He pauses. He's can't believe that his wife, the quintessential "perfect mother," actually needs his support in parenting their daughter. Until now, he had assumed it was all effortless for her. Seeing this, he grows a newfound respect for the importance she places in actively protecting their daughter's well-being every single day.

"I hear you. Honey, I'm sorry. I heard you before, but I guess I never realized how important this was to you. It won't happen again."

Amanda walks over and kisses him with gratitude, "I'm going to freshen up for our date night." Don feels proud of himself for handling the situation with a cool head. He's happy an argument was avoided, feeling himself more like a partner and source of support for his wife, he's looking forward to a pleasant evening with his Bride.

When we hold the priority of maintaining connection first to seek win-win outcomes, we rebuild the trust that had formerly been eroded by relating in a power-over paradigm. Being authentic to your feelings and needs, and learning how to make observations free from the undercurrent of judgment, or criticism, co-creates a profound quality of connection that uplevels all of your relationships. Rather than both parties having to occupy positions of right/wrong, good/bad, what you or someone else "should" or "shouldn't" do or be, as well as not get stuck in dead-end unhealthy patterns of withdrawal, blame, shame or guilt, this power-with model has both people on the same side of opposing needs. This enables the flow of communication to remain open, expressing observations, feelings, needs, and requests, in a dialogue of energy exchange that is focused on everyone's needs being heard, while exploring win-win possibilities so that everyone's needs can matter and be heard.

This communication process is more than a new language application. Relating through this power-with relationship model creates an internal paradigm shift. Learning any new language or skill takes some time to learn and master.

However, once experiencing your relationships in this way, you'll open up a whole new realm of possibilities in creating powerfully authentic and connected relationships.

Whether your relationships are of a personal, business, or even global nature, this choice to see needs as our common universal connection that unites us, creates an internal paradigm shift of understanding and compassion within us. It is not the needs, but the strategies we employ that create feelings of mistrust and disconnection. Even in the face of disagreement, anger, or even rage, even in the most trying of confrontations, even when our diverging beliefs or needs seem so opposing, and may have been ignored for years or decades, staying connected to one another to listen for the unmet needs attempting to be heard and met, can restore the trust that has been eroded in your relationships. The results are truly game-changing. The experience of this quality of connection to life is so worth the effort. The only war between lovers, friends, and nations, is our judgments and the opposing strategies we choose to meet our needs that block the flow of our connections. Our natural desire is to contribute to life being more wonderful for one another. This happens when we listen to, and honor, our interdependent connection to our common needs.

OUR CONNECTION TO NEEDS

We are all connected. Yet, at times, you may still think, act, and communicate in ways that belie this reality. Because you have been conditioned to believe that having needs, and expressing your deepest longings and desires to have them satisfied might make you feel or seem selfish, needy, or lacking; most of us have also been conditioned to develop and use strategies to meet those needs by operating indirectly, in-authentically, or outside of integrity when it comes to having our needs met. What this does is cast the whole subject of "needs" in an unnecessary dark light.

As humans, what we share is our interdependent connection to our common needs, and the desire to live as the fullest expression of what would make life more wonderful and abundant. As powerful co-creators of your personal and universal experience, how you find ways to meet our irreducible needs to one another, you discover what makes this experience called life feel alive, thriving, yummy, and abundant; or constricted, limiting and separated. Survival is dependent upon our needs for adequate food, water, shelter, and rest. As infants, we needed all of these to develop and grow. Our needs for love, touch, safety, companionship, and community are just a few of the fundamentals that only other humans can provide, essential to building a strong sense of well-being that helps foster a balanced sense of autonomy and freedom. Then we have other fundamental needs, also paramount to our well-being including, but not limited to, connection, play, peace, companionship, support, physical well-being, sexual expression, meaning, creativity, contribution, self-acceptance, communion, and to be known and understood. There are many more needs that weave our inter-connected experience that makes life more wonderful for one another. A full list of our Universal Common Needs can be found on page 221.

Using the Language of Compassion, a power-with model of communication, you gain greater understanding of your own needs while growing your understanding and compassion for the needs of others. For it is not the needs themselves that are the cause of problems and disconnection in your relationships, but rather the misguided strategies you employ that become the source of so much commotion, disconnection, dissatisfaction, unease, mistrust, and war. Separation occurs only because of the strategies we employ, whether in our family systems or between nations. At the core of what unites us is our universal connection and shared needs.

Developed by Dr. Marshall Rosenberg, leader and visionary for world peace and President of the CNVC (Centers for Non-Violent Communication, www.cnvc.org), the Language of Compassion is based upon his belief that "Violence in any form is a tragic expression of our unmet needs." Included in such "violence" are certain patterns of speech. These include labeling the behavior of others as right/wrong, good/bad, or manipulating or encouraging others to do what we want them to do through the use of shame, blame, guilt, judgment, or statements that one "has to" or "should."

Also known as Nonviolent Communication or NVC, The Language of Compassion teaches people a language of honesty, connection, and empathy which increases goodwill, builds trust, and deepens our intimacy and connections. This process also shows us how to avoid language that creates resentment or rebellion, lowering self-esteem and eroding trust. Speaking the Language of Compassion, you emphasize personal responsibility for your choices by having your words motivated by compassion and a true desire to connect and contribute to another rather than to compete. These tools are readily applicable whether you use them to address matters of the heart, home or Matters of State.

Language of Compassion application strengthens your ability to:
1. Build relationships based on compassion and true understanding.

2. Accurately hear what other people feel and need, even when they express themselves in a hostile manner.

3. Make assertive requests that increase the likelihood of getting what we really want.

4. Prevent and resolve conflicts in ways that work for everyone.

5. Break patterns of judgmental thinking that leads to anger, resentment, and depression.

THE PROCESS AND PRACTICES

Learning this language awareness process is just like learning any other new language. It can feel awkward and frustrating but also very rewarding when we see the results of connection maintained and deeper intimacy and love created. It requires discipline and more moments of pause and reflection than we are customarily used to as we communicate back and forth. Creating a gap between your stimulus and response during this process helps to reframe your internal connection in a sincere attempt to listen to what's alive within yourself, while also staying connected to the needs that are trying to communicate themselves behind who is speaking to you. In time, your new language will become a part of you, like second-nature. Every relationship exchange offers you the opportunity to become agile and confident at using this very powerful and life-changing relationship practice to empower and uplevel every facet of your life.

When communicating using the NVC/Language of Compassion model you are operating within one of two modes. Either you are "empathically receiving" the **O**bservations, **F**eelings, **N**eeds, and **R**equests of another or you are "honestly expressing" the **O**bservations, **F**eelings, **N**eeds, and **R**equests that you have to share. The acronym OFNR (pronounced off-ner) is an easy way to remember the internal framing steps to model this new language skill-set.

Here's an illustration of OFNR in practice:

Scenario:

You have a friend who, despite their otherwise caring and compassionate nature, has a tendency to cut people off mid-sentence. You are going to a conference and have just discovered your friend is going too and would like to pal-around while you're there. Feeling your friend's behavior might impede your efforts at meeting other professionals and like-minded people, you decide to address the issue using the Language of Compassion. When he calls, you tell him:

Dialogue:
"Joe, when we have been in social environments in the past, I have seen you cut people off when they're talking (**o**bservation). This makes me feel uncomfortable around the person we've just met (**f**eeling). As you know, I need to meet and build mutually respectful connections to expand my professional and personal contacts (**n**eed). Would you be willing to consider changing this behavior (**r**equest)? I'm guessing you get excited and want to share as well and that you may not even be aware of this action, would you mind if I bring it to your attention when it happens? I really do value our friendship and all the fun we have together and would love to continue having a great friendship. How does that feel for you?"

Addressing issues in such a head-on way may feel awkward and difficult, especially at first. But consider the alternative of not speaking to what is alive in you, what truthfully happens is you cut off the flow of connection in your relationships? Over time, the cycles at play in power-over relating becomes painful and we lose the desire to connect, and soon we find that resentment and separation builds. You may find yourself resisting the other's company, withdrawing, or no longer connected enough to be excited about maintaining the relationship. When you deny your own needs to authentically be known and express what's alive in your heart, you negate the opportunity to speak your truth so that your needs can be celebrated, valued and met. Can you see that it is first your own disconnection to your needs being expressed that blocks the connection, trust, intimacy and authenticity, which compromises and contaminates the relationship? This kind of relating not only takes courage, but also perseverance on your part. This is the missing link essential to co-creating relationships that are authentic, alive, and thriving. Any less-direct option and strategy is only a temporary band-aid solution that masks the underlying problem—your unmet needs—until you try another approach under a slightly different guise. How's that working for you?

Life becomes connected when you stay true to what's alive in you, while making clear requests that exhibit the energy of invitation which opens the possibility in all your relationships to hear a "yes," without the underlying currency of shame, blame, demand, guilt or "have to" or "should" motivating false compliance. You are much more likely to empower another to meet your needs when you make a clear heart connection to express what need they are meeting and how it contributes to you.

As you learn to trust your true nature, natural capacity, and motivation to contribute to one another, suddenly you see how powerful you are in co-creating authentic and exciting relationships.

The objective is to make a connection to your feelings and needs, make clear requests, while maintaining a free exchange and connection, which allows spontaneous possibilities to occur. This contributes to the result of staying connected to one another, while finding win-win solutions.

If you stay fixed on only what it will take to meet your need, you not only lose connection to the other person and the world of their needs, but you cement yourself into a finite box of scarcity, belief and expectation, that kills the mutual co-creative energy available in your relationships. Life is meant to be lived in the constant exchange of energy in (e)motion. Feelings of scarcity and lack occur only when we are attached to the belief that only one person, or one thing, is what's missing or responsible for meeting our needs for our internal fulfillment.

Observations:
When you are formulating the observation you will be communicating, it is important that it be free from any opinion, criticism, or judgment. A good way to check that what you are saying is a judgment-free observation, ask yourself: "Is it something a video camera or tape recorder could record?" If not, it likely includes an evaluation. When we mix the two, others are likely to hear criticism. So, for example, we would not say: "When you spoke disrespectfully to me..." Instead, we would just quote the words the person said, "When you said '...'" or "When you said '....' in that tone of voice..."

Be cautious about the use of the word "too" as in:

"too much" (e.g. "That's too much salt")

"too little"

"too loud" (e.g. "You're playing the music too loud")

"too soft"

"too fast" (e.g. "You're driving too fast")

"too slowly"

With The Language of Compassion we might express the above by saying:

"That's more salt than I would like."

"The music is louder than I enjoy."

"You're driving faster than I like to be going when it's raining."

Also be aware that words like "enough," "always," and "never" impede connection and are divisive and likely to provide an argument.

Enough implies a criticism or judgment. Whereas, something like: "I'm uncomfortable with you having more cake because you asked me to be your accountability partner in losing 10 pounds." If you were communicating with a child, "I'm uncomfortable with you having more cake because I have a need to make sure (protect) you eat healthy so you don't get sick," expresses the need which helps to maintain connection.

When we choose words like enough, always, and never that, by nature, cut off the flow of connection, we are likely to provoke a defensive response or argument. Using "always" and "never," as in "You always come late," and "You never listen to me," unless there are clearly no exceptions, are also word choices which are likely to provoke a disconnection of hearts. Using such finite words leaves little room for our hearts to focus on open connection to allow for possibilities to be explored that make it possible to get everyone's needs met.

Using the model below, it is important to maintain emphasis on "How are you?" rather than "What are you?" Sticking to the "how" guides the conversation toward a constructive resolution, whereas statements saying "what" someone is leads to evaluation of some sort and steers us off course.

LANGUAGE OF COMPASSION COMMUNICATION MODEL
It helps us to keep our attention on four questions:

How am I? (Rather than What am I?)

How are you? (Rather than What are you?)

What would make life more wonderful for me?

What would make life more wonderful for you?

COMPASSIONATE CONFRONTATIONS

Understanding that you may be the stimulus, but not the cause, of another's reaction can help you to activate your capacity to be more compassionate. When you can see someone's reaction as an expression of an unmet need, even in the face of rage, anger or disagreement, you can remain open to be proactive in shifting the negative spiral that occurs when you also become defensive. Remember, defense is the first act of war. It is helpful to maintain a healthy distance to not get sucked into the draining energy vortex of another's anger, so you can remain in your heart to listen to what is being said behind the fear-based reaction of anger. Maintaining presence allows you to offer empathy by listening, even guessing for the unmet need that might be crying out, so you can respond with love. Stay connected to hear what's alive within them which needs your heart of compassion. Attentively listening to yourself, and others, keeps you connected to an open flow of connection between your hearts, so possibilities can arise that contribute to meeting one another's sometimes opposing needs.

An unmet need is always at the basis of a highly triggered reaction. Behind that reaction, flows a river of deep heart feelings and emotions that rise up in us as needs that are trying to speak, be heard, and trust that they matter.

Choosing love to respond with empathy stops the mirrored reaction of defensiveness. When you don't take on their emotions personally, you can open up your heart compassionately to hear what need(s) are at the bottom of their volatile reactions, by guessing what need is not being met. You'll be surprised how intuitive you are and that you'll come close to what need is there at the root of the reaction. Your sincere attempt allows their hearts to soften, opening up a possibility. They'll likely respond by sharing what needs are at the bottom of their reaction, opening up a genuine ground for fostering authentic connections, that create deeper feelings of intimacy.

This one tool alone has the power to stop the cycles of relating that create feelings of hopelessness, resentment and separation.

There are many other tools at your disposal throughout this book. Use the FreezeFrame™ Technique you learned in Chapter III to create a gap and then act in love rather than react in fear. Remember, the only freedom you will ever have is not being controlled by the rollercoaster of emotions that is your own internal response to another's experience and reactions to life. Exploring the full range of your experience to your feelings and needs, while maintaining conscious connection of guessing what may be alive in another person, allows you to take ownership and responsibility as powerful co-creators of that relationship. Nothing neutralizes the situation of anger, or other volatile emotions, more than really listening and empathetically "feeling with" the person that is experiencing the pain of an unmet need. Marshall Rosenberg says: "We don't have to guess right, just human." Be present and be genuine. The point is to show your desire to connect to their heart need to be heard and know they matter. The worksheet Expressing Empathy at the close of the chapter has more on this.

CELEBRATING HEARING A "NO"
Let your "yes," be yes, and your "no," be no. The Language of Compassion empowers you to come to a "yes" only when your truth and inner-aligned integrity can allow for a real, pure and resolute "yes." When you say "yes" you do so knowing you are contributing to the enrichment of another person's life, without conditions. When you say "no" in a way that still maintains the flow of connection you actually foster, build trust, and set parameters for a whole new way of authentically connecting within your relationships. This frees up any conditioned patterns of relating based on beliefs of "have to" or "should." Doing this implicitly demonstrates what you have with the other person is not contingent upon having to agree or having to be something or do something, opening up new possibilities that build trust. Maintaining your connection, independent of the finite constrictions of conditions, fosters a co-creative energy in which you both can interdependently seek possibilities to meet your needs within your relationship.

If you've lived with a history of punishment, withdrawal of love, or control in a relationship, or if you have grown up in a subconscious core fear belief that saying "no" is "selfish," or isn't safe, saying no can feel impossible because of the fear that by saying no, we cut off the flow of connection between us and the other person. It is because of this past conditioning of relating, that using the word "no" blocks the flow of connection and can act as a powerful trigger, introducing a whole host of subconscious obstacles that block meaningful communication and connection. Offering your "no," clearly stating what needs you have that prevent you from saying "yes" at that time, is a powerful way to maintain connection while still honoring your needs.

Also realize, whatever no-request you state, this may prompt a twinge of pain in the other person, especially the first time they experience this with you. Their pain is a rejection fear-based response that may also trigger all the other associations that "no" brings up in their mind and heart. Stay connected and committed to your truth. Give them time to process your response and then tell them you are committed to seeing that all needs get met. Give every indication of confidence by your demeanor and behavior that you believe this is possible.

So what do you do when you really want something from someone and they tell you "no?" Answer: receive their "no" as a gift.

Learning to say no with compassion allows you to learn to receive the other's "no" as a "yes" to their own needs to stay connected and in alignment with their truth. You empower your relationships when the free flow of "no" and "yes" can be shared together, without manipulation, withdrawal, or judgment. If their "no" triggers you, whether by content or the manner in which it was said, you have probably located some stored trauma or limiting belief. Work through what their "no" brings up for you by using the clearing statements and meditation. Do you see only one person as the source of your "yes" or "no" to feel happy and have your need met? Check in with yourself that when you "offer" your no, that it is free from control by withdrawing, which is always divisive (an act of passive violence), and erodes the need for safety and trust in a relationship.

Often times, when we first begin the healing work of introspection to look at our unhealthy and sabotaging relating patterns, we might stand behind the catch-all psychological phrase of "boundaries," and "use" our no with someone as a wall, perhaps even subconsciously, which is a passive-agressive form of power-over control, and detrimental to building any healthy relational connection. Learning to offer your no, without cutting off the flow of possibility is what builds powerful, co-creative feelings of intimacy and of being deeply connected to the enrichment that relationships can bring to this journey called life.

The most change in your relationships will come when you allow your relationships to trust that you only want their "yes" when they can truly offer it from their heart. Be prepared to be on the giving and receiving gift of hearing "no" more often as your relationships are released from the fear of conditions. Giving someone permission to say no will lead you to a profound new dynamic of trust and freedom. "No" really is a gift!

A SOUNDING TO SELF

So how is it exactly that the Language of Compassion enables you to really come to know yourself? In one word: echolocation. This inborn technology found in whales, dolphins, and bats allow them to chart their course with pin-point accuracy. They transmit a signal that moves out into the area they are searching. The signal goes out and echoes back their surroundings as feedback which enables them to navigate their course. It is much the same way for us. When you engage in your sounding-out via real, authentic communication within the mirrors that relationships offer your life, your own course and needs location becomes clearer to you. Through the reciprocal process of engaging with others and locating your observations, feeling, needs, and requests, you discover what will make life more wonderful for you and for others. Authentically sharing in this very present moment of where you are, sounding-out what is alive in you, dispels the fog of unspoken needs and requests and pin-points with GPS-like accuracy your connection to the needs within yourself and within others. You now become more fully capable of partaking in the co-creative reality of the present relationship, taking part in an economy of interchange, inter-exchange, and inter-relatedness that makes your experience to life respond by expanding your awareness into a 4D reality of emotive experience that makes you a powerful co-creator within every relationship to experience deep love and intimacy.

Through the LOC process of interacting with others, you begin to have a much deeper understanding of who you are. This process collapses the rigid life-negating process where most of us defined our identity during adolescence by trying to deduce, through comparison of "what I am" and "what I am not." This connection process takes you from the finite beliefs of limitation in your mind, and moves you into living from the truth and possibility that is alive within your heart.

Commun(e)ication is to be present to commune with one another. Trusting how intrinsic to our nature the Language of Compassion is you can be empowered to know you can co-create, in every moment, a new possibility of relationship. Sharing your observations, your feelings, your needs, and making clear requests, adds this super-boost, game-changing ability to not get locked into the very same cycles that had, in the past, caused so much pain, feelings of separation and suffering. Using this language process is the most powerful communication tool and life skill that will shape-shift your internal experience and the living reality of experiencing deeply connected and authentic relationships. For me, this form of relating was the missing link in 25 years of searching for a way to express the river of life that lives within us to feel the power of two hearts connecting, making life more meaningful and wonderful!

The mechanics to learn the LOC is very cut and dry. You will discover that as you apply these powerful communication tools in your relationships, all your feelings of confusion, misunderstanding, and feelings of separation that lie at the bottom of your unspoken needs and requests, will allow an opening within yourself. It is your sole responsibility of having your needs met. When you expand your connection and awareness of truth to see that we share a common interdependent connection to one another, through our needs, we become free to celebrate this essential part of our connected humanness.

Magically, often times, just by uncovering your unmet needs and giving voice to them (either privately or within your relationships), you will often find that is enough to quell whatever pain or discomfort you are feeling because of your belief and societal conditioning that every need we have has to be met to feel happy. Coming to know yourself by speaking candidly and expressing how important a need is to you, while also knowing no one relationship could ever meet all the needs you have, vastly enriches your relationships. You will see that like feelings, needs are also fickle and transient. As you go deeper to unpeel your perceived needs, you will arrive at understanding what fundamental need is really yearning to be heard within you. A genuine openness releases you from any rigid, fixed, and finite beliefs of what someone should or shouldn't do or should or shouldn't be to allow a fluidity to create more ease and trust. By making requests of someone to meet your needs, not because they have to, but because in doing so they are contributing to enriching your life, you empower yourself to create the possibility of communing in our interdependent world of relate-tion-ship in an authentic state of being that makes life more wonderful.

The more you trust in the experience of expressing and owning your inner needs, the more you will come to respect and appreciate the various needs of others. Empowering others to honor their needs yields thriving relationships that are energetically authentic (truthful) which vibrate at the highest potency, which creates treasured moments of deep connection. Even with people you may have previously had difficulty connecting with, an honest attempt to hear their anger or unmet needs, by "empathically receiving," their needs without judgment, most oftentimes shifts the vibration between you. You will actually *feel* their internal emotion-transfer before another word is said. Feelings of animosity, grudges, and pain between you will ease into a more accessible trust because you will know that you can always return to this heart connection to seek ways to diffuse opposing needs that create feelings of separation.

The Language of Compassion can heal the damage and deeply rooted mistrust that has been created by living in such power-over paradigms. A single moment of heart connection to our common needs possesses the power to melt away years, decades, and even millenniums of division. Un-forgiveness, pain, suffering, hatred, judgments, withdrawal and false beliefs have blinded us to the truth of who we are. While our needs for autonomy, freedom, and our intrinsic need to learn, create, and express is what makes you uniquely you. Your connection to our universal common needs to live in peace, choice, mutual respect to know that all needs matter, builds the safety and trust necessary to bridge and weave the threads of diversity together so we can all experience life in a way that makes it more wonderful. When you seek what unites you, rather than stay locked into patterns of relating that divides you, your connection to the living energy that comprises your relationships, your families, and even our nations will never be the same.

THE CHOICE FOR CHANGE

The choice to transform the power-over ways in which we have all been conditioned to interact within all relationships takes considerable commitment. You are not just learning a new language skill you are shifting your inner experience to reality. Embracing The Language of Compassion let's go of the negative conditioned habits of speech and the perceptions that leads to the judgment, dividing beliefs and life-alienating strategies we use to meet our needs that are at the root origin of all disconnection and pain. There is a moment of experience when you will *know* that you have passed through and touched a knowing of relating that is not governed by law, should or have to, or constrained by limitations of our subconscious or intellectual mind.

In that moment, you know that we are irreducibly interconnected, and suddenly everything becomes clearer. Then, moment-by-moment, experience-to-experience, as you exercise your freedom to stay connected to chose your responses of love, you create the gaps that contribute to what we all want in life: to experience the essence of harmony, and love, within everything.

Each of us learn differently, but expect about a year of consistent LOC dialoguing effort to experience the internal natural reconnection back to responding with love rather than life running you by reacting to the triggers of life. During this time, you will be unlearning your conditioned tendencies of reaction, judgment, withdrawal, and other life-alienating patterns of relating when you or someone else is triggered. It is your close relationships that provide your best classroom of learning. This is where you have become the most entrenched in these power-over cycles of relating.

It always helps to let the people in your life know you are committed to experiencing your relationships in a more authentic and connected way and to request that they provide you with the grace of their patience. As you stay committed to speaking the truth of what's alive in you, give them permission and instruction so that they can do the same. Be patient with yourself and others. Use the tools. Be compassionate.

As you sincerely attempt to connect to the language of needs, your sincere desire will bridge hearts and ease the discomfort. Becoming fluent in the Language of Compassion, you can be the change you want to experience in life. Making the choice to live in compassion will open you up to authentically engaging with others to feel the fullness and appreciation that abounds in you as you give and receive. This deeply interconnected way of commun(e)icating is the gift of a lifetime. Through the mirror of your relationships you discover the truth of who you are. By remaining connected to your truth as you meet others in the exchange of seeing theirs, you enter the reality of authentic exchange to discover what unites you. To become truly alive with a flow of life that contributes toward making life all the more wonderful for everyone involved.

The following worksheets and models are founded by Dr. Marshall B. Rosenberg of The Center for Nonviolent Communication (www.cnvc.org), a global organization dedicated to the sharing of nonviolent communication, whose mission is to empower people to peacefully and effectively resolve conflicts in personal, organizational, and political settings.

TWO PARTS AND FOUR COMPONENTS OF
THE LANGUAGE OF COMPASSION MODEL

	Honestly Expressing	**Empathically Receiving**	
How are you?	**O**BSERVATIONS **F**EELINGS **N**EEDS **R**EQUESTS	**O**BSERVATIONS **F**EELINGS **N**EEDS **R**EQUESTS	How am I?
What would make life more wonderful for me?			What would make life more wonderful for you?

COMMON FORMS OF LIFE-ALIENATING COMMUNICATION (BLOCKS TO COMPASSIONATE CONNECTION)

※ Applying labels, moralistic judgments, interpretations, diagnoses of people or situations

※ Language denying individual choice and responsibility

※ Demands

※ Language that implies someone deserves to be punished (or rewarded)

I have just **three things** *to teach:*
Simplicity, Patience, Compassion.
These three are your greatest treasures.
Simple in actions and in thoughts,
You return to the source of being,
Patient with both friends and enemies,
You accord with the way things are.
Compassionate toward yourself,
You reconcile all beings in the world.

—LAO-TZU

The following Expressing Empathy Worksheet will help you begin to understand the internal reframing necessary that helps you maintain connection as you empathetically connect to how someone else is feeling and what they might need that is triggering their reaction. This is a powerful tool to not only help them identify their feelings and needs, but also bridges the disconnect that happens in relationships when we have opposing needs. Through identifying the core feelings and needs we are more likely to co-create solutions that will contribute to making life more wonderful for one another.

EXPRESSING EMPATHY WORKSHEET®

EXERCISE 1

1. Imagine a conversation that created a disconnection. Using the four components and LOC model of OFNR: Observations, Feelings, Needs, and Requests, imagine the responses from that person when it became difficult for you to feel loving and connected to them.

2. Write below what that person said in response to what you said:

3. Now receive the person empathically by connecting to what you believe is creating the feeling(s) and need(s) behind the person's words and actions. Express your empathy by saying back to the person:

Are you feeling...?

Because you are needing...?

EXERCISE 2

Now practice expressing empathy towards someone that makes the following statements. Use the format, "Are you feeling _____, because you are needing _____?"

1. The people I cook for are really picky.

2. What makes you think you can walk around the halls without a pass?

3. The superintendent is a racist.

4. I feel so ugly.

5. Be quiet!

6. I can't stand the way my daughter argues with me.

7. The cardiologist acts as if he's the only one who understands the complexity of this diagnosis.

8. They're not going to give us a raise just because we're nice to them!

For additional copies of this worksheet, go to www.THETRUTHMOVIE.tv/empathyworksheet

NONVIOLENT COMMUNICATION

SUMMARY OF BASIC CONCEPTS

COMPASSIONATE CONNECTED COMMUNICATION	LIFE-ALIENATING COMMUNICATION
Power WITH others	Power OVER others
Win/win (I/Thou)	Win/lose or lose/lose (You or I)
Process language	Static language
Focus on HOW people are, i.e. how they are feeling and what they are needing	Focus on WHAT people are: labels, diagnoses, interpretations
Value judgments	Moralistic judgments
Requests	Demands
Purpose: to create & maintain a certain quality of connection necessary to enable everyone to get their needs met	Purpose: to get what we want, regardless of long term costs of relationship
Inspires compassionate response	Tends to produce aggressive or indifferent response
Force used only to protect life	Force used punitively
Acceptance of choice and responsibility for one's actions & feelings, viewed as originating with one's met or unmet needs	Denial of choice and responsibility for one's feelings, viewed as originating with actions of others or situations outside of oneself
No blame of self or others	Blame of self and/or others
Motivation based on seeing how one's actions contribute to life, meeting the needs of self & others (intrinsic motivation)	Motivation based on guilt, shame, fear of punishment, hope for reward (extrinsic motivation)
Interdependence AND Autonomy	Dependence/Independence

The following Feelings Inventories List is an effective tool in helping you bridge "the gap" that can happen when we are trying to express the river of emotion that is alive within us. By improving your ability to connect within, to what's alive, to express your feelings and needs, the more likely you will be able to identify and make clear requests, so that life can become more wonderful for you. As humans, our need to contribute to one another becomes joyful and free flowing when we remove the underlying conditions of implied demands.

FEELINGS INVENTORY
How we are likely to feel when our needs are being met

absorbed	contented	exuberant	interested	rapturous
adventurous	cool	fascinated	intrigued	refreshed
affection	curious	free	invigorated	relief/ved
alert	dazzled	friendly	involved	satisfied/faction
alive	delighted	fulfilled	joy/ful/ous	secure
amazed	eager	gay	jubilant	sensitive
appreciation	ecstatic	glad	kindred	spellbound
aroused	effervescent	gleeful	love/ing/ly	splendid
astonished	elated	glorious	mellow	stimulated
blissful	electrified	glowing	merry	surprised
breathless	encouraged	good-humored	mirthful	tender/ness
buoyant	energetic	grateful	moved	thankful
calm	engrossed	gratification	optimistic	thrilled
carefree	enjoyment	groovy	overwhelmed	touched
cheerful	enlivened	happy	overjoyed	tranquil
comfortable	enthusiastic	helpful	peaceful	trust/ing/ful
complacent	exalted	hopeful	pleasant/ure	warm
composed	exhilarated	inquisitive	proud	wide-awake
concerned	expansive	inspired	quiet	wonderful
confident	expectant	intense	radiant	zest/ful

How we are likely to feel when our needs are not being met

afraid	despair	frightened	jittery	skeptical
aggravated	despondent	frustrated	keyed-up	sleepy
agitation	detached	furious	lassitude	sorrowful
alarm	disappointed	gloomy	lazy	sorry
aloof	discouraged	grief	lethargy	spiritless
angry	disgruntled	guilty	listless	startled
anguished	disgusted	hate	lonely	surprised
animosity	disheartened	heavy	mad	terrified
annoyance	disinterested	helpless	mean	tired
anxious	dislike	hesitant	melancholy	troubled
apathetic	dismayed	hopeless	miserable	uncomfortable
apprehensive	displeased	horrified	mopey	unconcerned
ashamed	disquieted	horrible	nervous	uneasy
aversion	distressed	hostile	nettled	unglued
bad	disturbed	hot	overwhelmed	unhappy
bitter	downcast	hurt	passive	unnerved

blah	downhearted	impatient	perplexed	unsteady
bored	dread	indifferent	pessimism/tic	upset
breathless	dull	inert	puzzled	uptight
brokenhearted	edgy	infuriated	rancorous	vexed/ation
chagrined	embarrassed	inquisitive	reluctant/ance	weary
cold	embittered	insecure	resentful	withdrawn
concerned	exasperated	insensitive	restless	woeful
confused	exhausted	intense	sad	worried
cool	fatigued	irate	scared	
cross	fear/ful	irked	sensitive	
credulous	fidgety	irritated	shaky	
depressed	forlorn	jealous	shocked	

Adapted from *A Model for Nonviolent Communication*, Second Edition Revised, Marshall B. Rosenberg, Center for Nonviolent Communication, 1983, 1999.

NON-FEELINGS OR PSEUDO FEELINGS

The following words often follow the phrase "I FEEL" but are neither emotions nor sensations, but are judgments about what others are doing or have done to us:

abandoned	manipulated
abused	misunderstood
accepted	neglected
attacked	patronized
betrayed	put down
caged	rejected
cheated	ripped off
criticized	threatened
distrusted	tricked
dumped on	unheard
ignored	unseen
insulted	unwanted
invalidated	used
left out	violated

(There are many more words of this sort, often ending in –ed)

HIDDEN JUDGMENT WORDS

The following examples follow the words "I FEEL" but are images or judgments we have about ourselves:

> inadequate
> stupid
> unimportant
> unworthy
> worthless

When the phrase "I feel" is followed by the word "that" or by proper names like Mahatma Gandhi, nouns like, my brother, or pronouns like, I, you, he, she, it, we, or they, no authentic personal feelings are likely to follow. Instead, what tends to follow are thoughts, judgments, evaluations, opinions, or criticism. For example: I feel that capital punishment is wrong, I feel Mahatma Gandhi was a great man, I feel my brother is troubled, I feel you are correct, or I feel it is outrageous the way people are treated in that country.

Additionally, using the word phrases, "I feel like…" and "I feel as if…" what is likely to follow are thoughts. For example: "I feel as if I am about to be crucified."

FEELINGS THAT ALERT YOU OF YOUR JUDGMENT THINKING

* ANGER (Thinking what's wrong with others)

* GUILT, SHAME, DEPRESSION (Thinking what's wrong with ourselves)

> *"All (moralistic) judgments are tragic expressions of unmet needs."*
> — MARSHALL B. ROSENBERG

ABOUT NEEDS

Needs are at the core of Language of Compassion communication.

We want to link our feelings to our needs, indicating that we feel the way we do because our needs are or are not getting met.

An example: "When I see…I feel…because I am needing…" When you relate using the Language of Compassion model, we never want to imply what someone else does is the cause of our feelings, although it may be the stimulus (trigger) for our feelings. In the words of the ancient Greek philosopher, Epictetus: "Men are disturbed not by things which happen, but by the views which they take of things."

The Language of Compassion views our Universal Human Needs as the divine energy seeking fulfillment within us. Contrary to the conditioning many of us have received, our needs can be viewed as a gift to others, giving someone the opportunity to contribute and nurture us. When this opportunity is presented without any coercive element, and people do not have other pressing or conflicting needs, it is our natural response to desire to contribute to the needs of others. Doing so meets our mutual intrinsic need to contribute to life.

Needs are universal. All human beings have the same needs, although we adopt a wide variety of strategies to try to meet these needs. (The strategy is included in the REQUEST part of the Language of Compassion model.)

When we express needs using the Language of Compassion we include no reference to specific people doing specific things. For example: I need physical nurturance, but I don't need you to get me a pizza. When we confuse our needs with the strategy for meeting them (specific people taking specific actions) we are apt to be heard as making demands. There are always many ways to meet each of our needs. If we believe that only a specific person can meet a certain need, we narrow and view an abundant Universe as one that is limited and creates feelings of extreme scarcity.

NEEDS INVENTORY
Some of the Basic Needs that We All Share

Autonomy
- ☐ choosing dreams/goal/values
- ☐ choosing plans for fulfilling one's dreams, goals, values

Celebration
- ☐ Celebrate the creation of life and dreams fulfilled
- ☐ Celebrate losses: loved ones, dreams, etc. (mourning)

Integrity
- ☐ Authenticity
- ☐ Creativity
- ☐ Meaning
- ☐ Self-worth

Interdependence
- ☐ Acceptance
- ☐ Appreciation
- ☐ Closeness
- ☐ Community
- ☐ Consideration
- ☐ Contribute to the enrichment of life
- ☐ Emotional Safety
- ☐ Empathy
- ☐ Honesty (the empowering honesty that enables us to learn from our limitations)
- ☐ Love
- ☐ Reassurance
- ☐ Respect
- ☐ Support
- ☐ Trust
- ☐ Understanding
- ☐ Warmth

Physical Nurturance
- ☐ Air
- ☐ Food
- ☐ Movement, exercise
- ☐ Protection from life-threatening forms of life: viruses, bacteria, insects, predatory animals (especially human beings)
- ☐ Rest
- ☐ Sexual expression
- ☐ Shelter
- ☐ Touch
- ☐ Water

Play

Spiritual Communion
- ☐ Beauty
- ☐ Harmony
- ☐ Inspiration
- ☐ Order
- ☐ Peace

MAKING REQUESTS

If I am making requests, I want others to do what I ask only if they can do so willingly. To check if I am making a request or a demand, I can ask myself if I am as interested in the other person's needs getting met as my own, and how I might respond if the other person says, "No." Would I seek to punish the person in some way, or would I honor the person's response by offering empathy?

Using the Language of Compassion we want to express requests in clear, specific, POSITIVE ACTION LANGUAGE.

Make it clear **who** you want to do **what** and **when** you want them to do it.

By using **positive** language, you generally want to say what you **do** want the person to do rather than what you **don't** want the person to do.

By using **action** language, you want to request an action that is **do-able** rather than say what you want someone to **be** or **become**. (If you do want the person to be or become something, for example, be more affectionate, you need to indicate what action you want the person to take to demonstrate that request or what you anticipate and hope will help the person to become that way.)

When making a request you also are asking someone to do something **now**, in the present moment, the only time anyone can do anything.

You want to avoid language that will likely be heard as making a demand. Avoid phrases like: "You should," "You have to," "You can't," and "You must." To help insure it is heard as a request, we might include a phrase such as "…if you are willing," while also checking our delivery tone to make sure that it is held in the pure energy of a question.

Some Initial Requests Using a Language of Compassion Dialogue:

1. Would you be willing to tell me what you heard me say, so I can see if I have made myself clear?

2. Would you be willing to tell me how you feel about what I have said? This is especially important after we have revealed our feelings and needs, to be sure we have a heart to heart connection with the other person.

3. Would you be willing to meet me on Tuesday to discuss the problem? **A specific action now request helps to insure your needs will be shared.**

We don't have to guess right.
We only have to guess human.
    —MARSHALL B. ROSENBERG

EMPATHY

Empathy is the total presence with which we attend to someone's being. It is expressed through the quality of our attention, which may take the form of silence, gestures, or words.

"Empathy is a respectful understanding of what others are experiencing. Instead of offering empathy, we often have a strong urge to give advice or reassurance and to explain our own position or feeling. Empathy, however, calls upon us to empty our mind and listen to others with our whole being."
    —MARSHALL B. ROSENBERG

"Each person has a sacred uniqueness which requires of us a reaction which cannot be prepared beforehand. It demands nothing of what is past. It demands presence, responsibility. It demands us."
    —MARTIN BUBER

SOME COMMON AND HABITUAL NON-EMPATHIC RESPONSES:

Advising
Agreeing
Educating/Correcting
Consoling
One-Upping/Telling Our Own Stories
Sympathizing
Asking Questions To Satisfy Our Own Curiosity
Explaining
Saying "I Understand"

(Instead Of Demonstrating Our Understanding Verbally or Non-Verbally)

Keep This Model in Mind When Offering Empathy:

Are you feeling...

because you are needing...

and would you now like...?

When empathizing, you want to focus your attention on what is alive now in the other person and adopt a tone indicating you are guessing what the other feels and needs. If you are mistaken, you let the other person correct you. When they do, this closes "the gap," and the bridge of connection is maintained.

It is the integrity of each individual human that is in final examination. On personal integrity hangs humanity's fate.

—BUCKMINSTER FULLER

Integrity is not a 90% thing, not a 95% thing; either you have it or you don't.

—PETER SCOTESE

INTEGRITY

Integrity is aligning our word with our action, which anchors the cornerstones of establishing relationships built on trust.

Integrity is a character trait that is an internal choice that honors your word even when no one is watching. Integrity is what leads you to stay internally disciplined to honor your commitments to yourself and others. How can you expect to operate in integrity in your relationships if you fail to meet your commitments in the relationship you have with yourself? Everything begins as an internal reflection. If your relationship has been breached by lack of integrity, offering acknowledgment of your breach between your words and actions, as well as making amends re-establishes your connection and commitments. You will often be blessed by the Law of Reciprocity in action.

The sincere attempt to connect and to honor your word is how trust is maintained in all relationships.

When you step into your integrity as well as take responsibility and be accountable to make amends for your co-creation to feelings of sepration, you allow someone else the ability to connect with their own human condition to recognize: as an ever-evolving human we all don't always internally align our hearts wishes and desires with our actions. We all want to receive grace, so it is a natural act to reciprocate that which we would also enjoy.

WHAT TO DO IF YOU CAN'T HONOR YOUR WORD:

First, acknowledge that you made a commitment and that you didn't honor your word. Ask the other person what you could do or suggest what you could do to make it up to them? For example: If you made a commitment to be somewhere at a certain time and are running late, call ahead and let them know. Ask if your "lateness" will still meet their needs for time efficiency and respect. Or, if you've said you would do something and you don't honor your word, acknowledge that by asking what you could do to make it up to them and wait for their reply. Your internal and external breaches are a direct access point of reflection to see how often you are not present with your own needs and cannot therefore be present with the needs of others.

Second, take the time for inward reflection, you may find that you are most often late. This reflection allows you to look at areas you may be over-committing or acting out in a subconscious rebellious passive form of violence to make the necessary shifts in your schedule or your internal beliefs to reduce your commitments to meet your needs for more peace, mutual respect, ease, flow, and time efficiency into your life. This, in turn, becomes reflected into the quality of presence and peace you co-create in your relationships.

Saying (and hearing) 'No' cuts the flow of communication I want to have with you.
—GARY BARAN

When I hear your 'No,' I celebrate you saying 'Yes' to you.

SAYING "NO" WITH THE LANGUAGE OF COMPASSION

What NOT to say:
"No," I can't," "I don't have time," "I don't want to."

What To Do Instead:
1. Receive the other's request as a gift (an opportunity for you to contribute to their life).

2. Say what needs of yours prevent you from wanting to comply.

3. Give empathy to the other person, if needed.

4. Express commitment to finding win-win solutions and express your confidence about that possibility.

5. Continue the dialogue or make plans to do so.

Instead of hearing 'No' from others, hear what they are feeling and needing that makes them reluctant to say 'Yes.'" This allows you to initiate a dialogue that sincerely communicates your desire to search for a way to find win-win solutions to meet our mutual needs to be heard and know we matter.

FULLY EXPRESSING ANGER

Notice and enjoy it… there is a message and an unmet need in it. Breathe into and through it

Absolve the other of responsibility for your anger

Identify the stimulus for your anger

Identify your thoughts and beliefs that are the root cause of your anger

Identify your unmet needs and associated feelings

Express (and perhaps get empathy for) those feelings and needs

Transform anger by using the Releasing Anger Peacefully Mindfulness Practice (see page 148)

EXPRESSING APPRECIATION/GRATITUDE

- Say what the other person did that contributed to your well-being

- Say how you feel now when you think about that

- Say what need of yours was met by what the person did

There is a moment when you will pass through the threshold of intrinsic knowing. When your actions are no longer governed by reaction or the law of "shoulds," "have-to's," coercion, manipulation, or conditions, but rather by authentic choice and connection, that is independent from the limitations and conditioning that once governed your relating, and reactions within yourself and with your external relational world.

In this moment, you *know* within every cell of your experience that you are deeply interconnected to life, as a living flow of energy that happens between the reflection that is possible within all relationships. Suddenly, what once was only captured as only glimpses of deeply living connected to your truth and to another now becomes a crystal clear expression of what this entire journey called life is all about—to experience a deep connection and reflection of love.

Then, moment-by-moment, experience-to-experience, you exercise your freedom to create a gap between your stimulus and response to choose love. As you expand your awareness to see that only when you release your finite beliefs and judgments of what you believe you need to "feel" happy can only happen a certain way, or with a certain "someone," you open an experience to life that sees the infinite possibilities awaiting everywhere.

In a world of 7 billion people all so uniquely amazing, infinite, and diverse—at the core of who we are there is one ultimate universal truth. There is only one Power. That Power to move spirit into matter is love, and the one reason we are here. One language—Our Universal Language of Needs. There is no us versus them. No man versus woman. No you versus me. No borders, walls or boundaries that can separate our interdependent connection to one another. When you see the truth of what unites us—our Universal Human Needs—you drop the illusion that we are separate. Now you are living in truth of the infinite possibilities to explore what would truly make life more wonderful.

Somewhere between the right doing, and wrong doing there is a field. I will meet you there.
—RUMI

VII

Relationships—The Perfect Mirrors

> *It's not what we eat but what we digest that makes us strong; not what we gain but what we save that makes us rich; not what we read but what we remember that makes us learned; and not what we profess but what we practice that gives us integrity.*
> —FRANCIS BACON, SR.

All relationships lead you back to the Self and are, by their design and very nature, reflective. They offer you a mirror that enables you to see just what is alive within you, both dark and light. Seeing your negative thoughts, patterns, and beliefs, from the mirror of your relationships provides you with the possibility to heal yourself of the limiting and sabotaging beliefs that are constricting your capacity to experience life as its highest truth of potentiality. By clearing away the old negative patterns, entraining new set points of beliefs more aligned to the truth of who you were created to be, you create healthier attitudes and relating behaviors, deepening your connections to life at every level. For this reason, even when relationships are no longer serving love, and are no longer sustainable in their current form, relationships are always a gift. Leaving one relationship for another because the grass seems greener with someone else, until you begin the inward journey work, nevertheless, ultimately leads you back to confronting the same problems and life-negating patterns present within you until you make that crucial choice to see your own co-creation, to learn, to heal, and to grow.

The only way out is in!

Every relationship, by design, is interconnected and everything we receive is an essential gift (pre-sent) for you to discover your highest truth. Choosing not to confront the pain and heartache that certain relationships may arouse in you is not unlike the man who went into the hills for years in order to overcome his anger only to find, the moment he returned to his village, the anger had never left. Relationship is an intrinsic part of the journey within, an integral part of your transformation to becoming more. Oftentimes, it is only through the mirrors provided in life's most challenging relationships that we discover our greatest gifts.

To discover the present inside, we must first unwrap the gift.

THE TIES THAT BIND US

Viewing familial relationships as a gift can be challenging, particularly if you now find yourself in the depths of disconnection and pain. While precious, these relationships can be hot spots of commotion and turmoil which wreak havoc on our nervous systems and negatively impact our overall health and well-being. By exercising awareness, you can take ownership of your own well-being and implement the necessary changes to enable a shift within all of your relationships, even the most disagreeable ones.

Central to all familial relationships is the co-creative roles we play. Our roles, experiences, and related expectations arising from our understanding and limiting conditioned beliefs we hold about these roles are what leave us feeling stuck, put-upon, anxious, frustrated, claustrophobic, unappreciated, insecure, playing out old records of unworthiness, and feeling unheard or unloved. Ultimately, it is our own limiting thoughts, beliefs and conditioning that lead to all feelings of separation, pain and suffering.

As a quick exercise, take a pen and paper and jot down the various roles you play with each and every member of your family: husband, wife, father, mother, son, daughter, brother, sister. Then jot down the many "shoulds" and "have-to's" that arise in that relationship whether expressly stated, implied, or assumed. You will likely find there's a lot to write down! Deepening your own awareness of the roles you choose to play and the subsequent expectations that arise from these roles is the crucial first step to taking back your internal power and voice of truth Doing the work by applying the tools you've learned will put an end to any confusion, pain, hurt, discomfort, feelings of separation, or unease you may feel in these relationships and open up the potential for upleveling all your mutually committed relationships to the experience of being deeply connected, intimate, and in a co-creative, authentic, and loving exchange.

Genuine and supportive systems of relating can and will arise as part of nature's design, apart from the illusions, beliefs, and models that have to date, shaped your relationships into their current power-over dynamics, only when you stop seeing your relationships as separate. While accounts vary as to the exact divorce statistic rate, due to the fact that four states—California, Colorado, Indiana and Louisiana—do not track statistics. The last U.S. reported statistic was 2005[10], reporting the alarming 6.2 year average median duration of marriage is evidence that something isn't working in the way we interrelate and build our relationships. Because marriage involves two people and statistics are tracked on one person filing for divorce, any statistic you review becomes more meaningful when you look at the per capita rate of failing relationships. Taking that one step further, upon examination, we take those same relating models of our current power-over dynamics from our bedroom into our boardrooms, then into our current business models and governmental systems. Which comes first, the chicken or the egg? Is it any wonder these systems that run counterintuitive to the truth of who we were created to be are collapsing? When you build any model of relations on a false system of belief—that we are separate—the foundational building blocks that comprise that system are set up to fail.

When we add the burden of role expectations, the "shoulds" and "have-tos" and passive forms of violence of withdrawal, conditions, shaming, guilt or blame that we're all so well-acquainted with and conditioned into, we can see other system models like; our education and economic systems who are also all driven by the same power-over energy of relating. This contrived and fear-based model of relating is built on our

---

10 http://www.divorcereform.org/rates.html

conditioning of doing what the "big people" tell us to do: be it our parents, our teachers, our bosses, their bosses, "the board" or President, and our government and governmental law agencies, all by-products of power-over relating. We become, until we don't, nothing more than hostages to a system of relating that creates division, mistrust, and resentment, all leading to more feelings of separation, isolation and suffering. This mentality is tragic as it denies the heart of humanity the truth of our interconnectedness and our capacity to contribute to life, and one another, as powerful, potent, and co-creative possibilities that intrinsically are wired to work together to see that everyone's needs are heard, and to seek what would serve the highest good to begin to restore the trust to support building long-term goodwill for everyone involved.

If you attempt to create any new model or continue to relate within a system that dictates a hierarchy of judgment of what is right or wrong, good and bad, you deny your natural inherent capacity to honor life. We were all raised expecting to "do" or "be" something, without ever really appreciating, or questioning, why we do what we do or is it aligned to our "who."

As children, many of us ventured to ask our parents, for example, why we had to kiss or hug Aunt Edna, even though we didn't want to. Your parents did what they knew. Acting as enforcers of societal directives or mandates, and as victims of their own "unknowing" of subconscious conditionings by their role models, they may have forced you to comply by insisting we kiss or hug Aunt Edna. Watch out if you didn't, you may have been punished, rebuked, ignored, or rejected by withdrawing their love and support until they gained your compliance. On the other hand, when you listened and did what they told you to do, did as you should, you were accepted, rewarded and/or praised for your behavior. The fact that you didn't *want* to kiss Aunt Edna was non-essential, for your feelings, needs to know you matter or you are heard, or your need to express your feelings, hear your inquiry or needs, if ever, found a voice with the "big people."

In essence, you tragically learned to disconnect from your own truth, intuition and feelings and found reward when you acted as a "good" little boy or girl when you did what you "should," as you outwardly complied as a strategy to meet your natural universal needs for love, reward and reassurance. As a grown-up, you've long since learned to do what you believe you should "do" or "be" regardless of how it makes you feel, growing resentful as you have separated yourself from your own needs and truth, which creates an on-going disconnection and fracture from your creation consciousness Self which becomes reflected in the life-negating behaviors you act out to have your needs met within your relationships. Does that sound like emotionally healthy, or connected living to you? Does it promote living in authenticity in which you are connected and aligned to your heart-based feelings, thoughts, and emotions? And does such forced conditioning truly teach you to listen to the real integrity and truth within yourself to build deeply connected relationships that yield authentic intimate, loving and powerful co-creative interactions with others?

Two stories follow, where two different individuals use the skills they've learned to promote transformation in their relationships. They adhere to four key fundamentals focusing on:

* Maintaining Self-Awareness and remaining in a compassionate state

* Speaking and implementing the principles found in The Language of Compassion

* Staying in the present (not dwelling on the past)

* Choosing love, truth, transparency and forgiveness, without withdrawing

BREAKING OUR ROLES: DAUGHTER AND FATHER

Celeste is in her early thirties. She and her father, Fred, a successful well-polished attorney, have a custom of meeting for a nice dinner for just the two of them on the first Saturday of every month. Although her father has never instructed her to do so, Celeste has always felt it necessary to dress accordingly, wearing either knee-length skirts or dresses, pumps, and her hair straightened and pulled back. The look is completely unlike her usual natural curly hair, slacks or jeans and comfortable tops.

So much so, that on two occasions, when she bumped into friends when dining with her father they nearly didn't recognize her. Nevertheless, she still finds herself wanting the approval of her father. He certainly seems to look forward to their dinners and enjoys doting over her, not unlike the way he had over her mother, who had passed away more than a decade ago. Although Celeste senses that she may be filling a void her mother has left, she relishes the attention she gets from her father. Attention she never felt growing up. Sure, it's seldom that they ever really speak in-depth about anything, but she's long-since decided that such closeness between them just isn't possible. If love means nice dinners and polite conversation with Fred, and not much more, Celeste has learned to accept whatever she can get.

But the more Celeste encounters her self-work, the more she senses and is increasingly sad about the dichotomy between who she truly is in real life: a single, artistic, sexy, free-spirited woman, and who her father sees on their "dates." Even though her life is not as peachy keen as she has often made it seem, she yearns for her father to know her as she really is, to connect deeply with him and have him see and share more of her real life. After meditating one morning, she knows what she has to do. She makes a vow to herself that the next time she meets her father for dinner she will not do anything that makes her feel unnatural or less authentic to the truth of who she truly is.

Arriving for dinner, Celeste realizes she is nervous and anxious. Though Fred says nothing about her curly hair and jeans, she's sensing his energy toward her is not as warm as usual. Rather than be hurt by this, she remembers her vow to herself and places her focus on staying present in being with her father. By the time the appetizer arrives she realizes the emotion she's sensing from her father is not so much disapproval as it is nervousness, perhaps even a little vulnerability. Seeing this, her heart goes out to him. By looking other than what he has become accustomed to expect, she has signaled to her father that she is not playing according to his rules.

As if sensing this, Fred says, "I like what you've done with your hair."

"This is my real hair. It's how I usually wear it," she responds. She reaches across the table and grabs her father's hand. "Dad, I just want to tell you these dinners mean a lot to me. I'm always happy to have this time with you," she says smiling and looking into his eyes.

A slight blush makes its way across Fred's face. He quickly changes the subject. He is uncomfortable with speaking on-point or from a feeling place and almost never does. Celeste smiles and adjusts to the change in topic. After a few minutes have passed, she sees her words have penetrated Fred's buttoned-up demeanor and she senses her father is more at ease.

As Fred talks, Celeste remembers to listen and receive what her father is saying even though he's talking about his golf game and the meeting he had with an old associate, both topics she would have gladly tuned-out on before. Breathing and taking-in his expressions, his cadence, the way he tosses and sticks out his chin when he wants to emphasize a point, a funny thing starts to happen. Right before her eyes she starts to catch glimpses of just who this well-dressed, expressive, witty man named Fred is aside from being her father. Though, of course, she's long understood the fact that her father had a life apart from hers, somehow she never felt just what this meant. Suddenly her sense of him is expanded and as this happens her appreciation and connection to these other aspects of him seems to grow too.

When their dinner plates are cleared and Fred begins to ask his usual, customary questions, Celeste responds not as she has been accustomed to, namely, by telling him what she presumes he wants to hear and glossing over the rest. This time she slows down, she connects to how she's feeling and answers from the heart.

Sensing this, Fred soon changes the content of his questions. He's surprised to learn more about Celeste's business and happy to learn she's working toward becoming more fulfilled in her life.

Celeste registers the happiness on Fred's face as he smiles at her and realizes that he too has noticed a shift.

While lingering over coffee and dessert, Fred says he has something he's been too nervous to tell her until now, she is happy to put him at ease and reassure him, because she too feels connected to her father as well as Fred, whom also is a man.

"I'd like to hear whatever it is you have to say Dad. I want you to feel you can speak your truth," she says.

Fred responds saying, "I've been living with someone for the past five years and we love each other very much."

Though it's a lot to process, Celeste breathes in this new information and tastes her love and her fear. Having created the necessary gap, she chooses to speak with love and says,

"I'm very happy for you Dad and I'm grateful you felt you could share that with me."

Hearing this Fred reaches his hand across the table. Celeste responds by sliding her hand towards his until they embrace.

BREAKING OUR ROLES: SON AND MOTHER

Brandon is a hardworking twenty-eight-year old man and is married with a newborn daughter. Growing up, Brandon witnessed his mother, Linda, being abused by his father, who eventually walked-out on the family, and later, by two subsequent boyfriends. Once he became a young man, he decided that he would never let anyone hurt his mother again. For this reason, he lives just a block away. Nearly every day, he still stops by to check-in at his mother's house after work. For the past two years his mom has had a boyfriend, Paul, who seems to love her and seems to have his act together. Nevertheless, Brandon cannot find it within himself to like or approve of this man. Despite his mother's pleas, he finds he can barely even acknowledge his presence.

Although Linda loves her son, she feels nervous every time he comes to visit. She wants for him and Paul to get along but senses just how defensive her son is. She can't even rub Paul's shoulder without sensing her son is getting upset or making a comment. He still treats her house like he has free reign, coming and going as he pleases. This affects her relationship with Paul, who feels disrespected. She wishes she could just be herself with her partner and her son. Instead she feels like she's two different people with the most important men in her life.

His anger has deeply affected his relationship at home as well. Things finally came to a head with his wife Marissa the last time Brandon's temper got the best of him. Seeing his baby daughter in her crib and knowing Marissa would leave if things didn't change soon, Brandon finally agreed to try things her way.

Since then he's learned to create the gap. Doing so, he's seen for himself just how triggered he can get, with his temper flaring up the moment Marissa starts talking to him. But, by taking the time to acknowledge his anger, then freezing the frame and choosing to act in a loving way, he's slowly beginning to reinstate trust and calm in their relationship. Now that he's come to realize there's a great deal of anger operating just below the surface, he's practicing the HeartMath Attitude Breathing® technique (page 111), something he, undoubtedly, would have made fun of just a few weeks ago, and he's surprised that something so simple could actually be working. Having tuned-in to his feelings, he can choose to feel into what he may be suffering from. He's pretty sure his unresolved anger has been the cause of his heart palpitations and chest pains. Though he laughed when he heard Marissa say there were only two emotions, love and fear, now, as he's become more accustomed to creating the gap, he's starting to sense that this might very well be true.

Already having what he'd like to say in mind, Brandon pays a visit to his mother's when he knows Paul will be there visiting. Paul answers the door with a grimace. Though Brandon feels a twinge of anger he simply breathes through it and takes a seat at the kitchen table, acknowledging the truth that he's been rude and distant towards Paul for years. When Linda enters the kitchen he tells her he would like to talk to both her and Paul. Hearing this, Linda shoots him a look full of skepticism.

"Don't worry Mom, I come in peace," Brandon says, smiling and lifting a peace sign, putting both her and Paul more at ease.

After Linda pours them all a cup of coffee, Brandon begins, "Mom, it seems to me that you and Paul are pretty happy together," he says. Paul looks astonished at hearing this.

"Yes we are," Linda answers.

"Good," says Brandon. Looking at Paul, he addresses him directly, "I know I haven't been the most welcoming to you, Paul, and I'm sorry about that. I'm just starting to realize how much I've been trying to protect my mom. For as long as I can remember, I've been afraid of someone hurting her. I also noticed as I've been reflecting more, how exhausting this has been for me and how it has caused hurt and discomfort to everyone I deeply care about, including my wife. After having my own daughter I suddenly have realized how important and committed I am to being the best Dad I can be to her."

Hearing this, Paul's heart fills with compassion. Suddenly he understands what was behind Brandon's behavior.

Turning to look at his mom Brandon can feel tears rushing to his eyes. Though he's feeling slightly embarrassed, he continues speaking, "Mom, I just want for you to be happy and to know that I'll be there for you if you need anything. If I can trust if you really have a need you'll ask, I can get the peace and relaxation I've needed that has been invested in worrying about you all the time."

Seeing his tears, Linda feels instant compassion, "I never asked you to do that."

Realizing there's truth in what she's saying, Brandon responds compassionately, "I know. All I can remember wanting is to protect you and keep you safe."

"You're an amazing son," Linda says. Brandon nods his head receiving and accepting what he's just heard. It's nice to hear. He continues, "I just want you to know I don't think it's a good idea for me to be coming by all the time. I have to take care of my own family."

Paul responds, "Have you ever considered she didn't ask you?"

Hearing this triggers Brandon. He holds up his hand and breathes. Paul looks stunned. He takes a few seconds and lets the feeling of anger run through him. He replays what Paul has just said. He laughs realizing he may have been misunderstanding the situation all along.

"Mom, is it true that you don't want me coming over here to check-in on you?" he asks.

"Well honey, you know I always like seeing you," Linda responds.

"Mom, it's okay to just tell me your truth," Brandon says calmly. He smiles and she feels safe to speak her mind. "Well you don't need to come every day. You could call too," she answers. Paul can see how much Brandon loves his mother and senses how hard he's been trying to protect her. Knowing how much they both love the same woman, he decides to bury the hatchet with him.

"Okay, Mom. So from now on I'm leaving it up to you to let me know how you're doing. If you need anything, I need for you to ask me for help. This will help support my habit of feeling so preoccupied all the time," Brandon says. Linda nods her head in agreement.

Feeling a great deal of relief, Brandon takes a deep breath. He feels lighter, as if a weight from his shoulders really has been lifted. "Can you guys make it over for dinner this week?"

Paul answers, "We'd love to."

Brandon slaps him on the back, and says, "I think we should get to know each other better since it looks like my mom seems to like you, okay?"

They all laugh, letting whatever tensions there may have been fall away. Anticipating good things ahead for all of them, Linda asks, "Who'd like more coffee?"

THE ROLE-COMPLEX

The core foundational relationships you have with your family members, especially those with your parents and siblings, can offer you tremendous opportunity for your deepest growth and healing. This is because these relationships form the very ground from which you have developed specific sabotaging patterns, behaviors, thoughts, limiting beliefs, and habitual traits. The triggers you encounter in your closest relationships most often stem from your early formative relationships that have molded you. All negative patterns of rebellion, withdrawal, and limiting beliefs that lead to life-alienating subconscious behavior is what creates the feelings of separation that permeate every relationship until you begin the inward journey. It is from the debris of these mindsets and finite programmed beliefs that we act out well into our adult relationships. During these developmental years, aspects of your truest Self are often fractured or left behind, denying you of the chance of truly stepping into your unique purpose, power, and truth you were created to be. The good news is that through interfacing with your family members, opening your heart to ask them to show you your blindspots, and earnestly expanding your awareness to areas you're asleep within your intimate relationships, you unlock the treasure within you to crack the code of what I refer to as the "role-complex" and thereby repattern and release whatever subconscious conditionings inhibit your further growth and the experience of true intimacy and love within your life.

In the example of Brandon, as a child and adolescent he felt it was necessary to become his mother's protector. Those qualities of his real and true nature didn't correlate to his notion of what it meant to be a big, strong, man. He loved and his whole life felt passionate about art. Because his false belief that an artist wasn't "big and strong," his life gifts were negated and never given room to develop.

The development and portrayal of Brandon's role-complex of seeing himself as his mother's protector is inconsequential. What is of consequence, is that at some pinnacle moment in Brandon's history, his own interpretation of what it meant to be a son (and man) limited his truth of "who" he is from fully being recognized and lived. The traumatic events in which Brandon witnessed his mother being hurt and felt powerless to help, created limitations and constrictions in all the relationships within his life. Brandon's prototype version of himself as "the protector," created a big, strong man which kept his mind/body/heart system locked in a perpetual cycle of being ready to protect and fight.

Because of this deep trauma, any perceived disruption or heated emotion, whether it is coming from his mother or wife or directed *toward* them, causes Brandon to automatically react in a triggered and defensive state. Remember, his subconscious still believes he's witnessing someone hurting his mother. The anger he feels is a long ingrained mechanism for masking his fear. As a son, he felt it was his responsibility to be strong for his mother, so he adapted a fierce shield and armor, which also denied others who loved him the ability to penetrate that armor. This also constricted his mind/body/heart to really relax his defenses so that he could enjoy the deep intimacy, connection and co-creative gift that adult relationships provide for. Anger was adopted as the "stronghold" emotion and fear hid undercover, masked as the shield and protector.

In the space of demand, implied or not, healthy human beings will generally respond in a state of resistance. This is natural as it protects our deep needs for autonomy and freedom. When we authentically express a need and inquire from a place of question, it puts us in a vulnerable and very powerful position. It is our natural desire to co-create a win-win economy of interchange and interdependency when we understand how our contribution can make life more wonderful for one another.

When roles impede on your fullest development as an individual, as was the case with Brandon, positive and loving impulses can end up misdirected, often towards hostile and destructive ends. Consider Brandon's situation with Paul. Brandon always looked over his mother's welfare. Imagine what would happen if Brandon were to come over after work and witness a dispute between Paul and his mother. He might physically attack Paul with little to no provocation.

THE "SHOULDS" AND THE "HAVE-TO'S"

Use of the words should, have to, blame, shame, and guilt, all work toward creating a gap, a fracture, between our true Self and the expressions of the ego structure Self. This causes you to choose life-negating strategies to meet your needs that perpetuate a spiral of more pain, separation and feelings of suffering within your Self, which are mirrored within your relationships. Just because they've lasted as emotional manipulative tactics for thousands of years, because they're highly effective at controlling others' behaviors, can you see the damage they have caused? All power-over strategies are short-cut band-aid remedies of gaining immediate compliance, with a pseudo effect of getting our interconnected needs met at the expense of others, in lieu of building real self-ethics, integrity, trust and self-governance. When you act outside your intrinsic capacity to contribute to another, by doing what you think you "should" be doing to show you care, gain approval and love, you unknowingly pass on, and perpetuate, these conditioned life-alienating tribal mindsets onto future generations.

The truth is when you strip away living in the "have to," "should," "right and wrong," "good and bad" habitual strategies to have your needs met, you will soon find that you are naturally wired to want to co-create powerfully connected relationships that contribute to improving the lives and well-being of others, particularly when you know how your contribution is serving making life more wonderful for them.

Inquiry into your own "shoulds" and "have-to's" can often pin-point the exact areas where you're acting out of alignment with your true nature. When you catch yourself being triggered and feel compelled to do or be something that leads you to act outside of your own integrity, you will find that upon reflection it is all designed to serve love, leading you right back to the point of creation where the limiting belief was installed. When you can clear and heal areas of trauma, hurt, misunderstanding, behaviors and life-alienating strategies you've developed as a child, and carried into your adulthood, in order to get your needs met to know you matter, to be heard, for love, for connection, for sexual expression, and the myriad other interconnected needs we share, every relationship will uplevel.

Between actions and reactions there are your thoughts, feelings, and emotions that drive that behavior. If you create the gap of inquiry, you will begin to see how many roles you play. Creating awareness is the first step to experiencing freedom from living entrenched and obligated to live outside of the truth of who you truly are for anyone or anything. The next time a non-emergency situation arises where you must make a choice, first consider the following questions:

How am I feeling? Am I feeling a "should" or a "have to?"

If so, ask yourself: "Can I do this out of love?" or "What would love do?"

If you cannot do it out of love, in that particular moment, then don't do it, because ultimately no one wins. Using The Language of Compassion, you can begin to reframe your internal reactions to share what needs of yours are not being met, then state what needs of yours need to present for you to truly say "yes" to other's requests. Once you find that you do want to do whatever is being asked of you out of love, make a conscious effort to anchor your action back to your heart. When you drop down into your heart, rather than reacting from what your head says, you extend your actions from your highest thought and loving-kindness. If you need mutual respect or trust, consideration, gratitude, or reassurance, express that need be met in the form of making a clear request and you will likely discover how much we love to contribute to meeting our interdependent needs of one another. Remember, In the space of demand, healthy human beings will generally respond in a state of resistance. This is natural as it protects our deep needs for autonomy and freedom. When you learn to contribute to another's need with a true understanding of how meeting that need contributes to the enrichment of life, without an implied demand, or fear of rejection, withdrawal from love, shame, blame or guilt, or other unhealthy and divisive choices of relationship, you will find that we naturally desire and want to exchange positive emotions in return. This powerful relating tool allows the relationship to relax into a deeper trust and intimacy.

Learning to ask for your needs by making clear requests is not a selfish behavior. This is simply the natural win-win economy that arises when we are free to give and free to receive.

Becoming aware of the times you are feeling governed to act by "should" or "have to," allows you the freedom to choose the what and how you may choose to respond. For instance: if you are taking a loved one to a doctor appointment that is at an inconvenient time for you, you can see if it can be rescheduled. Or, if the drive on the surface streets takes longer but is less stress-inducing than taking the freeway, perhaps you can plan accordingly knowing less stress will result in a greater feeling of peace and well-being.

If you feel there are things that frustrate you that you don't honor yourself to share, you will naturally move away and withdraw from being able to give openly and feel good about what you're doing. It is easy to know when you are operating in truth and love—it feels good, light, celebratory. You are the co-creator of your life experience, so set the stage in your relationships to feel good and joyful. Let your actions come from love and let yourself feel your own loving presence as you are being loving to another. It is a lie to believe the tribal mindset that being in relationship means you have to suffer to show or receive love. Suffering never yields love and it does not prove love. Suffering only creates more pain, resentment, disconnection and leads us down the path of acting out other life-negating behaviors.

When you give from a sense of wanting to make another person's life more wonderful, you feel joy and light in your steps at being able to freely give and receive. This joy is not present when we feel we "have to," or "should." Feeling joy and gratification from doing something that contributes to another's sense of well-being is part of the natural desire of economy of interchange and interdependency we all share between one another. Being able to receive this joy is just one powerful life change that enriches and empowers living your life aligned with your creation consciousness truth.

INTEGRITY AND TRUST IS PARAMOUNT

Integrity is the congruence between your words and your actions. Stemming from the Latin adjective *integer*, at its root, the word means whole or wholeness. In this context, integrity may be understood as "wholeness"—a sense of completeness and agreement between what one says they are going to do and what they do. When you act in alignment with your words and actions, trust is established within your relationships, deepening your experience of intimacy which uplevels the experience of all of your relationships who have made the commitment to build authentic, transparent and thriving co-creative connections within yourself and with others.

Integrity is the one critical influencer in all relationships. Without it, over time, trust is eroded and resentment builds. With it, your inner connection between what you say and do is in harmony. This is a simple recipe to establish trust and peace within yourself and your relationships. Simple but profound, this reaps great dividends when it comes to creating the kind of life experience of deeply intimate, powerful, and loving relationships— co-creating the experience and purpose of the reason we come to this experience called life · to learn, give and receive love.

Integrity is always an inside job. It is the hidden variable and missing link to serving your highest desires, passions and dreams! Have you ever made a commitment to yourself like losing weight, stopping smoking or discontinuing other negative habits only to find yourself eating just the same as before, maybe even more, rationalizing your lapse by telling yourself you'll start the diet next week? Then, next week turns into yet another week later and 2 more pounds to lose. When you stop to pause, creating the gap between stimulus and response, you create the opportunity to ask yourself if making the choice to eat your favorite burger is actually serving your conscious choice to be healthy and get into sexy shape. Each time you choose to honor your integrity, you raise and empower your highest truth. This releases your own resentment and conditioned judgment statements that erode your confidence and self-worth. When you choose positive affirming statements such as, "I choose to eat meals that support me feeling sexy and healthy today," you become the powerful co-creator of a new reality.

Do you or do you know someone who rarely shows up at the agreed upon time to meet? How you choose to address your needs for order, time efficiency, and mutual respect is what will build or erode the quality of connection you have with that person. Will you say something about their lateness? What does that say to the trust you have about the authenticity of that relationship? If you choose to say nothing how will you be honoring your own needs to know you matter, are valued and respected? In the event that you are the one who will be late, how do you choose to handle your own breach of integrity with yourself and the person with whom you have made the commitment? What you choose will either strengthen or erode the trust between you. Once the underlying foundation of integrity is questioned, the mutual trust, prosperity, and goodwill in your relationships is replaced by a level of uncertainty, and mistrust that will create feelings of resentment.

Stepping into the power and truth of who you are requires that first you acknowledge, to yourself, when there is or has been incongruence between your words and actions, or inquire within to see what needs are not being met by the actions of another that are creating distance and damaging the goodwill between you and them. Trusting that authentic relationships can be upleveled and can withstand your speaking your truth, you can then speak to those in your life acknowledging how their acting out of integrity to their word has infected and affected your relationship with them. When you choose to compassionately confront this conversation, remember to check in to see if they are open in their heart, in that moment, to receive your truth. Use the Language of Compassion O-F-N-R model, and trust it is how you express your need or unmet need(s) that contributes to the result of deepening the authentic connection you co-create. When you take the time to frame their action in a way that shares how it impacts you, without judgment or criticism, staying heart-centered to express what unmet need is not being met by their behavior, making a doable request that could co-create a win-win exchange of celebrating our interdependent needs for love, for connection and mutual respect that our needs do matter, gives you the key to co-creating powerful and dynamic relationships. Oftentimes, the hand of grace and understanding is extended also to you when you acknowledge your breach to another and moves you closer to rebuilding trust and deepening your connection. Grace is the natural exchange because we all have been at the receiving and giving end of not being aligned to our words and actions. By holding yourself and others accountable to align words with action, you shine the reflective mirror as a gift that contributes to our mutual need to learn and grow. If the relationship is grounded in integrity, we will value the truth of how our actions impact and infect our relationship with them. Conversely, if you speak your truth and someone continues to choose the same patterns of "lateness" or some other breach of integrity, you can choose another friend or redefine your relationship to seek relationships where there are mutual commitments of integrity that value the gift of your time, your presence, and your love.

WITH OUR PARTNERS

We are all heavily conditioned in our culture to think that romantic love is the "be-all, end-all love of loves." It is not. Romantic love is a powerful, beautiful love capable of showing you what it means to love another at a deep emotional, physical, and spiritual level and to experience what it is to be known through your reflection within one another. It is through this love that you get to taste what the soul yearns for: to reconnect to creation consciousness which deepens every experience to love and to life. Through this reflective experience of relationship, we come to understand what is alive in us, what is beautiful in us, what still is creating limitations in our ability to receive and give love, and what longs to be known and expressed.

Creation love is a reunification between the best parts of romantic love and authentic source love. It is limitless, asexual, unconditional, and free from expectation for it simply is love. All other forms of love forever lead you to reach-out and act-out in life-alienating ways to quench an insatiable thirst to "have" something that we believe exists in the external. All along what you thought you found outside of yourself can only be fueled and generated internally, from within. The nucleus of your life journey is to live the truth of who you are—love. You are love and were created to give and receive the experience of love. Tapping into the creation source of love changes every experience you create.

To discover your connection to self-love, deepening your experience and understanding through quiet times of inquiry, meditation, Self-discovery, and nurturing yourself awakens your deepest version of your highest you. As you clear and repattern your limiting beliefs to align to the integrity and truth of the infinite unfolding miracle that is you, you now have entered into your ever-expanding version of the truth you were created to be. Even in the routine hubbub of everyday life, once you experience your inner world love affair, everything you bring to the relationships of life is a pre-sent gift—you offer the "all in" authentic-ness of you!

WHEN YOUR PARTNER IS UNSUPPORTIVE OF YOUR CHOICE

If you experience resistance from your partner, do not relent. His or her disapproval can be regarded as a physical manifestation that is trying to derail your conscious intentions. Understanding that monitoring your thoughts is a lifetime process which does become easier as you continue to question and uninstall your limiting thoughts and emotional response patterns which will help you stay single-focused to ignore the voice of chatter. Your previous relationship patterns naturally create a resistance, and perhaps even a mistrust, in the faces of someone you love, because they have been hurt by your "unknowingness." When you change your energetic vibration of relating, it forces the dynamics of that structure to, by default, also change. This can cause fear and resistance in your partner. When you bring light into darkness, the patterns or cycles of the negative density that life-alienating relating and thoughts patterns create becomes a bright, sometimes uninvited beacon, to shine light into the darkness of that which is required to uplevel the relationship to match this new energetic pattern. Everything in life is participatory and reflective. Be patient and kind to your relationship, but don't buy into the resistance or the "pout" of another, or deny the reality of your new steadfast and growing determination to stay the journey. Stay focused and committed on centering your need for support, reassurance, and accountability outside of your relationship in a community that is also committed to living in their highest truth.

Continue to stay vigilant in your journey to co-creating powerful and connected relationships that make life more wonderful. This is your life and every breath to co-create what you deeply long for and desire is yours. Don't let anyone or anything stand in your way. Find creative ways to honor life responsibilities while creating new time, sacred time, for your practice. If you know that your change is a hot topic, then don't go near the fire! You need not talk about it nor involve your partner if it induces a negative response. Actions speak louder than words. As your energy shifts and your wisdom and intuition expands, slowly day-by-day, your compassion and understanding grows. We all do not know what we do not know, until we do. Love is always a choice. It is an individual journey to choose to "wake up" or not, until we do. Simply make time and do your work. Creation love holds the grandest feeling of joy. You are simply growing sufficient space, time, and establishing new habits, discipline, and routine. Remember, it takes around 30 days of consistent discipline to build new neural pathways that reinforce any new habit or routine and instill focused awareness to maintain it.

Thanks to societal conditioning, oftentimes it is male partners who will act as naysayers to their female partner's journey and may resent the change if they aren't ready to change themselves. Sadly, most boys have been conditioned at a much younger age (3-5 years) to hide their feelings, losing touch and connection with the truth of who they truly are! Having already witnessed a change in you, they may be afraid of losing you, of being emasculated, of you losing respect for them, of feeling rejected by not being the most important person in your life, feeling different or disconnected from the "old" you, or afraid of acknowledging and moving through all the hurt and pain they harbor and are feeling called to see. Sometimes the thought of facing the pain is the biggest fear to face. Know that there might be loads of issues at play. Take nothing personally. Their life is their own journey and responsibility. Remember, if you're in someone else's business, who's monitoring and upleveling your experience to love and life?

Let your heart be filled with compassion and remember...

* We all do not know what we do not know until we do!

* There is a great likelihood that your partner is speaking out of fear. The only antidote for fear is love.

* Unkind words said in anger are usually an appeal for love.

* You may be the stimulus, but you are not the cause of their pain.

* **Everything** you get from the external world, including pain and painful circumstances, is both a symptom and a gift, directing you within, waking you up to becoming more of the truth of who you really are.

* *The same is true for your partner or spouse, even if they do not know it yet.* Your partner is filled with enemy thoughts disguised as thoughts they believe will protect them, make them wise to the world, strong, untouchable. They may also have thoughts that tie them into their stories of victimhood, thoughts that make them misunderstood, and the list goes on and on. These thoughts and stories zap power and leave your partner feeling drained, desperate, unworthy, inadequate, unsatisfied, unloved, separate, etc.

Exercise your empathy and compassion. You know how difficult it is to stay the course; waking up is bar none, the most challenging, courageous and rewarding path anyone can choose. Your own triggers will act as humbling confirmation that becoming more is a process. At times it can be a painful process. Your awareness is an ever-expanding journey. As you come to experience yourself as a potent and powerful master creator, a part of the infinite power of the Universe, part of the Divine, part of the Grand Unified Field of the All That Is, remember that judgment is at the root of all dysfunction and feelings of separation. Each one of us are on different paths and journeys. Like our handprints, no two journeys are ever the same. We're all perfectly and imperfectly human. Being human can be messy as we're navigating a new story. Stay in love and speak your most crystalline truth.

As you interact with your partner, let your stance be powerfully aligned with the strength and goodness that is within you. Doing this, you appeal to your partner's intrinsic connected heart of goodness and institute an open structure of possibility that invites their support. This puts you both on the same side; in power-with the other.

VOW TO SHARE WITH LOVED ONES

I, _____, (your name) am an incredible gift to the world. I give myself full permission to be completely authentic with my truth, authentic to myself and everyone I have in my life.

I stand fully seeing and loving myself for the beautiful imperfectly perfect person I am.

I release myself from my need to judge or criticize.

I release myself from the need to control the outcome of giving love to myself and to others.

I release myself from the need to control the outcome of giving love in my relationships.

I show up for my love and my truth.

I create this vow to commit to stretch myself and to open myself to any limitations I may have that will block my experience of life in the pursuit of my own deep knowing. I bring and offer my truths and I trust you, _____ (your name or loved ones name) to honor the covenant I have made between myself and my truth.

Signed: _____

Date:_____

LET THEM ASK THE QUESTIONS

Trust the process of your journey and give it time. Modeling through action is how we empower others to be attracted to what we are. It is the unfolding and the consistency in our words and actions that create a curiosity in our friends and loved ones.

Creating and maintaining a supportive community also actively seeking their own awareness is so important, because there are times when we will navigate off course. Seeking approval outside of your own understanding is a futile and painful experience. Over time, the authenticity of your heart will allow for others to come to you. It is your *being*, not what you are *saying*, that will encourage others to discover the truth of who they are. It is natural to want to share our new awareness with those we love. They may be unwilling to hear us or we may have to make our own amends to foster new levels of possibility and goodwill. Treasure and trust in your newfound love affair with your own expanded awareness to open the possibilities in your life.

Creating a new network of healthy relationships with friends who are also committed to discovering and living their own truth is how you give yourself support and permission to make whatever necessary changes your heart is calling you to make. Regardless of the individual support you have, or don't have from your partner, your trusted accountability partners can support you by supporting role-play models and dialogues that help you maintain your new modes of being and relating. Co-creating peaceful conversations to have with the most difficult of relationships in your life, completing your responsibility to your relationships where you have hurt others on your way to deepening your own experience to love is the gift that community will provide you.

Today, there is a conditioned tendency to put too much responsibility on your partner to meet your needs. When you make your own internal shift of understanding that there are a myriad of ways to meet your needs, this opens up the space to allows for the relationship to adjust. The sense of freedom and autonomy you gain works to free you from traditional patterns of codependency, love addiction, and the roles that keep you attached to a finite belief system that believes there is only one way, or one person, or relationship, that can meet the deepest needs of your heart. To be known, to be heard, to contribute, to know we matter, these needs can be met in so many healthy and fulfilling ways. By releasing any constrictions for your natural needs for autonomy and expression, you open and encourage a free exchange of endless co-creative ways to excite possibilities in all those you choose to invite to the party of awareness.

When your partner does express a curiosity, invite them as a powerful ally, and friend, both on the same journey. There is a fine line between being the sage that can create possibilities in the heart of another, where they may be blocked and blinded from seeing truth, and acknowledging that we are all students as well in this journey to becoming more. It is far more moving, motivating and inspiring to have your loved ones see you serving love by aligning your integrity by walking the walk, not talking the talk. Share the movie and the book. Let the same impulse that has birthed through you be the ignition switch for them. Then you can join together in this ever-expanding journey to becoming more. Life gets yummy when we surround ourselves with infinite beings who live as the experienced truth of who they are.

If your partner or friends want to join a community of support together, here are some basics to get them to a place where they are ready to take the quantum leap for themselves:

The Basics for Better Understanding:
1. Creating the Gap using FreezeFrame™ Technique

2. Basic understanding of only two emotions: love or fear

3. The Language of Compassion, O-F-N-R model

4. Open the freedom and power in your relationships to say "no." Share with them how to say "no" without cutting off the flow of connection between you, until they can authentically offer a resounding "yes" from their heart

5. Uninstalling and Reinstalling new default truths through the Temporal Tapping Process

6. Thought Monitoring Exercises

7. Subconscious Clearing Exercises daily

8. Encourage your partner and give them permission to fully feel their anger, sharing that anger is nature's catalyst to create the impulse for deep reflection into what is the source of our pain. Direct them to HeartMath Attitude Breathing® page 111, and the Mindfulness Practice #5, Releasing Anger Peacefully without Damaging Relationships, page 148.

WITHDRAWING FROM PAIN CAUSES SUFFERING

Relationships of every kind are essential for personal growth. By learning to recognize the gifts that emotional triggers provide, we can find freedom from the false core beliefs that block us from experiencing the ecstasy of deep intimacy and connection—that relationships are designed to provide.

When we pull away or see the other person as the "cause" of our pain in the relationship, we cut off the flow of intimate connection, creating destructive and toxic patterns of communicating and relating between ourselves and others that create all feelings of separation and suffering. In essence, there are many ways we kill others off when we cut off our connection with them. Withdrawing from love and connection is a passive act of violence. There are many forms of passive violence that lead to all acts of physical violence. While this form of passive violence may be insidious, we must not underestimate the damage, emotional pain and suffering we impose when we say through our withdrawal and silence, in fact, bleep you. When you understand that all feelings of conflict and separation are simply opposing needs seeking completion, it can help you re-write your own withdrawal patterns to see a new possibility of your own victory and growth. By communicating your actions that have co-created these feelings of pain and separation, you uplevel your relationships on every level. Requesting a time to reconvene and taking time out in healthy ways, that maintain connection, to spend time in your heart to deal with what's alive in you, presents a whole new world of experience and an opportunity of co-creating win-win possibilities that grow more intimacy, respect and love. When we kill each other off with excuses like: "I've been so busy," "I need time away (with no reassurance of reconnection possibility)," slamming the door or leaving the house without any reassurance of when the possibility to connect may occur, these slight or more in your face forms of bleep you are at the heart of the long-term damage that withdrawing our love causes in our ability to experience deep connection and intimacy. Authentic love never places conditions or withdraws. Any form of withdrawing ourselves from another places conditions on love and is a powerful display of control that is an insidious way we violently kill each other off by withdrawing our love. In the end, we really kill ourselves, because we can never really "disconnect" from own consciousness. You deny yourself your own growth to learn, forgive and heal.

Because of core wounds from childhood, many have established a pattern of withdrawing too quickly from painful reactions. This is destructive and damaging to your body systems and relationships. Not only because it releases many forms of toxic neurochemicals into your body system, but it is also detrimental to your own growth and to the experience of authentic love as a human. Shutting down, through withdrawing, blocks your capacity to acknowledge the symptom of pain as the gift that guides you to your direct path to healing the core wound that the trigger and reaction provides you. It is through the conscious choice of using a mindful process of clearing that, by design, allows the "trigger" to be the gift and access point to find the point of creation source when you locked a limiting belief into your being. Without the reflection of our most intimate relationships, how could we heal and clear the runway to live empowered to the experience of deepening love in our lives? Learning to listen, and embracing these painful triggers as opportunities, rather than blaming the person or circumstance as being the "source" or "cause" of your suffering will deepen your capacity to be present with "what is," trusting the experience to guide you inward to release the limiting beliefs that are cutting you off from the full experience of what being human is all about—to return to the reflective One experience of true intimacy and love.

Freedom, and the experience of deep and connected relationships, comes in the moment you choose trust and intimacy to accept and relax into the painful feeling, rather than deny, resist or withdraw from the feeling. This gives rise to something larger than the tape recorder's subconscious limitations of fear-based patterns and cycles of relating that were modeled from your role models, environment and from your early childhood core traumas. By relaxing into the gift of all emotions, your natural intelligence provides you with an invitation to learn how to move through the feeling, to expand your consciousness from the limitations holding you back from experiencing true love and real intimacy. This wisdom within you, if you learn to listen, will naturally teach you how to breathe, will naturally allow for the blocked emotion to move through your body— to notice what's alive within you and expand your capacity to see things that you were not able to see, even a moment before, when you were locked in the fear-based conditioned cycle of withdrawal, judgment, victimization and suffering.

By trusting the wisdom within you, you allow your natural intelligence to unlock the negative and dense energy stored in your emotional body that slowly depletes your mind/body/heart system of the capacity to experience and share ecstasy and deep love. It is because of this withdrawal and separation from yourself—your truth—and your relationship that all feelings of being alone, feelings of pain and suffering, and feelings of being separate exist. We can never separate ourselves from our experience. It is the gift of our triggers that leads us to the doorway of our greatest healing, and connection to deep intimacy and freedom.

Love doesn't withdraw from anything—love is intimate and connected with all feelings. Love trusts and honors our feelings to be the reflective mirror to one another which teaches us that which we most need to learn. We are wired with an intrinsic capacity to experience and handle every emotion we are facing, including deep pain, which moves you closer to understanding what the emotion is telling you. We can then trace where it is locked in our emotional body, discover its origin, then release the false embedded beliefs to open and allow for our heart and consciousness to expand its capacity to love, to forgive, to return to the experience of deep intimacy and connection, empowering you and the relationship to uplevel greatly beyond what you knew just a moment before.

Breathe through the emotions that rise up in you, and you will discover an opening that allows the pain, grief, sorrow and feelings of being alone to dissolve and dissipate, opening your heart to see a new possibility, making this painful experience worth the journey into your reactions, created from the stimulus that our most intimate relationships provide. This allows you to uninstall the negative attitude or false belief about yourself and install it with a more healthy and regenerative attitude and belief, one more aligned to your highest truth of who you are, fostering your capacity to experience a deeper intimacy within all of your relationships. See the FreezeFrame™ Technique on page 92, the Attitude Breathing Technique on page 111, or the Mindfulness Practice,s 2, 3 or 5, in Chapter IV, beginning on page 127.

Nature wired us to shut down emotionally when our body systems have truly been put in shock, like being hit by a car, or attacked in life threatening ways. Shutting off your feelings and emotions is your natural survival response to run away from the pain to stop it, when it feels extreme. When you have been emotionally or physically attacked and abused in your youth, or watched caretakers be abused, even if wasn't a verbal exchange, but an energetic attack by someone withdrawing love or nurture, these false installed "truths" like: "love isn't safe," "I'm not worthy," "I can not trust those who love me," "he/she will cheat on me," and other false installed beliefs will continue to play out as viruses in the relationships of your life until you locate and release the original point of creation trauma, and will cause detrimental consequences to yourself and to your loved ones. Being on the receiving end of how painful it is to have love or nurture withdrawn, or energetically observing how impacted a significant role model was from experiencing love being withdrawn means you could also likely find yourself repeating the same unhealthy and sabotaging forms of withdrawal patterns that block the experience of real intimacy and growth that relationship triggers provide. Withdrawing denies you and the relationship the opportunity to listen to what the pain is telling each one of you, so you can grow from the lesson. As you learn to relax into each feeling, you will find an opening of heart where the suffering and feelings of being alone will dissipate into an acceptance and allowance of what is that supports the feeling of deep reverence for the gift of healing that the pain brought to us. Once you release the fear, driving the limiting core beliefs and move through the emotions, from this place, you can tap into something larger than your current experience. Each time you choose to inquire into the pain, you will find a much deeper place within you, where your "all knowing" intrinsic wisdom gives you the capacity to see with your conscious wisdom where the original core trauma occurred, how the pattern and cycle is playing out in your life, practice releasing judgment and forgiveness, and open the heartspace that reconnects you and establishes deep intimacy and connection. The result is a deeper connection of compassion within, which naturally reflects compassion and love into the relationship itself.

It is from this place of forgiveness and inward reflection that we heal, grow and find our compassionate true nature; first, with ourselves, and then with others in our relationships who have triggered what we believed was the source of our suffering and pain.

Our most triggered relationships, where we love the deepest and experience the most joy, and are the most vulnerable, are also the same relationships that can be the source of our greatest pain and healing. Being aware of this truth allows you the understanding, and trust, to not run from, but rather extend gratitude and lean into the reflective gift that these relationships bring up within us, calling forth the light required to see our own blindspots and destructive and limiting relating patterns that have lied buried within, that are now bubbling up through our consciousness to clear and heal. This is the master's key to understanding the gateway to your grandest experiences of love.

When someone has been deeply hurt by our actions, it is important to remember to listen to the unmet needs crying out behind the appearance of judgment, rage, or expression of pain. The reciprocal grace that we also ask for when we have been hurt, is what frees the hearts to dance in the gift that our righteous anger calls up when we've been hurt by the actions of another.

Everyday, in some way, either through thought or deed, we create acts of passive violence towards ourselves or another. We must tend to our gardens by watering the seeds of love within us, and with our loved ones, to not allow the seeds of resentment to infest the roots of our hearts and relationships.

We all do not know what we do not know, until we do. For our creation consciousness to expand, to know itself as it is—love—it must add to its experiences through the mirror of relationships. It is from this place that relationships offer us the pre-sent gift of opportunity to heal and grow.

The truth is that all relationships are a gift and path to our own freedom.

> *"We assume that violence is only in the physical form, that as long as we don't fight and kill people we are basically nonviolent. Grandfather said we have created a whole culture of violence, which is so deeply rooted it has taken over every aspect of human life. Our language, relationships, behavior-in fact, everything about us—To bring your body and mind into a place of harmony and to fully embrace, observe, and process the emotions that reside within us is what this journey of being human is all about."*
> —ARUN GANDHI, GRANDSON OF MAHATMA GANDHI

CREATING AN OPEN SPACE TO RECEIVE/GIVE

Picture a glass that is full to the brim with water. What happens when we try to add more water into it? There is a wonderful reservoir that can be created to receive and give when we check in to see if the heartspace is open to receive or give. However, trying to add even a drop to an already full container is futile.

It is mission critical to the experience of co-creating deep connection and intimacy in our lives that we learn to check in to see if the heartspace of our loved one is open and ready for the possibility of sharing our heart needs in a way that our need to be heard is ready to be received. Also, in reciprocity, when we are being asked to listen, it is important to check in to see if we have the capacity, in that moment, to offer our gift of full presence to deeply listen to the needs of our loved one. We have been conditioned to dump our thoughts and needs onto the table of our relationships, without checking in to see if their cup is overflowing. Also, we have been conditioned into the believing we "have to" or "should" listen just because someone wants to share what's alive in them. To participate in a subjugative or oppressed role of our pseudo presence, we deny one another the healing power that our true presence can offer to learn and enrich one another's life. Requesting from one another the time to open and prepare our heartspace is a gift we give, and receive, when we don't use time as an excuse, avoidance, or as a means to control through withdrawal.

Dear One, I want to share, do you have an open heart to hear is a powerful question? Staying connected to expressing your request for your loved one's heart, providing reassurance to each other of your desire to connect, even if it is not in that moment, agreeing on a time when the heartspace is open to the possibility to hear what is alive within us, is an act of love. This is how to co-create powerful relationships that honor our mutual needs for autonomy and freedom, that also deeply acknowledges, values and fosters building dynamic co-creative relationships of profound communion and shared intimacy that honors and builds trusts that our needs to be valued and heard do matter.

Learning to exercise the gift of compassion and true connection is what will open up a powerful trust that everything we need to share can be heard when the heartspace environment has been opened to freely give and receive.

CAREFRONTATIONS

All relationships are designed to provide perfect mirrors that help us see areas where we are blind or asleep. Operating in the understanding, "We do not know what we do not know, until we do," can help us come from a place of compassion to our relationships embracing mutual respect and love to speak our truth of how someone's actions have affected us, without judgment or criticism. When we choose empathy, we support our innate reciprocity, because we too would also want someone to tread gently on our hearts when we are sharing areas wherein we may be vulnerable, asleep, or harboring life-alienating beliefs or reactive patterns formed from childhood wounds. When we are triggered and react, these reaction patterns actually can cause suffering in others, damaging the mutual needs of respect, trust and goodwill in our relationships, through our actions.

All relationships are co-created. Thriving and trusting relationships don't just happen, they are a choice. You now have everything you need to engage the powerful internal language tools from the Language of Compassion, to openly inquire into the needs, met and unmet, that will uplevel your capacity to build trust, integrity, transparency, greater intimacy and deeper connection in all your relationships.

The single most damaging act that causes feelings of heart separation, divorce, conflict, and war within, is when we recognize an action where we have been hurt by another's choices and feel the "ouch" or stick of it (remember it's the lie), yet deny ourselves and the relationship growth because we ignore needs not being met by actions within ourselves. When you drop down into your heart courage to choose love for yourself to speak to that need, in truth and transparency, you will build dynamic and intimate relationships as well as quickly discover other relationships that thwart co-creating your life-living reality of relationships filled with authentic intimacy and love.

We have a conditioned tendency to ignore grievances and small actions (maybe even larger actions), that cause our hearts to grow, over time, hardened toward another person. When we do this, eventually our mind forms stories that cause suffering and feelings of separation that play out into (from within) our relationships that co-create the reality of life. Even worse, because we feel hurt, we may gossip to others about this person before sharing our unmet needs with the only person who can make a difference, that person, thus denying our relationship the chance to uplevel from our truth. From there, you embed stories in your mind that support your choice to separate from that heart, which can begin a mindset that justifies acting out in strategies to meet needs that are damaging in an active form of passive violence, which will destroy the goodwill and trust of that relationship.

This is what we must avoid if we are to live with the pro-active choice of living love over fear. We can always choose to drop down into the courage that comes from within – the wisdom center that connects us at our heart. It is mission critical for experiencing authentic love to live aligned in word and action; to build powerful relationships that honor and love ourselves enough to speak to areas where we have been triggered and/or hurt by another's actions and also acknowledge and be grateful when our loved ones expose an area where we have been blind.

Most of us have been conditioned by being shamed, guilted, feeling the loss of someone withdrawing their love when we tried to share our heart feelings of truth. Somewhere along the way, through childhood subconscious conditioning, we learned to deny our feelings and needs, which created a fracture within us and the false truth that it is not safe to share or selfish to speak to our feelings and needs. This began a series of sabotaging belief mindsets that separates us all from the very thing we yearn for—to experience the celebration of authentic love. The magical elixir to attaining this lies in learning to speak your truth, thereby co-creating trusting, intimate, dynamic and deeply connected yummy relationships.

Once it is understood that we may be the trigger, we can learn to listen from our heart to see if we may be experiencing a projection from the other person. However, if you find that another's offering causes you to trigger, thank them for providing a gift, because quite likely, this is an area where you are asleep and carry a deep core wound or false "truth" that is creating conflict, division, and denying you the experience of authentic love in your life.

Prepare your heart by turning inward to understand what needs are not being met by another's choices. Check in to see if the other is open to receive your heart, and if so, bravely love yourself and bring your heart truth to the table in your relationships. If the receiving end is unwilling to open their heart to co-create a powerful win-win possibility where everyone's needs can be heard, matter, and mutually valued and respected, it may be time to redefine the role that relationship plays in your life.

Always give thanks for someone having the courage to speak from their heart. You do not have to own their words. Try them on, take their words into silent reflection, asking wisdom to show you the truth of areas where you may be blind and causing suffering in your relationships, sabotaging both yourself and your relationship from growth.

Remember, you co-create your reality. If you want a thriving and powerful life, choose relationships that also share in the commitment of seeking truth, above fear, by living in the infinite possibility that comes from the trust that everyone's needs do matter, are to be valued, and deeply held in love, with the heart of compassion and care.

You can always be right, but you may be alone.

THE DANGER OF GOSSIP

Gossip is one of the most damaging, oppressive, and divisive acts of passive violence. There's a story about a man who went to an elder and said, "I have hurt someone that I care about deeply by speaking poorly about them, how can I fix it?" The elder replied, "Today, go take a down pillow, open it and shake it out in the park and return to me tomorrow." Upon returning the next day, the elder said, "Now, go back to the park and retrieve the feathers from the pillow."

Because we are energy beings and our mind doesn't know if something is actually happening or not, when we run the same experience again in our thoughts in an area we feel grieved, hurt, or wronged by the actions of another, our entire physiological/psychological mind/body/heart system responds as if the event was happening again, further embedding that energy pattern and false belief deeper into our hearts, causing more feelings of separation. The only person that can heal your heart is you – through your own reflective work and then by sharing your truth with the person whom has caused suffering to your heart through their actions.

When you feel the ouch, trust the gift of hurt and pain and open your heart to inquiry. You will often be led to the core wound so you can apply one of the clearing techniques presented throughout *The Way 2 The Truth, the Journey Within* to allow you to uninstall the false "truth" of belief and reinstall your new truths aligned to your grandest and highest thought and belief about who you are.

Remember, you can never take back the damage that is done in one moment of trigger or as a result of the "feathers" of gossip. To empower and build thriving relationships, choose the courage that comes from the heart to stay grounded and connected to the truth that lies within your heart, and choose love through mutual respect and trust that the other person also "does not know what they do not know." It is only through this reflective gift that relationships bring the ability to offer our truths to one another. Each of our relationships must be given the chance to uplevel into something more than it was one moment before.

Life is made up of moments. Each moment we each have the opportunity to choose love and to become more than we were just one moment before. Therefore, every relationship is a gift to become aligned to live the truth of who and why we're here...

BEYOND FORGIVENESS & ATONEMENT

If we see that life is nothing less, and everything more, then an expression of experience seeking its highest form, through the mirror of our relationships; a spiral, never ending process of becoming, than forgiveness and atonement (at-one-ment) can become a lifetime practice that expands the infinite possibilities of freely releasing the debt, knowing where we've been a victim, we have also been a perpetrator. In exchange for this release, we experience the freedom, and intimacy, within ourselves that we so yearn for within the reflection of our relationships.

The act and choice of forgiveness does not mean that we condone an action that has caused us pain. Forgiveness is a process. Realizing that all acts of forgiveness are acts of self-forgiveness opens up a new possibility and freedom within the imprisoned heart that unforgiveness creates within us.

Learning to share our truth and experience of how another's choices have impacted us, or listen with our heart to how our actions have caused suffering to others, without making someone "wrong," in love, rather than judgment or fear, by using the skills in the Language of Compassion chapter, is how we empower our lives and relationships to become more wonderful, connected and meaningful.

Dr. Arun Gandhi, grandson of Mahatma Gandhi spent eighteen months under the tutelage of his grandfather as a twelve-year-old boy. During his summer with his grandfather, a profound lesson his grandfather taught him about the two sides of violence, passive and physical violence, forever changed the life of his young grandson. It was then that he decided to follow in his grandfather's footsteps and dedicate his life to teaching the principles of non-violence.

His daily lesson, as a way of introspection, was to build a genealogical tree of non-violence with two branches, physical and passive violence. Everyday he was asked to analyze all of the events of the day and see his own actions of violence. He was instructed to put his actions on a card and to place his cards on the tree, where his passive or physical acts matched his action. After a few months, he had filled up an entire wall with lists of acts of both passive and physical violence.

It was then that Gandhi linked the lesson of truth to his grandson's heart—that everyday we commit acts of passive violence, consciously and unconsciously. This causes righteous anger in the receiver (victim) of our actions, who may resort to physical violence to get revenge (an eye for an eye tribal mindset), or to get justice, or choose more passive acts of judgment, power-over, resentment, rebellion, withdrawal, and so on. All of these forms of violence cause suffering to the heart and are the root of all suffering to the human collective heart of love. Arun learned that passive violence is the fuel that ignites physical violence and that, within us, we each have the power to ignite or cut off the fuel supply.

Physical violence is easy to define: it is all acts of violence in which physical force is used. From slapping, to beating, violent acts of murder and rape, killings and war, and so on.

Passive violence is more insidious and often unnoticed, but nonetheless, is the perpetrator of division and root cause of some of the most atrocious forms of emotional abuse and disconnection. This permeates the cell walls of our homes, our business, our global inter-exchange of power-over systems today. Its actions, whether being on the giving or receiving end, simply put, causes anguish, pain, or emotional injury, and contributes to another's pain and unhappiness. Its footprint on the heart treads look like this: it could be mumbling anger under your breath at a loved one, slamming doors, demanding compliance through passive forms of punishment and withdrawing love, withdrawing sex, to wasting global resources such as food, overconsuming, judgment, discrimination, name-calling, disparaging self-esteem of another, teasing, or oppression, and so on.

The tree of violence below serves as a powerful word picture of how consciously and unconsciously we can both be a victim or perpetrator of a violent act, either passively or physically.

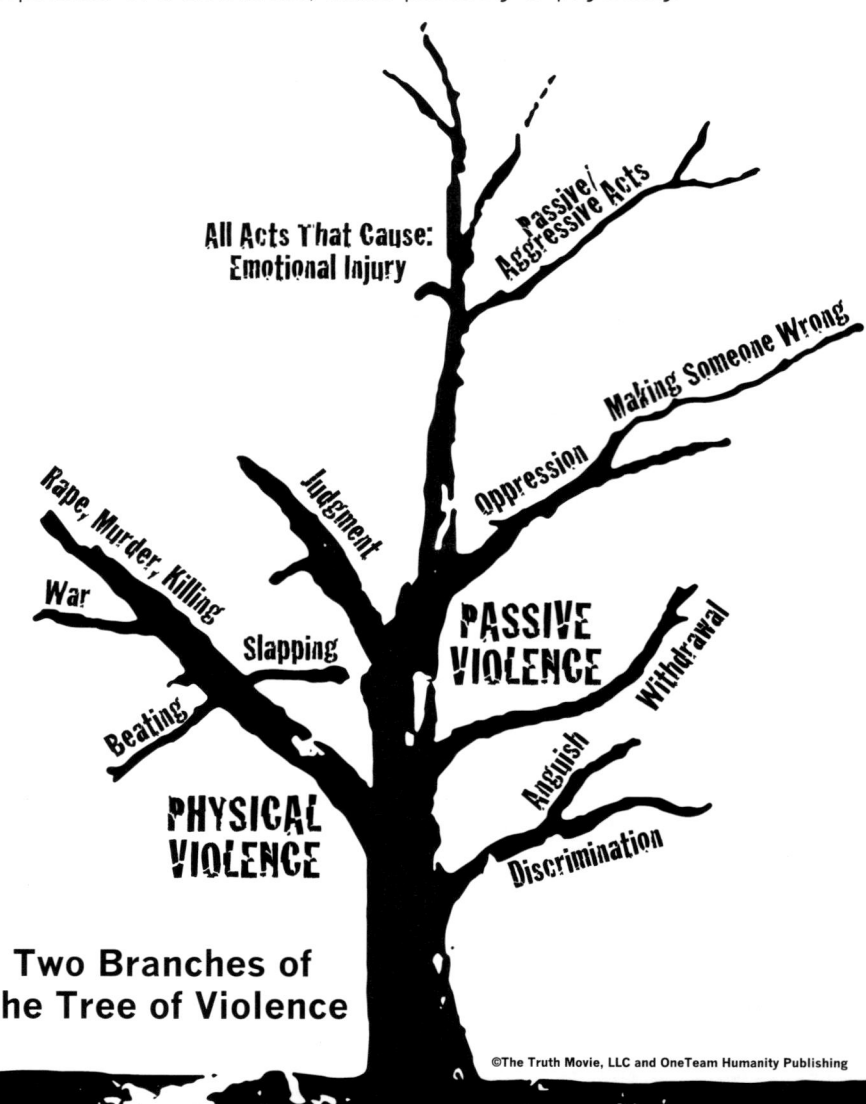

There is a famous quote by Nelson Mandela about forgiveness and resentment, "Resentment is like drinking poison and then hoping it will kill your enemies."

By now you understand that we live in a participatory and reflective world. If we are harboring resentment, trust issues, jealousy, judgment and unforgiveness, and other feelings that disconnect us from establishing deeply connected and intimate relationships, we are only blocking the flow of our own needs for connection, for the experience of intimacy and true love, of trust, to be forgiven, to know we matter, to be heard, and so on.

Compassion is a high form of love—an act that acknowledges that we all do not know what we do not know, until we do. Compassion grows from seeing oneself in another. It provides for an act of understanding when there is no understanding.

Forgiveness and atoning—making amends—for our choices and actions is what we also want the hands of grace to provide for us when we have been the perpetrator of hurting another from our own actions. This is how we learn and grow in our journey to becoming more. Life, through the mirror of our relationships, is how we discover who we are and who we are not. Only through accepting this truth, can we stay committed to trust that it is through our relationships that we learn to truly tap into the bliss and orgasmic ecstasy of what this journey of life is for—to experience love; to give and receive our highest expression of what we know in that moment, until someone or something opens up an awareness, by bringing their joy or pain to us, and then we know more, if we choose to listen, of what new understanding will expand our infinite ability to be love. Be kind with your heart, and the heart of another, for your heart is also a reflection of your divine beloved starring back at you.

You see, forgiveness and atonement are two sides of the same coin and can wash away the tarnish from the mingled tears of two hearts connecting in a pro-active choice of authenticity, of forgiveness, yielding the shining gift of giving and receiving unconditional non-judgment and love.

Not acknowledging your own culpability and co-creation denies you the experience of love, inner peace, connection, and true healing. If you make the other wrong and refuse to face the reality of your own co-creation and actions in hurting a heart and soul, you remain in denial and blinded to the possibility of restoration. On a more societal plane, we are each a single thread that together weave the fabric of our collective consciousness. Is our own complacency to not deeply examine our own hearts in relationships, and our actions, not contributing to having grown a culture of violence that does not accept response-ability for the systems that have perpetuated only looking at the end act, rather than opening our hearts to examining the systems that have created war, separation and greed that is the root cause of a society that reacts vs. reflects.

Forgiveness is an act that opens up the hearts to new possibilities for the fullest experience of love to express itself.

In the work of forgiveness, we are often not taught how to give or receive the unconditional healing gift of atonement—a gift where both the giver and receiver are healed by its heart of grace.

Webster defines atonement: satisfaction or reparation for a wrong or injury; amends. When our actions, conscious or unconsciously have caused the division of two hearts, atonement can allow for the debt to be satisfied in an irreducibly interconnected world, woven together by hearts, it is energy of exchange that unlocks the freedom to love "all in."

The essence of true love is an unconditional act that holds no judgment or belief of right/wrong, good/bad, and operates in the freedom to choose.

The internal shift of heart is the single most important healer of the self, the self perpetrator; and the self, the receiver of an act of violence, whether in physical or passive forms, we have been on both sides.

Holding anger in the form of resentment is re-sensing and re-feeling the division that keeps us imprisoned in a cycle of pain, disconnection, isolation and suffering.

The life skills provided throughout this work contribute to a way of being in the world that breaks the perpetuated cycles of violence within our own hearts to live aligned in the truth of "being the change we wish to see in the world."

One can always ask, which came first our culture of violence, our culture of materialism, or the tribal mindset of the grass is greener syndrome? Our current power-over systems of relating, seeking to control through fear, is the beginning roots of the inner conflict and incongruence we become as we attempt to live life in inner conflict of our core truth. Fear is the root cause of the greed, judgment, and all systems that seek an eye for an eye restitution mentality vs. authentic restoration and forgiveness, further perpetuating hatred, division and war. All of this is due to the tragic unawareness that this is simply because we have created systems which deny the truth of our irreducibly interconnected core connection to our Universal Common Needs for mutual respect that every heart and that every life matters. Of most importance, our healing individually, and collectively, begins when we offer our sincere presence to listen to a heart that has a need and mutually seek understanding and connection above the illusions of separation.

Pure love, the truth of who we are, evokes a smiling heart of willingness, positive thoughts and feelings, mutual respect, seeks understanding in the form of compassion and forgiveness, and when exercised, uplevels our relationships by authentically sharing in the mutual exchange of what is alive within us. Because we all are co-creating our experience to reality in every moment, are on this same journey to becoming more, we're wired and possess the capacity to pro-actively experience co-creating love within our lives; we each can, in our own way, moment-to-moment, choose love.

Like the good wolf story, the choice is always yours to set your heart focus on what feeds love.

Relationships shine the light of reflection into the blindspots that we can not see. When we are blind and in the dark, if we can't see a wall in front of us, we can fall or bruise ourselves, or others. Our relationships help us to see what we can not see.

Byron Katie shares in the *The Truth* film, "How loud does that person have to get before I realize that's an area where I'm asleep?"

An integral part of living a life filled with intimacy, deep connection, and meaning, that honors and reveres the gift that every relationship provides you requires a courageous and open heart to inquiry into areas where you have fallen asleep? Seeking or releasing the debt that forgiveness provides, and to then offer your open heart by seeking amends where we have caused emotional pain in the heart of another is why we are here and what makes the journey matter.

May the gift that righteous anger brings into our awareness the awakening of our deepest truth, give us the courage to speak, to heal, and restore our relationships to one another; to co-create something deeper and more meaningful than just one moment before. May our choice to be the change we wish to see in the world also act as the wildfire to spread the gift of compassion, to end the injustice of living in power-over systems of both sides of violence, and relating in ways of being that knows not what it has done, until it does. The magnitude of damage and carnage is evident, while the source roots may be untraceable on an external plane, the answer—and our freedom lies within our own reflection to see how these roots have invaded our own lives within, so we can restore the experience and imprisonment of living as a divided heart.

When you finally "get" that there is only one heart and one creation source of consciousness that feeds the truth; you "get" that there is no where to run from the chaos. You have everything tool you'll need, within you, to be set free and return to love.

If you seek the experience of living a deep and richly meaningful life you must choose love, to seek equitable solutions in your relationships, and in our society; to co-create a thriving world that works for all.

It is not enough to know a principle of truth. We each possess the capacity to re-organize our minds into expanded levels of creation source consciousness, to create enough entropy within, oftentimes through pain, to create a bifurcation point in your neural pathways which uninstalls your limited beliefs, tribal mindsets, and cycles of conditioned violence and unforgiveness—to re-member and install new somatic markers of beliefs that empower you to live aligned to the truth and core of who you are as your kindest interconnected heart.

What will matter as you look back on this journey called life, as we will each face the imminent ending of this body, is how many moments were spent in the inquiry of open examination of your own heart? To co-create a richly meaningful life requires daily seeking your inner wisdom that knows what contributes to making life more wonderful for one another, and to apply your heart's wisdom, discovered only through quiet times of reflection and silence, to awaken the life living experience of reality as a powerful co-creator of life as love.

We fear death because we are forced to look back in the rear view mirrors and see that perhaps we have not experienced a living experience of reality that was deeply connected and lived aligned to what truly matters—who we love and who reflected that love back to us. The journey begins to authentically embracing and co-creating a meaningful life when we authentically seek the truth of who and what we truly are—and honor one another by celebrating our irreducibly interconnected one heart of conscious love seeking itself through our mirrored reflection.

Soon, one-person-by-one-person, one-heart-by-one-heart, one-relationship-by-one-relationship, we will become a critical mass of consciousness that truly lives aligned to living the experience and truth of who we are.

WHEN TO SAY GOOD-BYE

Awakening to your awareness can mean that the closet full of old and comfortable relationships, even love-relationships just do not fit you anymore. It is a powerful and deeply personal choice to move from complacency and comfort to choose the uncharted territory of the unknown. When you have expressed your commitment to live your truth, and given the relationship "sufficient" time to uplevel, which only your heart will know, being comfortably sized with someone is never sufficient reason to stay.

Remember, like attracts like. Life is an ever-evolving journey which is constantly adjusting and changing. In order to experience life in full-throttle living, to experience the infinite truth of who you are, you must be willing to let go of any attachments, beliefs, and people who are constricting your life due to their own limitations and unwillingness to experience life in the infinite possibility that it is.

In the Bible, Matthew 10:14 shares: "If anyone will not welcome you or listen to your words, shake the dust off your feet when you leave that home or town." In my own journey as I confronted difficult decisions in my marriage, I read two amazing books that prompted me to reach out directly to the author, Terrance Real, to gain some additional wisdom. His two paradigm shifting books, *How Can I Get Through To You* and *I Don't Want To Talk About It*, deal straight on truth. Terrance Real is known as an authority on marriage and referred to as one of the top leading marriage "fix it men." Terry shared his wisdom with me which is drawn from his life's work (paraphrased), "I've learned through years of counseling couples, I can know someone for 5 minutes or 5 years, but the minute I challenge their actions and behaviors, calling them accountable, I'll know immediately if they are or not willing to turn inward and do the tough work to look at their own destructive and damaging actions of relating. How will I know? Because if they are not willing to look inward to see the gift that the reflective mirrors of relationships provide, they'll bolt. They will refuse to see their own co-creation in the disconnection. They will make the other person wrong and withdraw from the gift, and lessons, that all relationships are designed to provide. I'll immediately know if there is any point for someone to stay. So I have learned to observe the relationship and speak the truth of my awareness." He goes on to counsel me by sharing, "You'll know when you'll know and I think you already know (and I did)."

Sadly, I too had become a victim of my own conditioning that had me seeking answers outside of myself to know what I already knew for sometime was true for me. Through much inward inquiry, I was able to see that I was locked into a false belief system, handed down to me through my religious beliefs and conditioning, I was locked in a finite belief that I wasn't free to leave my marriage unless my husband had died or committed adultery. Trying to do what I thought I was suppose to "do" to honor my vows and be a "good" wife, I use to literally pray for my husband to commit adultery or die, imprisoning and enabling unhealthy and destructive patterns of relating that kept us both locked into destructive cycles that denied us the experience that redefining our relationship provided individually. When we stay locked into these falsehoods and tribal mindsets of fear-based thoughts of being judged by our families, our society and peers, can we not see that staying for any reason in unhealthy relationships where one party refuses to turn inward for open examination, we perpetuate these unhealthy patterns of modeling to our children, and each generation, until we don't? **If any relationship is no longer serving love, then it isn't serving life.** We've all been so very conditioned to seek answers outside of ourselves. From the time we're children we see our parents, then our teachers, as having the "answer." This conditioned pattern is not where authentic wisdom lies! As you begin to reshape your fundamental understandings of why relationships come into and out of our lives, you will see the gift that each relationship brings to you. When you open your awareness to accept the irreducible truth that we are all interconnected and therefore really never say "good-bye," you no longer stay attached to the "role" and can redefine your relationships. Each relationship you encounter in life becomes an integral part of you, so you can grow your inner trust and awareness that unless a relationship is serving an ever-expanding version of the best version of who you are and are committed to becoming, then it isn't serving love. Rather, that relationship is holding you imprisoned to your own complacency, fears, and conditioned beliefs. Within you is your own perfect teacher and sage. No one lives the inner-dynamics of your relationships and no counselor, guru, or life coach, can possibly understand the Universe of all the unspoken body languages, spiritual lessons that are accessible through your own intrinsic wisdom, that when you quiet yourself to ask and confront the tough questions, that only your heart knows the answers to.

As you embrace your irreducible interconnectedness to others, you yield into a growing inner trust of awareness that all relationships are a gift to help you become more. In doing so, you can find a deeper sense of compassion for loved ones who are not yet ready to step into their own journey. Saying good-bye to the "role" you've played in that relationship opens the door for new patterns of relating with that person. It also opens you to the infinite possibilities of experiencing powerful new relationships that are more kindred to your own level of awareness to support you in your own becoming the truth of who you were created to be. Your choice to redefine your relationship may be just the catalyst they need to begin their own inward reflective journey.

We all share the same truth: in this body we all have only one life to live. Staying in a relationship that is resistant, dead, or stagnant imprisons you. Stepping into your power and truth allows you to embrace the uncharted waters of co-creating a mutual dynamic energy exchange that empowers and welcomes the fullest expression of authentically living and celebrating with others your truth is not really living at all. Relationships are our gift. They are designed to allow for an ever-yielding field of expansion. They are designed to co-create an on-going exponential growth of authentic relating, deepening intimacy and celebrating your highest truth of what makes life magical and more wonderful.

CUTTING CORDS OF CONNECTION IS CRITICAL STEP TO MOVING ON

When we say goodbye, sometimes long after a relationship has ended, as both parties are moving on and redefining the role we've played to one another, do you ever still felt connected to that person's energy or stuck in repetitive thoughts about that person?

This energetic connection is real and more than just the emotional ties and our body's need to break the physiological/psychological cellular habits of that connection that come from the natural grieving of letting go of the unlived dreams, hopes, and visions we shared together that only time can heal.

Quantum science confirms that we are all interconnected. There are energetic cords—the transfer of etheric and astral energy co-created between two people that are connected and attaching us. We can see this now on sophisticated GDV cameras and other neuroscientific measuring devices. Cords can be both positive and negative, and develop between anyone you've shared a strong connection and energetic exchange with—a lover, a friend, your pets, your parents.

A positive cord, for example, transfers loving energy and feelings of warmth, wrapping you in a blanket of support and love even if you're on opposite sides of the world or dimensional planes.

However, in the case where you had a highly charged sexual or emotional exchange, or experienced a life-alienating and toxic relationship, which is really a warp speed gift to heal some deep core wounds, it is detrimental to attracting any new relationship and moving on to clear your energetic heart field that is still connected and sending or receiving energy after the relationship has ended.

This exchange of negative energy subconsciously drains your energy supply. It is imperative that you dissolve and cut the invisible connection cords of attachment to become fully available to focus on loving yourself and open your heart field to the other infinite possibilities to create new cords with new lovers and friends.

The surest way to your healing is to cut the cords that are clogging up your heart field from a relationship that is not serving the highest good, whether it is with a friend or a lover.

Here's the cord-cutting steps:

1. See the other person in front of you, standing a couple of feet away from you.

2. See one or more cords of energy connecting you at your core and heart. Picture a sword, raise the mighty sword and with intention and strength cut the cord three times.

You may find yourself in painful memories or having resistance to cutting the cord. Stop and honor yourself, allowing you to fully grieve the dreams that were unlived, forgiving yourself for your role, returning to gratitude for the many life lessons, and see yourself co-creating that reconnection with yourself and with infinite new possibilities of love to enter your life, which will transfer the energy of connection, help empower you to cut the cords to free yourself to move on from the "unsafe" and "life-negating" relationship.

It is possible that after you have cut the cord, that person will feel the energetic disconnection, and suddenly try to reconnect with you. This does not mean they have done the work and are healthy, or safe, in their being to come back to you. This is a time to exercise your gift of discernment, loving yourself, to look for the accountability through action, not just words. Look for the actions of: authentic acknowledgement, forgiveness and a true desire to make amends; or beware that dancing with the hungry wolves and energy vampires trying to drain your lifeforce blood again could take you back down the rabbit hole of repetitive cycles of pain and suffering.

For the experience of true love and deep intimacy to become the experienced reality of your life, it takes two open and courageous hearts willing to be more, than even a moment before. When you've discovered that treasure which is there for the asking, you've opened the VIP party invitation and have began the dance into the sublime experience of full throttle "all in" living and authentic love.

Love is always a choice...and only operates in the freedom to choose.

VIII
COMMUNITY IS STRONG TECHNOLOGY
THE REASONS AND ESSENTIAL NEED

Competition becomes cooperation when we discover the 'community nature of the self'...
In the new systems worldview, we move from the primacy of pieces to the primacy of the whole, from absolute truths to coherent interpretation, from self to community...
—DR. PETER SENGE

There is more than a verbal tie between the words common, community, and communication...
—JOHN DEWEY

Today, the Internet, with all its technological applications and breakthroughs has literally connected us to one another in ways that no one could have imagined even 15 years ago. Billions of people use the Internet every day. For the first time in history, people from the farthest reaches of the world can meet and connect in mere seconds. Stop and think about it. The fact that we can send messages, receive messages and see each other to carry on conversations in real time even though we're thousands of miles apart, connects us for the first time to the infinite possibilities of interconnecting as a global interconnected family network. Just a few years ago, this possibility would have been considered pure science fiction.

LIFE IN THE DIGITAL AGE

And yet, isn't it surprising to find that it is the subject of pornography that connects 25 percent of total search engine requests and even accounts for 8 percent of total searches taking place in professional workplaces. This has become the foundation of the pornography industry, generating 12 billion dollars in revenue each year in the United States alone[11]. That's more than the combined revenues of professional football, baseball and basketball franchises all together. It is also more than the combined revenues of the major media networks: ABC, CBS, and NBC (6.2 billion). Other primary online activities include playing video games, going onto social media networks like Facebook and Twitter, searching the web, shopping, and paying bills.

In July 2007, The CDC (U.S. Centers for Disease Control and Prevention) released statistics showing adult use of antidepressants nearly tripled between the periods studied 1988-1994 and 1999-2000. The Internet was released in 1983 with most American households going online over the next ten years. Since then, antidepressants have become the most commonly prescribed drugs in the United States. They're prescribed more than drugs to treat high blood pressure, high cholesterol, asthma, or headaches, making medicating unhappiness a multi-billion dollar business. There are millions daily now medicated to treat depression. This numbing out to our authentic truth and feelings is doing little to curb divorce rates, with the average marriage lasting 6.2 years, nor contributing to creating a peaceful world of civil harmony.

These sobering statistics are not expressed to judge or condemn but to show how our choices and behaviors, fueled by our natural fundamental human need to connect, is detrimentally impacting our interconnected lives. There is no drug or external "connection" that can feed your universal needs for community, interdependence, creativity, authenticity, happiness, or peace. Human beings will continue to act out in either consciously healthy or unconsciously unhealthy ways in order to try to satiate an illusion of "connection," when perhaps what we need most is

---

11 Ropelato, Jerry. *Internet Pornography Statistics*, http://internet-filter-review.toptenreviews.com/internet-pornography-statistics.html

the return to our intrinsic, fundamental core needs for authentic touch and connection.

Consider the habits of mind that the very use of the Internet perpetuates. The information you get via Google is free and accessible to all. It can also be a psychological trap, unreliable, a time distraction, and completely void of context. Sure you may regard whatever you read with skepticism, thinking of yourself as discerning by doing so; but what mentality does this foster in you? And what about the voyeuristic aspect of so many of the stories and temptations that pop-up on your internet portal homepages? Are they not meant to entice you, distract and entrap you into reading half-truths about celebrities, people with whom you have no real relationship and lure you into the abyss of marketing "consumerism?" The media keeps bombarding us with these images again and again. Brainwashing us by embedding these images into our minds denying us from the experience of living a reality aligned to the real truth of who we are. In the world of the Internet, nearly everything is objectified and devalued.

FROM YOUR THOUGHTS FLOW THE WELL-SPRINGS OF LIFE...
I once heard a church message about the media and its effects on our lives. "Garbage in, garbage out" was how the pastor surmised it. This simple reminder makes you aware of the choice you have to stop reading or watching anything that feeds fear within you. You will find that as you prune back reading the newspaper, watching television, or your unguarded time on the internet, you will begin to feel more freedom in your days to pursue other activities and relationships that better serve life-affirming choices. This will bring more peace, calm, and happiness into your life. It will also open up more personal time to connect with you, to feed your intrinsic desire to learn and grow! To create a different life, you must create a different choice. The awareness of how important it is to guard the messages and people you allow into your heart, your body, and your mind is one of the greatest life skill tools you will ever know: the gift of discernment. Anyone who has been surfing the Internet knows how easy it is to get sucked into the infinite temptations, and abyss of life-alienating distractions, of candy-store-marketing, consumerism, lust, and gossip, all accessible within the privacy of our "passwords."

Value your heart, your time and value your mind. **If you don't guard your heart, who will?** Consider what you occupy your mind with when you're online. From your thoughts flow the wellsprings of life. What thoughts and messages do these images, stories, and information convey about you? Recent advances in technology allow neuroscientists to scan the brain and see the depth at which media's marketing messages are ferociously embedded into your subconscious mind. Are your choices life-alienating or life-serving? The more time you choose to invest in life-negating activities, the greater your addictions to these behaviors become, spilling into all areas of life: deeply affecting your children, your relationships, your families, and our collective society that continually adopts and perpetuates false identities and illusions via the media of what "authentic" connection and happiness should look like.

Consider what happens to your friendships when you rely on only social media to "speak" to your friends. There is an optical illusion of real connection, but texting, instant messaging and "connecting" online does not allow for much humanness. If you're texting a friend instead of calling him or her, isn't it common to skip the truth about how your day is really going, because authentic dialogue is nearly impossible by such an illusionary and time consuming means of connecting. Is your friend going to have the opportunity to hear the tone of sadness or joy in your voice? Can you hear what really is alive in their world? Reducing communicating to such elementary rudiments loses all texture and nuance. You miss out on your chance to really, meaningfully, connect with your full presence. You really can only gain awareness to the complex array of emotions through the use of all of your senses that we discover only through valuable inter-exchange. You miss the looks, the smiles, the tears. You miss invoking the sense of sound, which carries the energy of what is really alive in your worlds. Sharing authentic laughter has now been reduced to a black and white screen writing, LOL!

Neuroscientists have actually discovered that "multi-tasking," something we wear as a badge of achievement, actually fragments and detracts from our ability for concentration and to build our neurocircuitry to higher levels of memory, focus, and cognitive thinking. Sadly, with today's technology overload, teens are not developing their brain's essential cognitive "blocking" abilities. This is your brain's most powerful capability, which neutralizes distractions, and governs the trillions of synaptic connections vital for expanding your focus to access your higher cognitive learning and intuitive capacities.

Another alarming statistic is that because our children's brains are not fully developed and protected, the cancer causing EMF's (electromagnetic frequencies of radiation), being emitted, which are now hundreds of millions times more than that our grandparents received, from our technological devices are creating eye, brain and other cancers that are already being attributed to the use of the over 1.65 billion cell phones in use today, and is growing in exponential alarming rates. Because of our "unknowingness," we are allowing our children to sleep with their cell phones under their pillows, have their computers near their beds, and carry these EMF cancer causing devices near vital organs. Did you know these same related studies show that one-third of our young girls, ages 18-34, are checking their Facebook account before even going to the bathroom in the morning and that our young adults think that breaking off a relationship via the internet is perfectly okay? Can we consider the possibility of what our governed world will look like if we extrapolate out these disconnected ways of dealing with matters of the heart?

Getting connected to the truth of how disconnected we are?

The overwhelming rising statistics of depression and loneliness, often times difficult to pinpoint the tangible attributable reasons for, suggest that since the invention of our "connected" world there is a dramatic increase and correlation in the quantity and intensity of feelings of isolation that leads to human loneliness, suffering, and ultimately, depression. There are reams of data, evidence, and published research that exemplifies the truth: it is the quality of our connections, not the quantity of our social interactive connections, that fosters our feelings of well-being and happiness.

Are social media sites, that by "face" value seem to be connecting us, actually spreading the very feelings of isolation and loneliness that they appear to be preventing? Is this new societal behavioral pattern actually denying us and interfering with our ability to create authentic "friends" and deep intimacy and connection?[12]

There is a growing body of research and evidence that within our interconnected world of instant messaging and absolute communication, now only bound by our limits of time, we are suffering as a humanity from unprecedented feelings of alienation and separation. As a society, our "interconnected" world has never been more detached, separated and lonely. We intuitively know that loneliness and being alone are not the same thing. All psychological states are not measurable based on external conditions; they are an internal reflection of what is alive and happening within us.[13]

Technology is an amazingly efficient way to send messages to one another and to let people know they're in your thoughts. But as a steady diet of relating, it lacks and denies the very substance that can only be experienced through the deep connections established when we spend heart to heart time exchanging, truly communicating, and creating community with each other. As you learn how to give and receive true empathy and compassion, you deepen the bonds of trust, integrity, and authenticity fed by true connection. Cell-phones and internet devices can never take the place of face-to-face, heart-to-heart real time. Exercise discernment by honestly examining how your usage of any technology is either working to unite you or working towards separating you from your intrinsic need to authentically connect to yourself, to your own truth, and to share your life experiences with the heart of another. Any stimulus you allow into your heart shapes the thoughts, emotions and values that define the character and integrity you bring into the reflections of reality experienced in your relationships.

WHAT IS COMMUNITY? WHY IS IT IMPORTANT?

The great poet John Donne said, "No man is an island." As human beings we all possess a deep, intrinsic desire and need to be connected and feel connected to community and to

---
12 http://mashable.com/2010/07/07/oxygen-facebook-study/
13 http://www.theatlantic.com/magazine/archive/2012/05/is-facebook-making-us-lonely/8930/

one another. Yet, despite our intrinsic needs for expression, for authentic connection, to contribute to one another, to celebrate, to be seen, heard and known, have you allowed your relationships to become fragmented from your intrinsic need to experience deep connection? Do you maintain various friendships by which you get your various needs met, dividing out allotments of time for this friend and for that friend, yet find that your needs for deep connection and to be truly known, and heard, are not being met?

When you're with one friend, you might talk about arts or sports while with another, you might talk about relationships. Whom you decide to spend your time with is then predicated by whatever need you may have and want to have met in the immediate moment. While all of this neat, compartmentalized behavior may appear on the surface as fine, when we lack a sense of belonging to a wider network of supportive people whom really know us, and with whom we can be truly authentic and accepted for, we miss out on the valuable dynamics of interaction present in a vast and diverse world. When you relinquish rigid control and open yourself up to an array of different ways of relating with others, a fluidity, ease and acceptance of others reveals itself to you. You then learn how to really be transparent with others through practice, non-judgment, reflection, and authentic sharing—this is when your relationships take a quantum leap into a co-creative expression of a living reality of life that is deeply connected, genuinely intimate, ecstatic, and loving.

This is a fundamental building component to living your truth. Being committed to working on discovering your truth is what makes this journey amazing. Living your reality and truth means little if you do not learn how to walk, talk, breathe, relate and be your true and authentic Self with others. For it is always the mirror of your relationships that direct you to that which you still need to learn.

Community is the exponential tool that supports your growth. It is through building a solid, life-affirming community network that you can be supported to perfect your inner-potential to become powerful, potent and strongly aligned in your truth, while supporting others in finding their truth. Community can unite our common visions and become an exponential co-creative experience of living a different way that we bring into our larger world in our day-to-day lives.

The people you want to work toward building your community with are those who operate from a positive place and whose visions and goals also support contributing to the new emergent world you are creating within you. Create a diverse community that is blind to profiling by religion, politics, lifestyle, or socio-economic standards but rather for the inclusive greatness that allows for us to expand our understanding about the uniqueness of welcoming all sectors of beliefs. This grows your own capacities of awareness, for patience, developing non-judgment, compassion, and co-creative possibilities to emerge. When casting a wide net with a motley assortment of personalities and specializations, you exponentially increase your own awareness and learning, but also see a world that you might never know existed. You will be forever strengthened by the exponential power and collective voice that deepens your experience to life as the truly one global family we are. You must first see the possibilities to effectively co-create and live a new reality.

Strong communities do not rise automatically but through the commitment of each one of its members striving to serve the highest betterment through its choices. In the strongest of communities, each member can offer support to another by listening and helping our mutual accountability of taming our thoughts and emotional states when we are troubled and need support. In time of pain or crisis, it is your community that helps lighten the load by offering compassion, support, new awareness, accountability, and love.

Community is a network of friendships and relationships whose connections go beyond simply you and them. Community offers you the wisdom of elders and the support of those who have already experienced and overcome struggles or limitations where you may still be growing in awareness. Though it is essential that you do your own work, when you feel weak and tempted to fall back into old patterns and behaviors, community can be there for you and visa versa, to help you stay committed and focused to create your reality as your highest thoughts, dreams, and visions to stay on the path that creates an abundant and powerful life.

Communities such as Alcoholics Anonymous (AA) have been amazingly successful in overcoming the addiction of alcohol or drug use, because they are based on providing on-going support and accountability from like-minded people who come together with a shared experience to support and build a clean mind and sober belief system. They share accountability, responsibility, and an external support system, which in turn supports the on-going growth and empowerment of an individual's choice to choose love in new, life-affirming and empowered ways.

There is a powerful opportunity that happens in the group setting characteristics of community. You will find through the interactions and transparency of seeing another in pain, an interactive dynamic that can allow you to also locate other latent encoded pains and traumas within you. When this happens, having a loving, supportive family to shine the light on such blind-spots and subconscious strongholds is exactly how we experience exponential individual and collective growth. As you work through the traumas or fears you may bring or gain from the collective experience, you open up to feeling the joy that comes from being with people from all diversities, exchanging energy, expanding beliefs, and sharing and celebrating moments of life together, which defines a strong community at its best.

THE SOCIAL CONTRACT

At the crux of community is something called the *Social Contract*. It's a philosophical term that means we, as humans, tend to agree to certain morality, conduct and beliefs by consensus. We thereby create our shared reality based upon these beliefs and agreements. In a world that is rampant with disease, disorder, and gross disparities of wealth and quality of life, as well as false beliefs and judgments, the only way to remake the interior worlds of our hearts and minds to align with the exterior world of our planet Earth is through the collaborative and diligent effort of mirroring new impressions/co-creations of an emergent reality that is life-affirming and aligned to the truth of who we truly are.

Your "impression" is the vision you carry within you; the product of your perceptions of reality. Your "co-creation" is that which you impart and mirror into the relations of your world. If the impressions you carry within you are positive and life-affirming then the creations or gifts you bring into your world are also life-affirming. The evolution of your life-living reality and the evolution of our families, and our humanity, will occur only when what you are being and doing is nothing short of choosing to respond in love to set a default way of being that supports life-affirming actions to govern your life.

We can reshape a world when we stay focused on a powerful motivating factor—our children, and the generations of our future, who depend on us! By mirroring to our young children's malleable minds, through our inner-actions of new possibilities for relating, we co-create a future worth choosing. When your children witness life-affirming attitudes, and behaviors, through your living experience, they are wired to mirror your impressions of the world. They receive the signals through the messages they receive from their experience, which includes not only your actions, but also the impressions they pick up using their keen uncensored senses.

Through your actions of positive impressions, you mirror a pattern of relating and actions that teach them how they too can go about appreciating the beautiful gifts that our relationships are. When they see you co-creating heartfelt interchange, laughing, experiencing joy and even pain with others, and they see that the experience can yield more intimacy and deeper connections, this vast spectrum of possibility and richness of the human experience serves as a powerful model of impression for them. When they experience your words and actions aligning to bring life-affirming beliefs into the world, even when the world may not appear that way, they see with their own eyes and transfer that experience into their hearts that, indeed, it is possible to contribute something valuable and affirming into our world.

This is a powerful antidote to the societal devaluation of the Self, the pressure they will feel to conform, the dynamics of inclusion and exclusion based on external comparison, and to counteract the ever-pervasive media's constant audio and visual bombardment of influences your children will undoubtedly encounter as they move into their teen years and on into adulthood. Our human potential to exponentially experience our universal purpose for being love, evolves individually and collectively, one-person and one-heart at a time.

WHY COMMUNITY IS STRONG TECHNOLOGY

Through community you can apply the tools, knowledge, and practices necessary to institute wholistic systems in the micro, in your relationships and families that can support the implementation of these new models into the macro-levels of humanity. Creating this prototype of community that supports sustainable, life-serving, and equitable models rather than simply trying to fix more of the same retrofitted versions of unsustainable power-over systems is how we become the change we wish to see in the world.

To aim solely at changing what is broken does not honor our irreducibly interconnected world. Band-aid fixes are what we've been doing for centuries! They are not enough. We must spiral above the system that created the problem. It is not enough when our family is in crises, and band-aid fixes are not enough to our world which in crises. Although everything begins with your own individual transformation, it will take a collective and steadfast effort to set the stage for transformation to happen on a grand mass consciousness scale. When one person changes then the energy in that collective system is also pushed to change. Then suddenly, one day, a bifurcation point occurs, when exponentially a new emergent view is taken on as the predominant mass view. Together, we all contribute a unique puzzle piece to co-creating that reality as we each hold a new possibility and reality in our own lives.

There is nothing random about our world. There is an implicate order to which we all contribute a major role and part of. As energy beings, there have been billions of oscillating mutant fear-based brainwaves formed. As you do your part and live aligned to living/being in your highest truth, you unleash that exponential power and possibility into the reality of your world. It will, at times, seem overwhelming when we look at the mess and mistrust that has been created by living in the power-over systems that have taken us down this path to believe that it is impossible for anything that one individual can do actually to affect a real difference. As we prepare for a plane flight and are instructed in case of emergency to first put oxygen masks on ourselves, followed by reaching out to loved ones, we must also prepare and equip ourselves for what may be coming ahead in our lives and the new reality we create.

Our answers individually and collectively can only arise when you turn inward to clear the limitations, fears, and judgments you hold in your own heart. Listening to the silent language of your heart allows all spontaneous truths to arise. Trusting that we have exactly what we need individually, and as a community, to co-create a new world reality happens as each one of us lives in our authentic truth, and then reaches out to help empower and support our loved ones to turn inward to live their truth. Together, one-by-one, your reality of a different world is lived and co-created as you bring your grandest passions and dreams to your families and create your highest dreams as contributions and gifts needed in our reflective world.

TECHNOLOGY FOR A STRONG COMMUNITY
Albert Einstein said, "You cannot solve a problem from the same consciousness that created it." The level of consciousness and integrity you employ while connecting with others exemplifies language and power-with relating that co-creates life-affirming actions. By modeling this new possibility, you mirror your heart and enthusiasm to support a powerful way of living. Wired into your DNA, we as human beings have a fundamental driving desire to learn and grow, to perpetually seek a fuller expression of life. When you live in this inter-exchange of relating, you give permission and naturally encourage others to do the same.

Fostering your own growth enables you to exponentially shift consciousness away from the tribal mindsets and illusions that have lulled us, and our world, into a false sense of identity that runs counterintuitive to the very nature of existence itself. By being the integrity we wish to see in our connections in every form of technology we use, be it online or in the boardrooms and bedrooms, we open the space for meaningful dialogue that extends from us listening with full presence and speaking from our highest truth. Such inter-exchange will enable you to find and hone the unique gifts and contributions you come to offer your world as an intricate puzzle piece. As we each serve our highest dreams, a natural order of cooperation and hierarchy, unattached to previous titles and power-over ego structures, begins to emerge. This emergent wholistic system can then move into place in our family systems and our business systems, creating tremendous transformation in the reality of our world. You are the powerful co-creator of your life experience. You bring your reality with you everywhere you go in life. Your heart, living aligned to your truth, is how you move light-years past the debasement and devaluation of Self that has caused the pain and suffering we see out-pictured as the human experience that is so prevalent in all forms of media and technology today.

In the film, *The Truth, The Journey Within*, Dr. Reverend Michael Bernard Beckwith speaks of how our inherent interconnected web of technology can enable community to grow and thereby exponentially empower a collective voice to move life-affirming messages into humanity. The power and magnitude to spread game-changing messages like The Truth, to all four corners of our global family, is a possibility that provides the implementation of sharing forward new life skills and tools that have the power to co-create a critical mass shift of action that can now, because of the internet, spread globally with a viral and warp speed momentum, as our ancient wisdom shares, "in the blink of an eye."

"Community is very, very important, because when we're gathered there's a powerful amplification of what we are collectively in tune with. Ultimately, I have to know the truth, the person next to me, they have to know the truth for themselves to be a truly self-sufficient being…they have to have a revelation themselves…each one of us has to do our own work. In community… it becomes easier and a whole lot more fun for us to do our individual work."

This "amplification" Reverend Beckwith speaks of is how powerful we are as co-creators to draw from the exponential power of energy created when two or more are gathered together. When our energies are combined collectively, participating and supporting life-affirming practices and actions, we each raise our vibratory energies, and in doing so our world reality is amplified. Seemingly miraculous events occur when we harness the collective power of our hearts.

SYNERGISM

Wikipedia defines synergism as two or more agents working together to produce a result not obtainable by any one of the agents acting independently. Webster's defines it as conditions such that the total effect is greater than the sum of the individual effects. In the aftermath of natural and man-made disasters, we have witnessed or experienced the power of synergism in action as people ban together to help our global community during great tragedy. The word synergy or synergism comes from two Greek words: *erg* meaning "to work" and *syn* meaning "together." Synergism is "working together."

The Internet gives us an interconnected system through which humanity can work together to expand the collective evolution of consciousness. As individuals, as families, and groups, we can exchange and connect new models for interchange. As businesses, churches, governments, and organizations of all kinds, we can exchange valuable information among our communities to learn from each other in exponential ways that can yield new positive models of interaction, commerce, and communication.

By living, sharing, and spreading The Truth: a new world view message and story about who we truly are, we each possess the exponential power to contributing to shifting a critical mass of consciousness. We can be the tiny ripple that becomes a gigantic tsunami wave.

To start your own community now you can go to: www.MyHeartConnects.com. Creating a Mastermind group of support and accountability partners requires only three people to begin. Joining an internet community that focuses solely on supporting you in your journey to becoming more allows you to access an A-Z resource library. This library consists of eBooks, webinars, science breakthroughs, exercises, eLearning tools, apps, and mind-changing media. You can chat, post questions, share thoughts, and engage in live chat rooms where you can share your deepest fears and your greatest victories, all within the privacy of protected usernames. Your Mastermind group can set reminders and you can hand select specific accountability partners to share in the most intimate details of your journey.

Other accountability partners can be partnered with for tracking your intentions, to motivate you, provide empathy, and encourage you to stay the course. This will enable you to really experience the truth that you are not alone. Though we are all different, many of our struggles are the same. It helps to know that there is someone who has already emerged from the other side of your limitation that can provide support and reassure you that there is a greater possibility just around the corner when you stay on purpose.

As you begin to experience a new realm of possibility, your energetic thoughts will attract many new relationships to support your new awareness, values, beliefs, and life changes. Your community and accountability partners can help establish and reinforce new habits, helping you to utilize and practice new communication tools, and help you with grounding and expanding your constitution of inner trust. The role of sage and pupil, guide and guided, are not fixed but oftentimes interchangeable in accord with whatever it is you may be working and learning through at that particular time of your journey.

Connecting to the amazing matrix of pure potentiality that your internet community makes possible for you is a powerful tool that reaffirms the power you have to transform the limitations holding you back from being the life of your dreams. You co-create your life reality by driving your connections from a defined intention to meaningful connection. To live in your truth and build true community, your actions online must also extend from life-affirming choices. There are essentially three beckoning questions that can keep you on track as you move forward:

1. What is my unique purpose and how can my gifts and talents serve and play an intrinsic role in co-creating my new reality in my life of our new emerging world?

2. Who do I have in my life now that is also committed to living as a powerful and co-creative partner that I can invite into my community to get this party started?

3. How can living as my highest truth and purpose contribute to serving our new emergent world? The world that is within me.

If you feel that your life purpose is to contribute or support, through involvement or resources, a new global think-tank cooperative model dedicated to addressing and solving mankind's most critical problems, we'd love you to join OneTeam Humanity at: www.OneTeamHumanity.com. OneTeam Humanity is a new non-profit organism, committed to supporting humanity's needs, providing tools and life skills, techniques, education and resources to one another so that no needs go unmet. The foundational creed is built on a powerful new power-with model fostering natural leadership, supporting cooperation and new system models. The mission model is built on sacred geometry that honors the integrity and spiritual principles of The Four Agreements.

OneTeam Humanity is devoted to spiralling above and moving beyond the currently fragmented ways of solving the problems of our human family today to foster a new common vision of community and culture. We are committed to addressing the biological and intrinsic needs of all. The Internet now provides an ability to converge global minds, linking leaders, scientists and investors to breakthrough quantum and new healing energy technologies; linking like-minded organizations and communities to what they need to stimulate the necessary dialogue for creating new wholistic worldwide models and systems. This new emergent reality is our return to our intrinsic connected nature to serve the highest betterment of one inter-connected power and whole.

Lastly, *The Way 2 The Truth, The Journey Within* website, www.thetruthmovie.tv also has a catalogue of tools, life skills, exercises, and a full A-Z Resource library through www.MyHeartConnects.com, to support you with expanded knowledge as well as live demonstrations of practices and exercises, to support you with expanded knowledge as well as live demonstrations of practices and exercises. Peace in your world is but an empty wish until you eradicate the war waging within your own heart. Letting go of your finite and self-limiting beliefs takes courage, dedicated practice, mindful awareness, and divine minds entrainment of new life-affirming habits. You were born as a divine human masterpiece —a spirit into manifestation—born into this world to thrive. Discovering the truth of who you were created to be is what this journey called life is all about. Community is the strong technology to meet our Universal human interdependent needs for support, love, to be heard, for creativity, and to celebrate the victories as we each chart and navigate our individual journeys to become the potency and truth that only you uniquely were created to be!

Harness the exponential power that community holds to synergistically affect positive change in your life, the lives of others, and our world. Share forward with others through **MyHeartConnects** (www.myheartconnects.com) and **OneTeam Humanity** (www.oneteamhumanity.com) how your life has changed and commit to living as a valuable link to co-creating the critical mass tipping point. A point in time when the unexpected becomes more than expected, it *becomes* our life-living reality. When we each do our part, in creating the reality and life of our highest dreams and visions, we contribute to our collective intention of a new emerging reality. Living your truth enables you to be the reality you wish to see in the world. We reflect from our interpersonal worlds at the micro-level into the macro-level of a united collective consciousness achieved from the culmination of living as our greatness and truth.

COMMUNITY ON THE GROUND

The truth is, nothing can replace the needs for non-sexual touch, trust, our needs for deep connection, and our needs for transparent and authentic relationships. Reflection and inflection can only be met from the real time, face-to-face, heart-to-heart experience. This experiential relating is formed from building community on the ground. Today, such connection is sorely lacking everywhere. This lifestyle choice to be fragmented in our relationships, our commitments, our integrity, and our minds and hearts, is all due to the mutant fear-based matrix of systems built on false beliefs about the truth of who we are. These systems are not emotionally sustainable and perpetuate more feelings of separation and suffering into our world. As we experience the value of returning to community, returning to life in a way that honors and supports more times of silence, quality time for communing with other humans, we will benefit as a society in life and game-changing ways.

It is important that you strengthen the current ties you have to positive, supportive people in your life. Find and invite people with whom you can build community on the ground. Living, breathing, sensing, experiencing, intuiting, and feeling the energy of other life-affirming people is an essential part of our interdependent and irreducible human nature to be a part of a dynamic, creative, and strong heart-based community. We were not created to be alone. You are a powerful co-creator, connected to this One Power of our Grand Unified field of connected heart consciousness, the one mind/body/heart. What makes this experience called life rich, meaningful, and worth the ride is to be victorious in your ability to live as a fully autonomous and free individual, celebrating the uniqueness of you, yet remain profoundly connected to the communion of hearts coming together in celebrated human interaction. It is only through your relationships and relations with others that you can see the truth of your current awareness, revealed to you through the mirror of your relationships. Community is the gift that every stimulus of reaction you experience provides you an impulse and invitation to journey within.

"Be the change you wish to see in the world." Gandhi envisioned a new possibility. It is the false set of beliefs and conditioning that you are separate that feeds the finite and self-limiting beliefs you hold. Your disconnection from the reservoir of truth and power you have within to co-create your most unimaginable life is the only thing disconnecting your heart from living the truth of your grandest dreams and in your true power. Collectively, as individuals, we can be that change one-heart and one-person at a time. Share you revelations and experiences in co-creating your own community found at www.thetruthmovie.tv and become a TruthMaster and Share The Truth Forward Abundance Sharing program, where we co-create a new financial distribution win-win model that blesses everyone. Your transformation will inspire others. Together, we can co-create a future worth choosing. You can become a global community through which the emerging world is ultimately realized.

IX

OUR NEW WORLD, A CALL TO PEACE

Terror is in the human heart. We must remove this terror from the heart. Destroying the human heart, both physically and psychologically, is what we must absolutely avoid. The root of terrorism should be identified, so that it can be removed. The root of terrorism is misunderstanding, intolerance, hatred, revenge and hopelessness. This root cannot be located by the military. Bombs and missiles cannot reach it, let alone destroy it. Only with the practice of looking deeply can our insight reveal and identify this root. Only with the practice of deep listening and compassion can it be transformed and removed.

Darkness cannot be dissipated with more darkness. More darkness will make darkness thicker. Only light can dissipate darkness.... Those of us who have the light should display the light and offer it so that the world will not sink into total darkness.

—THICH NHAT HANH

Now that you have begun the journey by applying and integrating these practices into your daily life, you are growing in your awareness and trust that you truly are a powerful co-creator that can dramatically change your experiences of reality. By integrating this truth and wisdom into your being you are experiencing many more moments when you no longer see or experience the world as being separate. Does it mean that living in a different reality when the critical mass of our world and some of your relationships are resistant and lack your awareness is easy? The answer is emphatically no! In truth, *being* the change you wish to see in the world will be one of the greatest challenges of your lifetime, particularly because you live in a world that is filled with constant distractions, challenges, and systems of relating that are foundationally broken and corrupt at their core. There will be a time when suddenly you experience, by quieting the chaos in your mind, that you can choose through conscious intention to access coherence to creation source; to all knowledge and understanding—you can see this new reality once you have begun to lift the veil on areas where you have fallen asleep from your truth, even when it appears that the world around you hasn't gotten "it" yet. This is crazymaking you might say. You will feel your righteous anger rise up which is the power it will take to fuel you to stay the journey, to see the victory when most seem still blindly caught in the sea of illusion. This is when you must steady inward, focusing on connection to your source truth and power, and become that hope, that beacon of love reflecting out, living from the new possibility and new belief of who you know you are. This is the master's key—just you being you living in your truth—unlocking and unleashing the power to change and shift an entire mass consciousness.

This entire journey called life is about re-membering the truth of who you are and living it through you to inspire others to do the same.

We all come here for one reason: to learn to love. To give it and receive it as its fullest expression.

It takes courage to live from your truth, to stand up and speak what is alive in you in a world that has lost its way. When systems and the very means we use to relate within our relationships have been set up to deny the foundational truth of who we are—one participatory irreducible whole—then what we are really requiring is that we reconstruct an entire belief system aligned to the truth —to co-create the new story about us.

This will take more courage than war, more courage and strength than some of our greatest challenges and sufferings mankind has faced; it will take the will of the mighty warrior within us to emerge.

It is this perpetuated, contrived by the dark cabal, "power-over" system of programming that is unsustainable and broken. This mutant false belief system has formed the basis to which all systems have been established. We must look into our own hearts which is where all possibility and conditioned limitation exists.

You become the difference each time you are triggered by experiences in life and you turn inward to expand your awareness and compassion, to respond, in love, to help others see you model a powerful dynamic of relating that makes you a leader and beacon to show others the way.

How do you change a world? How do you change your life living reality? One heart and one person at a time. By moment-to-moment and day-by-day living committed to being your truth and counter-correcting your course when your new awareness tells you that you've strayed. You are offered everyday opportunities for expanding your awareness, to practice forgiveness, compassion and atonement towards your brothers and sisters, and ourselves, which is where everything begins. Everyday, we can live as the infinite potential defining, re-adjusting, and staying focused to chart your life in a manner that lives your integrity, your purpose, and as your greatest thoughts and visions of your reality—a pursuit and victorious journey that lasts a lifetime.

To entrain new habits into your physical, mental, and emotional reality aligned to the real authentic truth of who you are, makes everything you experience a real transformative change from the inside out. Every time you experience that you have the power to choose to co-create a better reality for yourself, each and every moment, you "create the gap" between your stimulus and response, choosing to act out of love not fear, inspires within you a profound inner trust that shifts your reality. Each time you choose love, you are reprogramming the limiting relating patterns that block you, opening within you, an expression to experience a new life living reality that is more aligned to your real truth and infinite possibility that you truly are. This heightens your discernment and awareness with each new choice you make daily to create your reality.

Ease and flow become more spontaneous as well as a capacity to maintain your sense of autonomy, equanimity, and power in your life, especially in the inevitable difficult situations and challenges that life holds. Once you access the ever flowing source of potentiality of the All That Is within you, life never will be the same. You can now manifest your deepest, truest desires and purposes into the world. Employing the Language of Compassion into your relationships and experiencing the interconnected dimension of reality supports the other collaborative tools provided throughout this book to deepen your connection to the life living reality expressing itself through you.

Each time you reap the results of co-creating relationships that feed your soul, you honor your authenticity, your integrity, reveal your truth, and empower yourself to expand into even deeper authentic connections that shape a new spellbinding reflective world. Incorporating everything you know in this moment, you can now begin to reach out and make connections that will inspire others to see a different reality that delivers the promises to thrive, live abundantly, and share in a cooperative model that celebrates a common vision and future of a global community that seeks what serves the highest goodwill for all.

THE RESTORATION OF HUMANITY

As we create a collective body and consciousness united by our own individual highest truths, then our synergism can return the world back to its people, back to its humanity. This happens as we take the quantum step to transform the current fragmented power-over systems of the planet into new wholistic power-with models. This isn't your job, nor is the weight that this possibility bears yours to carry. It is our collective job that happens one-person and one-heart at a time.

We have been conditioned to believe that until we reach our dreams we can not, nor do we have the time or financial resources, to contribute to serving the greater good of the world. So we leave the needs and crises of the world up to the "other people" feeling too overcommitted, overwhelmed, and separate from the "them" and "those" who can create a momentum for change.

In an infinite world, the truth is that your feelings of happiness, contribution, and abundance are lived and realized as you serve your highest thoughts, dreams and visions. When you're happy, your world is happy! Ultimately, when one person in a family or group models their grandest truth, that energy inspires, shakes up, and awakens possibilities, co-creating a collective action where the impossible becomes inevitable. You being your highest vision of you is enough to bring about great change in your world and that is how precisely we change our participatory world! Your fulfillment and realization of your unique purpose in life will ultimately, by design, tie back into the thread of the greater prevailing human tapestry of the One Power of The All That Is. That is a high reality to grasp, but it is the truth. Continue to live in the question of what possibility can you become, revealing an ever-expanding living truth. Know that right now, right this very moment, stored within your every cell of you is access to your original divine DNA blueprint, prior to your programming. As you learn to access pure consciousness and intrinsic knowledge to move you into being the reality of all that you were created to be is accessible when you quiet the chaos and distractions of your mind. This is the unique blueprint for your life and the life around you. Your blueprint is part of the grand architecture of the Grand Unified Field. The same life power that allows a sprout of grass to push through the concrete seeking the sun is also within you. As pure life is always in communication with our grand living matrix, you commune through the silent language in your own heart with the heartbeat that governs the truth of connection to all life, to live the expression of your unique gift of magic, of your greatest dreams and highest purpose to realize them into your life living reality.

Your mind is an open system with an ever-expanding ability to move into higher and higher levels of consciousness. Everything we know as creation: sciences, arts, beliefs, technologies and emotions, are constrained only by current limited mindsets and fears. Only you can choose to uplevel your reality to live unleashed as truth and love. As you live that infinite potentiality residing within you creating a new story about you, we each contribute to creating the new story about us.

CALLING ONE VOICE

The Language of Compassion gives you a perfect framework to engage new dialogues that value maintaining connection as their most important priority. It is through this valued emphasis on communication and cooperation to seek win/win solutions, not competition, that we inspire trust, deep communication and mutual respect. This procreative, active choice begins to mend the breach of trust that has seethed into the crevices of all our relationships and permeated deep into our society. The inward inquiry, through creating a gap, allows you to look into what is working ,and what is not, in your own world to prune the vines of the power-over systems within your own relationships and other relating structures.

As you begin to respond with more choices of love, you open the possibility for others to relax to create a new environment of trust and cooperation. A new possibility of solidarity and accountability emerges as we drop our defenses to collectively begin to create a unified voice that will seek co-creative ways to meet the critical needs now facing our world today. New wholistic models can be integrated and put in place, trumping the old, failing systems that subjugated the masses and enriched the few. This is a vision of humanity living in solidarity, in unity, and in mutual care and love. We will never be, or create anything more, or less, individually or collectively, than what we see into reality from the power of possibility that is the truth that is within your/our hearts. That is why the mission critical first steps to creating peace and love in the reality of your life, and our world, begins within you as you shift your inner reality by generating peace and love within you. Love is always an inside job.

WHOLISTIC SYSTEMS

The current power-over paradigms cause suffering to the human spirit, mistrust, unfulfilling relationships, hunger, homelessness, depression, addictions, separation, divorce and the displacement of children raised without a supportive environment or community. Our unsustainable ideological paradigms of government and economy have yielded systems that thrive upon the deprivation that perpetuates a gross disparity of wealth and quality of life amongst people across all geo-economic classes on a global scale. Meanwhile, under the guise of "freedom," wars rage, killing the innocent, perpetuating further hatred, mistrust, division, and sickness, while ravaging the planet of its resources. Everywhere you look, the failing paradigm models are evident.

Einstein nailed it when he said, "You cannot solve a problem from the same consciousness that created it. You must learn to see the world anew." Through discovery of your own empowerment for co-creating new relationships you are experiencing your ever-expanding consciousness. The only way out of the failing paradigms the world has gotten itself locked into is to re-conceptualize and re-member the truth of who we truly are, to create new power-with systems of cooperation that support a need to celebrate and encourage maintaining our strong coherence to one's truth. Your day-to-day interactions create the necessary momentum and drivers which contribute to the same intention going out into our Universe through action with others. You become the light that attracts others to a new way of being as you choose to stand in your courage and engage with your families and business systems. By offering new ways and models for cooperating, you stir new hope and possibility by staying true and aligned to your heart. To "see the world anew" is within our collective grasp as we become willing to let go of the things we thought we needed to be "okay." Your relying on the same mindsets that created the problems perpetuates more of the broken same. You create from "the space of nothingness" as you open access to "the everything" that accesses original conception of thought, to access the divine inspiration available to you—to all of us!

Then, existent knowledge can be added to and placed within a new context. Living from a new reality that acknowledges the whole spawns a total reconstruction of the sciences, arts, and all human knowledge operating within power-with consciousness models that replace the power-over models that were created under systems that by design, separate and divide. Releasing our mind's relentless linear game of control of "needing to know" emerges new models aligned with our truest nature that serves the highest betterment and goodwill for all. These models play a leading exponential role and leap in our achievements of living in a participatory quantum world that constantly exchanges energy and creation with us, that is both interactive, and reflective, to create a reality lived as the fullest expressions of our highest collective thoughts and visions. Organic in design, the testimony of these power-with systems will be the production of fruitful, inventive work, and equitable arrangements of power-with that support the possibility that there is "enough" abundance for all.

Envision a world where economy can be modeled around peace, healing healthcare systems and new energy technologies. These new energy systems already compose a multi-trillion dollar industry. There will be ways to invest in a future that allows for the flow of monies, or exchange for value to fund building these new technologies, yielding impressive returns that feed our world economy and the creation of new emergent systems. Scarcity is the lie! It is true that resources will always be needed to build these new systems, and to meet the growing needs of 7 billion people that make up our human family.

Continuing to allocate our precious resources to feed unsustainable systems in place today perpetuates the collapse of even more systems. If we continue to feed sick systems of relating, of governing, of economics, and of trade, it takes very little observation to yield undeniable proof of a fiscally and morally bankrupt government whose spending is threatening your very freedom and way of life. When do we say enough is enough? What, if any, level of accountability will you accept in co-creating the problems we now face today that threaten our very existence? When did your belief that you cannot impact change in a world so broken create the complacency in place of a collective responsibility we have to change our future for a quality and reality of life worth living? When will the excuse and comparison, "well, it's better than the other systems we have in the world," create enough pain that we step into our truth to empower the courage to call a collective voice, so powerful, millions growing to billions, to require full accountability and change? When did we close a blind eye to the truth that we've been downgraded and reclassified as "consumers," giving away our birthrights as sovereign citizens? We each can do our part to begin the dialogues. In our homes, in our businesses, in the boardroom, we can engage leaders, individuals, and corporations, to inspire and connect to our collective hearts of truth. Everything we need in our participatory world to co-create these systems is already here, waiting to make its way into our daily physical reality as we respond and act from love, not fear, as our governing default to raise the setting of the vibrational sequence and connection to institute the actions necessary to co-create a new living reality.

What does this looks like on the ground? You are a powerful co-creator to spark the impulse of possibility as you interact with new awareness in day-to-day life. This begins a positive chain-reaction that will give others a new viable model to adopt. We are drawn to positive people, because we connect to how we feel as a result of being in their energy. By living your truth, you inspire others to put down their old fear-based mentalities. The foundational building blocks for co-creating a new story about us are empathy, compassion, gratitude, humility, love and peace.

Be relentless in your pursuit and choice to live in this new story of reality, and give permission to others to stay grounded to their core connection of truth that can only be found by communing within the silent language within your heart. Watch what happens as we emerge exponentially, grounded to the universal truth and force that is so powerful, it unites us to our greatest truth of who we are within our collective field, bringing us into direct experience and manifestation of the highest vibrations—of being love. Let people feel the power coming from your heart and your truth as you co-create new experiences with them, relating in a way that though it may seem unfamiliar, resonates deeply with them and then catches and spreads like wildfire! It is simply the reconnecting and re-membering, the internal "hello" that recognizes the old friend of truth within you, immediately dropping its defenses. "Welcome, old friend," you will feel in your heart, "I know you, for you are me, we are the truth, let's celebrate!"

As you celebrate and acknowledge your interdependency and our common universal needs to be known, to be heard and know we matter, the collective voice of community is created, relentless in both our individual and collective pursuit to live in one accord to our truest nature and truth. Do not be discouraged when your bully friend, Fear, comes knocking (even bullies are crying out for love). It will.

Emotions aren't just reactions, they're choices. You now have all the tools you will need to return to your heart, always, to listen to the needs that are crying out to be heard. You have everything you need within you to calm the inevitable fears that come, and go, as you chart new territories, new economies, and new relationships, both at the micro-level, beginning with you, then moving on to your families, business systems and the world. Choose to respond in love, acting and trusting your own inner constitution and truth, and the Universe will always be there to bring you what you need.

Dr. Peter M. Senge, the founder of the MIT Center for Organizational Learning, shares in his book, *Closing the Feedback Loop Between Matter and Mind*, "Wholistic thinking or ecological thinking—sees into how everything affects everything else. Systems view sees the world in terms of relationship and integrated wholes whose properties cannot be reduced to those of similar units."

What this means is... Our current systems and modeling has produced an inability for mankind to appreciate the depth of our interrelatedness which has led to unsustainable systems in the world's economies, ecologies, and ideologies. When you dissect the source of our recent failures in the housing market in the United States, you gain access to a direct path of observance, through quiet inquiry, to see the truth of exactly what was at play—greed. These unsustainable systems will continue to infect the very fiber of what makes any system life-affirming and sustainable, if we allow the continuation of living in a false reality of belief that what one does for "self" does not effect and infect the systems of the whole. By looking into these systems, it is easy to see that it is time to look at ways we may address everyone's needs from a power-with co-operative perspective that focuses on seeing what unites us rather than continue to live and create more band-aid fixes to our false power-over systems that continue to divide us.

Said at the very beginning of this book, this emergent world is not a grand, utopian, pie in the sky world—it is the world that lies within our inherent nature. Man is joining to embrace new wholistic and interdependent systems thinking. As Barbara Marx Hubbard shares in *The Truth, The Journey Within* film:

> "There is no doubt that the old systems are collapsing. There's no doubt, that the new systems, new consciousness, new innovations are arising. Our crisis is painful. Instead of thinking and noticing only what's failing, are you noticing what is emerging?"

FACTS ABOUT THE EMERGING WORLD:

Industries supporting peace represent a trillion dollar industry serving the highest good and interests of the greater whole, our humanity, and Universe.

The creation of a healing healthcare system is a growing multi-trillion dollar industry. There are revolutionary healing breakthrough technologies, all harnessing the laws of quantum science and energy which are available to create a reality of vibrant, thriving, and healthy lives throughout your lifetime.

There is a world-wide collective base of over 90 million people, termed "Cultural Creatives," that are already contributing to a commitment of creating new communities to foster and educate us on new sustainable ways of living.

New energy solutions are already here, being contracted and installed in power plants around the world supporting fully sustainable and renewable forms of non-polluting energy to end our dependence on fossil fuel, and the depletion of resources as an underlying cause for war. These new technologies of energy support an environment for new business models, generating trillions of dollars of abundance whose collective spirit and intention serves the greater whole.

EMOTIONAL RESISTANCE AND FEAR OF MACROSCOPIC TRANSFORMATION

It is common conditioning to exhibit feelings of skepticism, denial, disbelief, mistrust, indifference, protectionism, bigotry, prejudice, and judgment that are rampant in today's world. False collective tribal mindsets have hardened our hearts into an acceptance that our world is irreversible. The chronic level of pain and unmet basic survival needs has now also penetrated geo-economic classes everywhere which helps us to bridge and empathize with others who are undergoing real adversity. "Others" can be someone in our own families, or someone we personally know who has been deeply impacted by the devastation and carnage of power-over living. This crisis is painful. Pain and the righteous anger we feel from the intentional acts of the few, affecting the lives of our entire world, is the exact fuel and power we need to stand up and be counted, heard, and take action. Every day, in some small way, we can learn about each other. Every day, in some small way, we will begin to see that we are not so far apart. As we choose to respond in love, we give to one another in such a way that we contribute, each in our own way, to collectively making our world a different place. We must start at the nucleus of where all division begins, within our own hearts, within our own mental constructs of belief that have created limitations and life-negating forms of relating to which our entire systems are based on. We live in a fast-food world that has become accustomed to band-aid solutions which we know do not work. There is a collective call, an impulse within us, that is ready to conceive, birth, and live the new story about us. As Dr. Reverend Michael Beckwith says in *The Truth* film:

People ask me, 'How are we going to save the world?' and I always have a tendency to say, 'What world do you want to save? Do you want to save the world in which kids are starving every single day? Where there's massive homelessness in the richest cultures in the world? Where there's bigotry and racism? Is that the world you want to save?' And inevitably they'll say, 'No.' We all want to save the world that is emerging.

When you continue to operate within power-over systems you implicitly tell the powers-that-be "it's all OK, we're not going to rock the boat." Consider not only what you do, but how you do it and choose to speak your voice by operating from a power-with model, aligned to your truth that inspires and encourages others to do the same. Our collective hearts, creating a gap between old fear-based patterns of reactions, choosing to respond in love by aligning your words with your actions, will reshape and contribute to the becoming of a whole new reality.

This choice to love is not easy. It is a noble and courageous choice to choose speaking against systems that have denied us our real connected power that comes from cooperation and open hearts.

> *Choosing to live in your greatness and highest purpose means choosing the opposite of the masses. If we look back to history we see that every new inventive work or possibility that life could be a different way than what was expounded from the "experts" was met with inquisition, ridicule, judgment, isolation, and even death from the masses that did not revere open examination of truth, above the fear of change. There is a truth of a participatory universe that is cheering us on to stand in our truth, rather than be locked into the patterns and cycles of false beliefs that now threaten our very existence. There is a new world emerging within us if we dare to see it.*

Fear is the greatest threat to real transformation in the world. You have been conditioned by a mutant fear-based multimillenial matrix of fear from the time you were a child. Fear is what closes and hardens the heart from the truth. There is no "us" versus "them." There is only "One." There is only One Power. We are not victims of a separate and random world. Playing small never serves. We are each powerful fully-individuated infinite creators. Only when you truly come to see, value, and act in accord with your true nature, as the precious and infinite being of pure potential that is an integral part of the One Power of The All That Is, will fear finally be allayed. Love is all there is when you center into your heart and be governed by this guiding truth. Love is the only antidote to fear. As author, luminary, and global human rights activist, Lynne Twist, shares in *The Truth* film, "Fear is not the opposite of love...it is the absence of love."

Master creating the gap in your conversations and relations with others. Quiet your mind to access "the gap" where all infinite potential resides. Become mindful of your own needs and love yourself by learning to make clear requests in the energy of mutual contribution of making life more wonderful. Speak with compassion. As you practice these things, you act from love. For only love brings light into the darkness of fear.

Through love you find a new path that leads you to your own emergence. Everything begins with you. You will know truth for its vibration feels good, feels light, and always seeks the highest good for all of humanity. Pure Love is and has always been hidden within you, within every cell of your primordial blueprint, accessed from the silent language within your heart. It is the beating impulse and small voice that you always somehow knew existed and was whispering within you—I am here Dear One, I am here... and have been waiting for you, always!

The power-over systems of the world have every reason to cling to their archaic, dying, pre-historic, life-alienating patterns and ways. Remember, they're invested deeply into seeing that the world remains just the way it is—in their master control and power.

As global citizens, we can eradicate war, terrorism, judgment, and hatred and remove it from where it resides—within our hearts. This is what the journey is for. Your heart is also where freedom, genuine happiness and peace reside. All external efforts to find love or create peace are in vain, unless you are connected and convicted from the truth and love that resides within you. It is an inside job to create love and peace within your heart. As the Indian guru Osho said, "Only when there are many people who *are* pools of peace, silence, understanding, will war disappear."

CRITICAL MASS

As more choose love as a way of being, aligned to our doing, to operate nonviolently within the emerging power-with systems will we co-create a different way of living, of interaction, and of being. Then, one-by-one heart, the echoes rising from living as your inner truth will create momentum, infusing others with your energy. Collectively, we will contribute to solving mankind's greatest problems by creating larger wholistic power-with systems that will overcome and heal the carnage and devastation that has resulted from centuries of living from the false beliefs creating scarcity, separation, and fear-based patterns of thoughts, actions, and relating.

Operating in non-violence does not mean we do not raise our voice to stand against the power-over systems that have single-handedly driven humanity to a real threat of demise. It does mean that we create new models, and communities, that demand accountability and change from the systems that have created and perpetuated these lies about living that are a godzillion times counter-intuitive to the truth of who we are and were created to be.

As these new communities begin to form in every part of our world, that are the reverent return to the sacred and deeply connected one heart of nature, honoring and living together within the organic systems of our ancient wisdom and quantum convergence of the new world truth—honoring that we are an irreducibly interconnected participatory world, we will co-create and begin the critical mass momentum of returning us to the truth; that we are nature, and nature is within us.

This moment is the grand "tipping point" described by author Malcolm Gladwell, as a momentum of critical mass "where the unexpected becomes expected, where radical change is more than possibility. It is—contrary to all our expectations—a certainty." Though we are all conditioned "gradualists," with "our expectation set by the steady passage of time," according to Gladwell, such change "happens not gradually, but at one dramatic moment."

The power of our collective, focused, coherent intention, thoughts, and emotions can create the energy of such consciousness and mass momentum that we can shift our collective reality, relative to linear time, "in the blink of an eye." Perhaps this is the moment the world's religions have been pointing to for millennia. Unearthing this new reality will be so powerful, so aligned to man's intrinsic desire to learn, to expand into our highest truth, that there will be no power-over paradigm that our conscious, evolutionary voice will not transform. Perhaps, the Second Coming of Christ is actually the light of Christ's consciousness coming to awaken the resurrection of it's one heart of love?

A CRITICAL TIME IN HISTORY

So what does it mean for us to have the privilege of living right now at our particular point in time in which the human race hovers on the brink of extinction, owing to the reality of modern day warfare, unsustainable economic systems of greed, and severe pollution and degradation of natural resources? This "blessing of unrest" can force humanity to pull together, to reorganize our collective ways of doing things. We stand at an absolutely critical point in time. As Gregg Braden shares in *The Truth* film:

> "Almost universally, ancient texts and spiritual traditions point to our time in history, and they say that it is now, in our lifetime on earth, that it is our civilization who is undergoing a rare moment, something that has not been seen on this planet for 5,000 years of civilization. This all centers around the year 2012, which marks the close of two great cycles of time.
>
> One of them is a 26,000 year-old long cycle that is called the Precession of the Equinoxes, which our ancestors divided into sub-cycles of approximately 5,300 years long. The ancient Mayans likened the 5,000 year cycle that we are completing now to the gestation of a living embryo in the womb of a woman and they say at the end of that gestation is birth, and our cosmic birth into this new world. It's not the end of the world, it's the end of an age, and by virtue of the end of one cycle being present, it means it is also the beginning of what comes next. The Mayans said this to us, they said, that we will begin a new world, a

> *new 5,000 year old cycle and they said that we won't recognize ourselves, and we won't recognize our world because of the changes at the end of our cycle appear to come so quickly."*

And so, at exactly this precise time in history, when the planet is crying out for intensive care and humanity faces the greatest challenges known in the last 5,000 years of history; we see breakthrough technologies for the human healing of our hearts, here now, to guide us and support us into new ways of seeing/being ourselves. You now have every tool you need to teach you how to move from the false belief that you are a powerless victim of a random world to clear out the lie of limitation holding you back to empower you to become empowered co-creators of a new reality within your world. These quantum discoveries speak to a world of infinite possibility in which we each have the power, through the silent language of the heart, to commune with the very stuff of which this world is made. Creating and being the pools of peace within our own lives that is then reflected back to us in the world we inhabit.

Although humankind has unknowingly participated in being the great perpetrator of the world's broken state, we are also the answer and technology we have been waiting for. We are the missing link, the manifestation and co-creator with the grand architect of The All That Is, The Divine, and The Grand Unified Field. It is through you, choosing love to be your greatness that you become potent intentioned vehicles of human energy, to live the truth of our universal irreducible connectedness, so that our Mother Earth and our species may survive. Within you there is an ever-expanding capacity to access your self-awareness, cognition, and self-actualization of the truth of who you are. It is now, as members of an Implicate Order, who have each received a Divine Mandate, an order by the Universe to live the universal truth that we are all one. It is time to come together as one family, to contribute to helping to heal our families and solve the critical problems facing humanity right now.

To dismantle and move from world systems that have been built upon the lie and illusion of separation, creating an "every man for himself" and "dog-eat-dog" world that continues to perpetuate more of the same scarcity, to co-create a world that instead seeks cooperation, that places our highest priority on good for all, we must begin from a place of open examination into what is working. We now have all the tools necessary to co-create the new story about us, aligned to the truth of who we are. Building this future together exponentially brings cooperation and restores hope to rebuild the trust that has been shattered from living in systems that are based on boundaries and walls of divisive power.

Along with knowing that you have, within your grasp, the capability and power to directly transform your world, comes a great responsibility. It is up to you to contribute, guide, and usher-in the birth of new paradigms for the emerging world. You must first reclaim your own citizenship by reclaiming your/our collective power and voice, so we can harness a collective exponential power to let that voice of our truth be aligned to the collective blueprints of all our unique purposes. As we each become connected to our inner declarations of truth, we unite together as a strong and powerful mind/body/heart. Once you understand who you are, nothing can make you return or accept the broken, fragmented world of before. You rise up to stand in truth, as the mighty warrior you are. We are the answer. We are the Universe's way of being aware of itself as infinite, potent, greatness, and truth living human "beings" on our divine Mother Earth.

A WISH FOR YOU AND ME

We at OneTeam Humanity, and each one of us have a brave and courageous choice to co-create a world where we can live the promises of our ancient wisdom—to live together as A Thousand Years of Peace —to live a reality aligned to the truth of who we were created to be. Science, as man, in search of truth and answers to the primordial questions of "Who am I" and "What is my relationship to our connected nature to the environment as a whole?" has split the atom and peered into the depths of the universes of man's mind to reveal truths, new truths about you and me as a participatory world, unto ourselves, where the observer affects that which is observed.

In a participatory world, our primordial desire and thirst for truth, to learn, to live, and to excel has led us to the answers and undeniable facts that we do have the power to change our life living reality and world now.

Our ancient wisdoms have been sharing all along that within you and me there is the power to heal, to inspire, to live as abundance, to live in peace—all created from the well-of-being that is within you, within me. And now that our science and ancient wisdoms have converged, we can integrate and *become* what our wisdoms have been telling us all along—the truth that we are all One... "I tell you the truth, when you did it to one of the least of my brothers and sisters, you were doing it to me!" In every part of you, there is a part of me. So, if even one child goes unloved then we haven't done enough. May their cries, become the salt we also taste to feed that fuel in our hearts to empower the mighty and fierce warrior within us, to stand up against the lie and illusion of separation. It is time to search within, find that connected part of you, who isn't just sympathetic to the man who goes hungry, but is willing to contribute to being the difference. If that hunger is for truth, then guide his heart with love. If that hunger is for nutrition, then feed that hunger with bread. For at the basis of all hunger in our world lies the need to return to truth.

All great wisdoms and scientific discoveries unite now at one universal truth and reason for being: to be love and reflect that love to share, and receive, what it means to live grounded to this truth. To build new models of cooperation, that contribute to one another in a way that honors our irreducible common connection to our universal basic human needs for: air, food, safety, for life and meaning, for touch and connection. Meeting just these basic needs opens the heartspace to rebuild trust that leads us to celebrate our united needs for freedom, autonomy, and peace, for creativity, inclusion and belonging. These needs being met support our united need for contributing to building communities that apply coherent hearts and minds to quiet the chaos, to listen within, to seek new constructs of wholistic systems that honor our universal needs for equality. We all have a unique contribution for co-creating something greater in this grand schema called interconnected life. We can each contribute in a way that allows for joy, communion, presence, celebration, creativity, learning, for rejuvenation, trust in primordial truth, and for the most important common universal need of all—to live united in the truth of who we are—love.

What man has proven is that he is capable of amassing great wealth and power, arrogant wisdom, and self-proclaimed glory, at the expense of others, and that all of "that world" is based on a foundation of false beliefs of "knowledge" that will never lead a man or humanity to the experience of genuine happiness, meaning and well-being. If our lives are filled with all the riches of an external world, and yet we fail to live as the truth of who we are—love—then we will continue to be imprisoned by a false lie of our world, filled with illusions, and fears that govern and decay life today.

Now, just as we face the real possibility of extinction as a species, we have the truth to empower a new story about us. Now, the only moment we ever really have in life to create a new world, comes a full spectrum possibility coupled with every self-tool you will need to clear out your subconscious mind from the prison of living in old, archaic, false systems of limitation, beliefs and scarcity. We each now have been invited to become an integral part of the greatest show on earth—we each have a front row seat and access pass to co-create living the grandest love story of truth and pure love on earth. The master key to the most precious treasure on earth has been hidden and always accessible within the silent voice and language within our own hearts.

We fear death because we might be forced to look back to see the truth that we have not experienced living a meaningful life, individually and together, that was fully lived aligned to the truth of who we truly are—united as love.

Birthing life, and death, is a painful process. Birthing new life through the gift of authentic reflections from our most intimate relationships is painful as well. But pain and suffering serves love...if it bends us over and gets us closer to our hearts. It is through our hearts, in coherence with our infinite mind, that we possess everything we need to empower a new reality, kindred to the heart of truth that lies waiting to be tapped into, as we quell the chaos of an unexamined life and mind.

How long will you accept the lies, illusions, and fears that have governed our world that have denied you from living as the powerful co-creator that can change your life living reality today?

One might ask: how can we change our world that has strayed so far away from truth? One person and one heart at a time, with millions growing to billions.

Lovingly commit to the journey. Transcend your limiting beliefs. Heal yourself to live free from the control that negative conditioning and negative people create that has blocked you from living as the infinite truth you are. Harness the power, potency, and connection to the truth that we are interwoven, irreducible, and primordially good beings and have the courage to spread the good news. Your world is your participatory, dynamic, and co-created ally and playground. Live in this realization to move into higher and higher levels of functioning, intelligence, consciousness, learning, focus, concentration, and healing. Seek communion with one another in ways that hold connection as your highest priority. Learn to break free from your own reactions, by creating "the gap," to listen first to the truth within your own heart. Listen to what is alive in others and then celebrate, forgive (for we do not know what we do not know, until we do), make amends where necessary, and encourage and support one another in our journey of becoming more. Encourage others to seek first their Highest Truth and only contribute from the pure intentions of their heart. This gift of grace to one another will always serve to align what serves the Highest Truth for All. Live to align your hearts in truth. Everyday, find times for silence to quiet your mind. Find times for silence to quiet your mind to live aligned to your heart; to speak to the magnetic fields of the planet, through the magnetic fields of your heart, to help quell the chaos present in your/our interconnected world.

Open your heart and live as your highest expression of life, living through you. This is your opportunity to unleash a world that is but only a heartbeat away. Gregg Braden shares in *The Truth, The Journey Within* film:

> *This invitation is for each of us to reach within our hearts to speak to the fields of the planet, the magnetic fields of the earth, through the magnetic fields of the human heart and to quell the chaos created by the stress and disconnection of 7 billion people moving through the greatest challenges in 5,000 years of recorded history. Now, we have the opportunity to transform ourselves and our world. That is what this time is all about.*

Your opportunity for freedom comes through the mirrors of your relationships. By creating the gap and choosing moment-by-moment to love, you have fulfilled the purpose we all have in life: to give and receive love. When you live aligned to this truth and reality, you will move light-years beyond anything before.

Located within the silent language of your heart is your greatest guide. Your own inner wisdom is everything you will ever need to discover and live as your highest truth, power, and greatness. Together, as we each live the truth, and join a collective voice to stand against the false world systems built on a lie of separation, we build a future worth choosing that co-creates a homeland security of authentic peace governed from our hearts, from our universal interconnected needs to live in freedom, to trust in the goodwill of our fellow man and woman, and to live life within the genuine fulfillment and community that converges within you and me. This power-with model for relating and living can only be experienced when you quiet your mind to listen to the one language, and electromagnetic power, that is united within our hearts.

What does it take to live a richly meaningful life?

To live a richly meaningful life, these three pursuits are profoundly and inextricably intertwined:

1. The Pursuit of Understanding, of Insight, of Knowledge, of Wisdom. If I let a day slip by and have made no effort...directed no attention to this pursuit, then that day is not complete.

2. To Cultivate Virtue: to be wiser, kinder, and have more patience.

3. To Cultivate a Deepening Sense of Happiness and Well-Being, from what I am bringing to the world, not just what I'm getting from it.

In the modern world, these three pursuits are often presented as being independent, unrelated, and even in conflict with each other. But at the deepest level, the pursuit of understanding must be inextricably intertwined for the cultivation and sake of genuine happiness and well-being. This pursuit leads me naturally to the avenue of cultivating virtue: intelligence, wisdom, sound judgment, and clear observation. So, for the pursuit of understanding to be as rich and deep as possible, it must be entangled, interwoven with the cultivation of virtue, to come to know myself and the world around me in the deepest sense of Happiness and Well-Being.

How can we do this if we don't know our own minds...? The nature of human existence...? Our relationship to the people around us...? Our connected nature to the environment as a whole...? All three pursuits are what naturally give rise to the experience of life, living as our deepest and greatest sense of well-being and happiness.

We've built a world with systems that deny and repress the discovery of our own essential nature. A world that is searching for love and for meaning in the lie and illusion of the insatiable desire and external quest for more; building a false sense of happiness that has led our world into an abyss of all types of addictions... a craving for stimulus, a certain type of frenzy.

To live a rich and meaningful life we must have times of silence. Times for reflection... Times of simplification... Times of solitude...to come to terms with our own identity, our own being, our essential nature, prior to and independent of the many roles that we adopt and release in this lifetime journey.

Will truth set you free?

Any discovered truth is simply knowledge. Without application and integration into your being, your life, it is simply wisdom that grows dust on the bookshelves of your life. We are human *beings*, not human doings. Is it time that we begin to live the truth of who we are...

The Truth is...In every part of you, there's a part of me.

The end of the illusion...

The beginning of the truth and the new story about us...

It is in the silence that everything gets created.
—INSPIRATION FROM THE VOICE OF THE TRUTH

Acknowledgements

Wow.... Life is this amazing, mysterious journey seeking itself through us!

Deeply humbled and filled with gratitude for every wisdom leader, visionary, scientist, and to the many new technologies and deep connections of hearts that have made their way into my awareness so that I could honor the message that came through me in the making of this book and film. Indeed, what a journey!

For each wisdom warrior: Rev. Michael Bernard Beckwith, Gregg Braden, Byron Katie, Jack Canfield, Paul Ferrini, Dr. Arun Gandhi, Dr. Elisha Goldstein, Dr. Henry Grayson, Azim Khamisa, Dr. Bruce Lipton, Lynne Twist, Howard Martin, Barbara Marx Hubbard, Lynne McTaggart, Arnina Kashtan, Inbal Kashtan, Miki Kashtan, Dr. Konstantin Korotkov, Dr. Mary Manin Morrisey, Marcia Martin, Dr. Rollin McCraty, Dr. Sue Morter, Freddie Ravel, Colette Baron-Reid, Dr. Deborah Rozman, Jon Symes, Max Simon, Sandra Anne Taylor, Joel Garbon, Dr. B. Alan Wallace, Mark Weill, and Dr. Darren Weissman. Each contribution of your passion, gifts, and life's study has helped to co-create a powerful game-changing message of a new truth and reality breaking through into our powerful emergent world. I want to express and acknowledge your irreducible contribution and celebrated shared vision—to empower and support humanity in our collective journey and vision to choose love and become more.

Special thanks and gratitude to the amazing Dr. Henry Grayson. Your life's work, friendship, wisdom, contribution to this book, and love has been the gentle wind of encouragement to support this book's unfolding.

To Straw Weisman, Ramin Rahmanpour, Timothy Patrick Cavanaugh, and to my soul sister, Heather Hart, whose belief in the message of The Truth was the fuel that allowed your gifts, passions, sacrifices, protection, and perseverance to be the pillar of community I needed to deliver this book and film.

To the many silent warriors who have individually contributed their trust, time, prayers, heart and resources: Mark Mueller, Tami Ralston, Dave Pixley, Cynthia Noe, Timothy Patrick Cavanaugh, Brittany Park Lund, Craig Park, Marcia Martin, Arielle Ford, Brian Hilliard, Shawn Galloway, Faith Rivera, Sheira Rosenberg and Wkwesi Williams, infinite love and gratitude for you. Your support and love makes this journey so yummy and worth it!

To Liya Swift, the Editor, whose gift and brilliant art form transformed my words into a coherent creation, supporting my need to honor the integrity of the vision I received.

And to Dawn Mena whose final editing touches added the fine detail and brush strokes of creativity that The Truth needed to get this party started.

To Robert Ireland Cudlip, "the everyman," whose contribution to language suggestions challenged me to share new concepts of information in a way that reaches every man and heart that will benefit from the message of truth on these pages.

To Itzel Damaris and Newton Bailey for anchoring and sharing the Principles of NVC/The Language of Compassion that were powerfully shared in the film. Casting you both over the phone provided just one more of the many miraculous synchronicities that guided my decisions through the making of this book and film. When I met you both, I saw the power of the truth to provide, once again, another unplanned real message about how much our judgments and limiting beliefs cloud how we perceive *everything* in life. I am grateful for your contribution in every way, and more. And, I am so grateful for the deep connection and friendship that has blessed my life since meeting you. Because of both of you, and the guiding message of non-judgment that prevailed from our meeting, I was allowed to see into my own fears, judgments, and limiting patterns within myself, that empowered my courage to tell the real story.

For the gift, energy, and strength of the powerful Kashtan sisters: Arnina, Miki, and Inbal. Your individual contributions to The Language of Compassion fill me with gratitude for your continued dedication to sharing the teachings of Dr. Marshall Rosenberg's *Non-Violent Communication* in our world. Our working together provided me a lifetime experience of understanding that we can come from four divergent backgrounds, belief systems, and still remain connected and focused on our common needs for contribution and create a synergy of trust to share a unified message.

To my parents, Ronald and Bettylee Johnston, and my sister Carolyn, I am grateful for the gift of lessons our lifetime together has given me. I appreciate every part of you that has become a part of me. To Mirage, Gizmo and Shadow, I am grateful for your unconditional tails on constant wag patrol. Everyday I smile and celebrate the moments in our journey together!

To my stepsons: Jared Mueller and his beautiful wife Maryam; and to Joseph Mark Mueller and his spirited wife Katie; and their children whose presence and innocence, light and spirit, has gifted me with laughter, joy, and clarity of why this journey to illuminate a future worth choosing is worth going "all in" for, thank you! Your precious and celebrated lives have touched my needs for deep, meaningful relationships, authenticity, trust, love, community, meaning, celebration, play and truth.

And to every relationship, event, circumstance and choice that has, and is contributing to my lessons on the journey of unfolding who I am, who I am not, and who I am becoming, I offer my Infinite Love and Gratitude to the reflection of me I saw within you!

Finally, to the humanity within me, thank you! For without your reflections from one heart to the other, our shared pain, sorrows, our united common needs, and tears, the light of truth would not have shined so brightly in my love for our freedom, and the truth, to contribute to honoring sharing a message with the power to break free from the lie and illusions; to begin the living experience of aligning to who we truly are. Because of you, I am "ALL IN" to pursue an unyielding burning desire to participate and contribute to co-creating a new story about us. Together, may our unity, shared vision, unique gifts, and common needs create unified inner reflections of experience that shape and co-create a powerful new story about us, fervently grounded and connected to our creation consciousness; the source that supports every system that gives us this amazing participatory journey called life. It is time to live the truth of who we are, to achieve the highest vision of who we were truly created to be—located where is has been hidden all along; accessible through communion with the silent language within our hearts.

There's an impulse and collective call beckoning us to the inward journey to return to the truth of who we are; powerful co-creators of a brave and victorious new world... can you feel it emerging within you?
—INSPIRATION FROM THE VOICE OF THE TRUTH

Sources & Endnotes

SOURCES

The download I received unfolded on these pages played the fundamental key role in connecting and explaining the full spectrum understanding of who we really are once we uninstall our conditioned "untruths" from our early programming. The sources noted below are a listing of the developmental references from the works of philosophers, scriptures, religions, and transformational books that contributed in my journey of reconstructing my identity formed from false "truths" of who I am, in my pursuit for understanding the meaning of life. I had no idea until that instant moment of clarity in 2006, that the truth of how to bring that wisdom into living a deeply interconnected, yet autonomous and joyful life was located where it had been all along; within the silent language of my heart.

While perhaps not referenced specifically in my conscious writing, these works are inextricably connected to both who I am now and who I am becoming. I'm citing them here in the order they come to mind from the beginning of my journey in my 20's until now.

I offer them to you for reference during your journey to becoming more…

Understanding Yourself and Others: An Introduction to the 4 Temperaments 3.0, Linda V. Berens, ISBN-10: 097437511X, ISBN-13: 978-0974375113. This is an updated version to a course that was centered around Dr. Berens' work when I was in my early 20's.

The work of John Bradshaw on *Homecoming-Reclaiming and Championing Your Inner Child*. This course brought powerful foundational understanding of how to heal childhood wounds, teaching us how to reclaim the innocence that was taken from our childhood conditioning, and to connect to the truth that our parents were also wounded children, and in their "unknowingness" also didn't know what they didn't know, until they do. It is only through life's journey that we are presented an opportunity of learning from our most reactive reflective core relationships. Our pain is the gift that turns us inward to make the courageous and heroic decision to seek the truth, and pro-actively develop the inner trust and courage to speak from that truth, in love, so that through our reflective mirrors of relationship, the possibility and experience of living the truth of authentic connection and love will deepen our compassion for one another.

Bible, Life Application Study Bible, Tyndale

Boundaries In Marriage, Henry Cloud, John Townsend

Love Is a Choice: The Definitive Book on Letting Go of Unhealthy Relationships, Dr. Robert Hemfelt, Dr. Frank Minirth, Paul Meier, M.D.

Conscious Loving: Finding Joy in the Real World, Gay Hendricks

The Verbally Abusive Relationship: How to Recognize It and How to Respond, Patricia Evans

How Can I Get Through to You?: Closing the Intimacy Gap Between Men and Woman, Terrance Real

I Don't Want to Talk About It: Overcoming the Secret Legacy of Male Depression, Terrance Real

Mindful Loving, Henry Grayson, Ph.D.

Love Without Conditions, Paul Ferrini

The Spontaneous Fulfillment of Desire: Harnessing the Infinite Power of Coincidence to Create Miracles, Deepak Chopra

Conversations With God, Neale Donald Walsh

Don't Be Nice Be Real: Balancing Passion for Self with Compassion for Others, Kelly Bryson, MFT, Elite Books; 2nd edition (November 10, 2011)

Being Peace, Thich Nhat Hanh

True Love, A Practice for Awakening the Heart, Thich Nhat Hanh

Peace Is Every Step: The Path of Mindfulness in Everyday Life, Thich Nhat Hanh

Taming the Tiger Within: Meditations on Transforming Difficult Emotion, Thich Nhat Hanh

The Energy of Prayer: How to Deepen Your Spiritual Practice, Thich Nhat Hanh

Going Home: Jesus and Buddha as Brothers, Thich Nhat Hanh

Buddhism Without Beliefs: A Contemporary Guide to Awakening, Stephen Batchelor

The Spontaneous Healing of Belief: Shattering the Paradigm of False Limits, Gregg Braden

The Divine Matrix, Gregg Braden, Hay House

The Field, Lynne McTaggart, Harper Collins

The Biology of Belief, Bruce Lipton, Hay House

Great Instauration (1620), Francis Bacon

Law of Compensation Essay, Ralph Waldo Emerson

ENDNOTES

Chapter I

Page 23: Deepak Chopra, *Synchro Destiny*, Random House (September 11, 2004)

Page 29: Bruce Lipton, Ph.D., *The Biology of Belief: The Biology of Belief: Unleashing the Power of Consciousness, Matter, & Miracles*, Hay House; 13 edition (March 1, 2011)

Page 30: Wikibooks, *Human Physiology*

Page 31: John Hagelin, Ph.D., http://www.youtube.com/watch?v=OrcWntw9juM, *Consciousness 1 of 2, Consciousness & Superstring Unified Field Theory*

Page 43: Gregg Braden, Interview from *The Truth, The Journey Within*. The Truth Movie, LLC. All Rights Reserved.

Chapter II

Page 37: John Hagelin, Ph.D., http://www.youtube.com/watch?v=OrcWntw9juM, *Consciousness 1 of 2, Consciousness & Superstring Unified Field Theory*

Page 51, 65: Henry Grayson, Ph,D., Interview from *The Truth, The Journey Within,* The Truth Movie, LLC. All Rights Reserved

Page 59: Allen Koss, *New Life Enterprises,* http://mindaerobics.com/, *Mind-Science Report*

Page 41: http://en.wikiquote.org/wiki/Albert_Einstein, Letter of 1950, as quoted in *The New York Times* (29 March 1972) and The New York Post (28 November 1972)

Page 61: Mother Jones, *San Francisco,* Nov/Dec 2003. Vol. 28, Issue 6; pg. 76

Page 63: The toxic mind: the biology of mental illness and violence. *Medical Hypotheses* 2000; 55(4): 356-368 E. Van Winkle

Retired Neuroscientist, Millhauser Laboratories of the Department of Psychiatry, New York University School of Medicine

Chapter III

Page 116: Dr. Herbert Benson M.D. and William Proctor, J.D., *Gene Expression, Relaxation Revolution: Enhancing Your Personal Health Through the Science and Genetics of Mind Body Healing*

Page 87: E. Van Winkle, *The Biology of Emotions: Self-Help for Anxiety and Depression,* Laboratories of the Department of Psychiatry, New York University School of Medicine, ©1998

Page 111: Howard Martin, Institute of HeartMath, http://www.heartmath.org/ Interview from *The Truth, The Journey Within.* The Truth Movie, LLC. All Rights Reserved.

Page 111: Dr. Rollin McCraty, Institute of HeartMath, http://www.heartmath.org/ Interview from *The Truth, The Journey Within.* The Truth Movie, LLC. All Rights Reserved.

Page 94: Gregg Braden, Interview from *The Truth, The Journey Within.* The Truth Movie, LLC. All Rights Reserved.

Page 90: Byron Katie, *The Work,* http://www.thework.com/index.php, Judge-Your-Neighbor Worksheet, is a transformational way of identifying your thoughts and questioning the thoughts that cause all the fear, violence, depression, frustration, and suffering in the world.

Page 90: Shonkoff, J.P., & Phillips, D.A. (Eds). (2000). *From Neurons to Neighborhoods: The Science of Early Childhood Development* National Academies' Press.

Chapter IV

Page 102, 103: Allen Koss, *New Life Enterprises,* http://mindaerobics.com/, *Mind-Science Report*

Page 142: Jack Canfield, Co-Author, *Chicken Soup for The Soul Series,* http://www.jackcanfield.com/, *Nasa Study of Habits,* Interview from *The Truth, The Journey Within,* The Truth Movie, LLC. All Rights Reserved.

Page 155: Lectino Devino meditation practice (adaptation), http://en.wikipedia.org/wiki/Lectio_Divina

Page 125: B. Alan Wallace, Ph.D., http://www.sbinstitute.com/, Santa Barbara Institute for Consciousness Studies, Interview from *The Truth, The Journey Within*, The Truth Movie, LLC. All Rights Reserved.

Chapter V

Page 128: Ian Rheeder, *Psychologies of Successful Leaders*, published 2010, http://www.markitects.co.za/files/book-short-chapters/Chap%202%20Neuroscience%20Power%20of%20Positive%20Thinking,IanRheeder.doc.pdf

Jung, CG: *Modern Man in Search of a Soul*, 1933, pp 253 – 254

Damasio, Antonio, *Descartes' Error*, 2006, p.87, p.223, p.229

Damasio, Antonio, *Descartes' Error*, 2006, p.227

J Nolte, *The Human Brain: An Introduction to its Functional Anatomy* 5th ed, Chap 11, pp. 262–290

Page 136: Lynne McTaggart, *The Field: The Quest for the Secret Force of the Universe*, Harper Paperbacks (August 5, 2003)

Page 180: Double-Positive Programming Technique, http://en.wikipedia.org/wiki/List_of_studies_in_neuro-linguistic_programming

Page 181: Robert Provine, a leader in research on yawning and psychologist at the University of Maryland. Among his papers on the subject are: *Yawning as a Stereotyped Action Pattern and Releasing Stimulus*, Ethology (1983), vol. 72, pp. 109-122

Robert Provine, *Contagious Yawning and Infant Imitation*, Bulletin of the Psychonomic Society (1989), vol. 27, no. 2, pp. 125-126

Chapter VI

Page 198: This powerful language process shifts our focus to find and connect with our Universal Connection to Human Needs in an effort to seek win-win solutions based on needs. The process dynamically shifts our internal conditioning and relationship of seeing ourselves as "separate," creating damage to our relationships when we employ strategies to meet our needs that cause division and separation, creating feelings of suffering. This internal shift ends our relationship of judging, evaluating, and communicating in power-over systems of relating, teaching us to instead look for our interconnected and interdependent connection we have to needs. This ends the damaging cycles of power-over conditioning that have, to date, kept us locked us into patterns of judgment and relating of what we should or should not do or be. Freedom and open relating comes when we release a heart from the "should's," "have-to's," "shame," "blame," "guilt" or conditioned demands and instead choose to co-create relationships based on freedom, and truth, by making requests of what would make life more wonderful for everyone. The Non-Violent Communication philosophy and relating model is built on the lifetime work of Dr. Marshall Rosenberg.

Dr. Marshall B. Rosenberg of The Center for Nonviolent Communication (www.cnvc.org), a global organization dedicated to the sharing of nonviolent communication, whose mission is to empower people to peacefully and effectively resolve conflicts in personal, organizational, and political settings.

Major contributors to this work in this chapter and film were contributed from Miki Kashtan, Inbal Kashtan, http://baynvc.org/ of Bay Area Centers for Non-Violence Communication, and Arnina Kashtan, http://meitarim.com. Gary Baron and Center for Nonviolent Communication

Chapter VII

Page 249: http://thomasdorrance.com/Documents/Understanding%20the%20Boy%20Code.doc, William Pollack, *Real Boys: Rescuing Our Sons from the Myths of Boyhood*, Owl Books; Later Printing edition (April 1999)

Page 272: Terrance Real, *How Can I Get Through To You* and *I Don't Want To Talk About It,* A Fireside Book/Simon & Schuster Trade Paperback; March 1998.

Page 208: David Kirsh, Dept. of Cognitive Science, Univ. California, San Diego. http://interactivity.ucsd.edu/articles/Overload/published.html, A Few Thoughts on Cognitive Overload

http://www.fritzhubbard.org/words/The_Multitasking_Generation.pdf

http://www.nais.org/publications/ismagazinearticle.cfm?ItemNumber=155242

Chapter VIII

Francis Bacon, *The Great Instauration,* 1620

Page 209: http://www.internetworldstats.com/stats.htm

Page 282: http://mashable.com/2010/07/07/oxygen-facebook-study/

Page 282: http://www.theatlantic.com/magazine/archive/2012/05/is-facebook-making-us-lonely/8930/

Page 285: Rev. Michael Bernard Beckwith. Filmed interview from *The Truth, The Journey Within.* The Truth Movie, LLC. All Rights Reserved.

Chapter IX

Page 306: Rev. Michael Bernard Beckwith. Filmed interview from *The Truth, The Journey Within.* The Truth Movie, LLC. All Rights Reserved.

Page 309: Malcom Gladwell, *The Tipping Point: How Little Things Can Make a Big Difference,* Back Bay Books, January 7, 2002.

Page 310, 315: Gregg Braden, Filmed interview from *The Truth, The Journey Within.* The Truth Movie, LLC. All Rights Reserved.

Page 239: B. Alan Wallace, Ph.D., Filmed interview from *The Truth, The Journey Within.* The Truth Movie, LLC. All Rights Reserved.

Page 278: Ropelato, Jerry. *Internet Pornography Statistics,* http://internet-filter-review.toptenreviews.com/internet-pornography-statistics.html